Economic Sanctions vs. Soft Power

Economic Sanctions vs. Soft Power

Lessons From North Korea, Myanmar, and the Middle East

Nikolay Anguelov

palgrave
macmillan

ECONOMIC SANCTIONS VS. SOFT POWER

First published in 2015 by
PALGRAVE MACMILLAN®
in the United States—a division of St. Martin's Press LLC,
175 Fifth Avenue, New York, NY 10010.

Where this book is distributed in the UK, Europe and the rest of the world, this is by Palgrave Macmillan, a division of Macmillan Publishers Limited, registered in England, company number 785998, of Houndmills, Basingstoke, Hampshire RG21 6XS.

Palgrave Macmillan is the global academic imprint of the above companies and has companies and representatives throughout the world.

ISBN: 978–1–137–52375–4

Library of Congress Cataloging-in-Publication Data

Anguelov, Nikolay.
Economic sanctions vs. soft power : lessons from North Korea, Myanmar, and the Middle East / by Nikolay Anguelov.
pages cm
Includes bibliographical references and index.
ISBN 978–1–137–52375–4 (hardback)
1. Economic sanctions—Burma. 2. Economic sanctions—Korea (North) 3. Economic sanctions—Middle East. 4. International trade. 5. Investments, Foreign. I. Title.

HF1586.7.A54 2015
327.1'17—dc23 2015002003

A catalogue record of the book is available from the British Library.

Design by Newgen Knowledge Works (P) Ltd., Chennai, India.

First edition: July 2015

10 9 8 7 6 5 4 3 2 1

Contents

Figures and Tables

Figures

Tables

Acknowledgments

This book's journey started in 2009 when two graduate students—Kristin Bryant and Bradley J. Hornback—invited me to be part of their capstone committees. They brought their passion for the subject of sanctions and their compassion for the people of Myanmar and North Korea into the research process. I am especially grateful for their unique perspectives, based on their personal experiences in South East Asia, that allowed us to discuss the rapidly changing economic dynamics of the region. During that time, the guidance of Dr. Holley Ulbrich for including the concept of rent seeking into the evaluation of sanction effectiveness was essential. We are grateful for her continued support.

The idea for developing the book must be credited to Brian O'Conner who spotted the potential of conference papers to be combined into an interdisciplinary volume on sanction mitigation. His continued support for the project was essential as the collaborations grew with the very important contribution of another graduate student—Tiffany Kaschel. I am also grateful to Joshua Botvin and Trevor Mattos for their editorial contributions. This book has been a truly collaborative project that has allowed me to encourage the passions of students for research, learning, and their quest to build knowledge applicable in policy dynamics.

Introduction

This book links together the literatures on sanctions, soft power, international business, and foreign direct investment (FDI). Following case study examples from Asia and the Middle East, an FDI analysis of incentives is offered at the firm level to explain how the growth of international business opportunities can diminish sanction impact.

Introduction

Economic sanctions—a tool of governments—directly impact the profitability of private firms. In this way, the imposition of sanctions can create market rents for competing multinational corporations (MNCs). MNCs from the "sender" nation are at a disadvantage while firms from non-participating nations can gain competitive market positions in "target" nations. The problem is that in a global marketplace, overall firm profitability is contingent on degrees of internationalization. The absence and/or late arrival in one market can have negative nonlinear spill over effects on overall firm growth. Such an outcome can occur because fragmentation of production necessitates the building of multiple linkages that are geographic in scope. Those linkages involve not only the sender and target sanction nations, but also their regional partners. Firms that are the first to build foundational linkages in any market can control entire supply chains and co-opt backward and forward linking business partners in resisting late arrivals. Such an outcome allows for significant profit maximization because it creates market rents.

The dynamic of rent extracting and protecting in international inter-firm competition can be used to explain the political rent-seeking behavior of repressive governments. Today, Russia, Iran, Myanmar, North Korea, and the Middle East provide examples of the increasing futility of economic sanction. The book examines the industrial growth of sanctioned nations in terms of their ability to foster trade partnerships with countries that choose to evade or not comply with sanctions. When the absence of firms from sender nations allows those "black knight" nations to find strong local market competitive advantages, incentives develop to support local political status quos.

For those reasons, the political resilience of rogue and repressive regimes is analyzed in terms of their economic incentives to remain repressive. The resilience is based on the fact that the local politicians are also the local businessmen who create systems for protecting self-interests. Growth of international production networks allows for the augmentation of not only their business opportunities, but also the rents associated with that growth. As business activity increases in the absence of competition, so does the amount of rent extraction and protection that local businessmen receive. Successful rent protection leads to strengthening economic and political leadership, because the wealth is used for creating further rents by providing economic benefits to the regime supporters. That reliance on economic rents provides strong political rents and lowers opportunities for the development of viable political oppositions.

Chapter 1

Economic Sanctions: An Overview

This chapter summarizes the extant literature on sanctions. The focus is on the evidence of sanction effectiveness that has led to their current popular use. Examined are ways to quantify sanction effectiveness historically and a discussion, if offered, of the applicability of those methods today.

Theoretical Background

The term "economic sanctions" refers to restrictions on trade and international financial assistance (Carter, 1987). Today, economic sanctions are at the forefront of international diplomacy. Their use as a means of achieving foreign policy goals has grown in popularity since the end of the Cold War (al-Roubaie and Elali, 1995; Dashti-Gibson et al., 1997; Hart, 2000). This growth is mainly due to the fact that sanctions are an alternative to military intervention. Other reasons for the popular use of sanctions today are: (1) a post–World War II awareness of the human cost of war; (2) the growing interdependence on the international economy, which has made nations more vulnerable to trade disruptions; and (3) the end of the Cold War, which has made more countries vulnerable to Western economic pressure (Rowe, 2000; Winkler, 1999).

Economic sanctions are "the deliberate, government-inspired withdrawal or threat of withdrawal, of customary trade or financial relations" (Hufbauer et al., 2009: 3). The "sender" is the country that is the primary originator of the sanctions. The "target" is the country that is the object of the sanctions (Hufbauer et al., 2009: 44). The four main types of trade limitations are: "(a) restrictions on the flow of goods, (b) restrictions on the flow of services, (c) restrictions on the flow of money, and (d) control of markets themselves in order to reduce or nullify the target's chance of gaining access to them" (Miyagawa, 1992: 16).

Sanctions may be intended to compel the target country to change its policies or government. They may be used as tools of punishment against the target country in two ways. One is when sanctions are implemented against the target country for specific policies it has enacted within its borders. Another way that sanctions can be used as a diplomatic tool of punishment is when their benefits are meant for specific policy outcomes in the sender nation. Sender countries can employ sanctions in order to demonstrate their opposition to the target country's policies in regard to specific domestic constituents, its citizens at large, other potential targets, and the international community (Carter, 1987).

As a leader in world affairs, the United States often imposes sanctions on less powerful countries. In many of these instances, the tactic is a credibility tool intended to signal the government's position to both domestic and international audiences. America uses sanctions to both demonstrate its power and uphold confidence in its position as a world leader. A combination of increasingly combative international pressures and political polarization on the domestic front compels the government to continuously prove its credibility in this manner. Therefore, the American government operates under an ever-increasing scrutiny of its willingness to lead through action. In this system, any loss of confidence resulting from the imposition of sanctions would be minimal compared to the possible harm that would result from the government's inability or unwillingness to act decisively in the face of international discourse (Hufbauer et al., 2009: 5).

Whang (2011) explains that in America, sanctions have become a convenient tool of political muscle-flexing aimed not at solving international disputes, but rather at showing local constituents and political rivals a strong presidential leadership initiative. The results of Whang's study indicate that the benefits of sanctions are felt directly at home in the form of both political gains and a positive effect on presidential approval ratings. However, it is unclear if America's approval rating increases internationally.

Drury (2001) put it bluntly by stating that domestic political gain is the hard currency behind sanctions. Such gain comes in several forms. As Whang (2011) points out, for the president it can be to the effect of both higher approval ratings and building important political coalitions. This outcome occurs when increasing presidential popularity leads to political entrepreneurship from members of Congress. Attempting to maximize their own political gain, the policy entrepreneurs show willingness to ingratiate themselves with a popular president. In the process, partnerships that can lead to building valuable political capital are forged, fostered, and cultivated. This process of building political capital has become very important in today's polarized congressional environment.

In America, economic sanctions can be an immediate tool of presidential legislative action because of the fast track authority rule. Fast track augments the president's power delegated to the office under Article I, Section 8 of the Constitution to conduct international trade disputes with other nations. The ambiguity of the statement puts sanctions under that scope, because they affect the direct trade of American goods and services with the sanctioned nation. Due to their authority to sign executive orders for the implementation of sanctions, presidents do not need congressional approval to impose sanctions as they see fit. The only exception is made in cases addressing disputes that deal with direct threats to national security. In those cases, the proposed sanctions are voted on by Congress within ninety days and they are either approved or rejected as proposed, without the ability of Congress to change specific terms (Kang and Greene, 1997). This provision is a safeguard against the lobbying efforts of domestic businesses that would be inadvertently hurt by the imposition of new sanctions. While it may seem like a rather long time for the deliberation of matters of national security, 90 days is considered a fairly short time period for the US Congress to act on anything, especially in the current climate of congressional partisan infighting that often leads to ideological standoffs. Kirshner (2005) argues that this polarized environment allows the president to conduct negotiations in a virtual absence of checks and balances. Both the awareness that Congress will have to vote within ninety days with the possibility of not having made any amendments, and additionally the strong possibility that even if Congress does not approve the sanctions the president will still be able to enact them by evoking the "failure to act" rule,gives presidents significant freedom to choose both the diplomatic issues and the nations with which to engage (Kaempfer and Marks, 1993). The failure to act rule allows the president to sign legislation through an executive order if he or she deems the issue to have implications for national security, even if Congress does not support the legislation. The overwhelming concern here is that, in this day and age, national security implications have become subjective, and therefore anything can become fair game for evoking the failure to act rule. The ambiguity of this provision put in place in an environment of increasing international interdependence provides a platform for augmenting presidential power. Therefore, it becomes foolish for a president not to implement sanctions. It is an immediate, easily publicized, powerful platform for showing leadership, building political capital, and creating coalitions. The United States is not alone in embracing the popular use of sanctions. The United Nation's Security Council has also increasingly deployed sanctions toward applying diplomatic pressure, mainly because sanctions are an easy and low-cost alternative to employing military force.

However, the effect of sanctions internationally is unclear. Recent studies show that their failure rate is relatively high. Sanctions, overwhelmingly, fail to produce their intended results, mostly because they seldom cause a change in the overall pattern of behavior of political leaders in targeted nations. Rather, sanctions can lead to unintended negative humanitarian consequences for the populations they intend to help. They are generally the marginalized and oppressed members of the targeted nation societies (de Jonge Oudraat, 2010). For these and many other reasons, there exists a disagreement over the use of economic sanctions today. Many scholars debate whether sanctions are even an effective means of achieving foreign policy goals (Galtung, 1967; de Jonge Oudraat, 2010; Doxey, 1971; Kaempfer and Lowenberg, 1988; Marinov, 2005; Pape, 1997).

The general theory of economic sanctions proposes that sanctions would result in economic hardships, which would lead to political instability, and the ultimate result would be local government compliance with the sender government's demands (Galtung, 1967). According to this theory, the main goal of economic sanctions is to lower aggregate welfare of a targeted state by reducing international trade. The justification is that the importance of trade has become so strong that it is a viable motivator to put pressure on a target government to the degree that it would change its political behavior (Pape, 1997). Therefore, the economic effect of sanctions is the most important predictor of their success (Dashti, Davis and Radcliff, 1997; Pape, 1997; Drury, 1998; Hart, 2000).

Supporting evidence of the theory has been found by Morgan and Schwebach (1997) and more recently by Hufbauer et al. (2009), who argue that often sanctions have an impact when they establish a significant level of economic hardship. A vein of research has found that in some cases measures of GDP growth, amount of international trade and capital, and FDI flows decline following the imposition of economic sanctions, while measures of unemployment, inflation, and debt rise (Manby, 1992; LeoGrande, 1996; Gibbons, 1999; Hufbauer and Oegg, 2003; Allen, 2008).

The degree to which sanctions affect the target economy depends on the target's vulnerability to changes in trade with respect to capital flows, and foreign assets flows, as well as the transaction costs associated with the target's response. Transaction costs of sanction response are the effort and resources governments must spend in finding alternative to the sender nation trading partners.[1] The uniqueness of the target's exports, the level of global demand for the target's goods and services, and the target's ability to evade sanctions, define the target's transaction costs of finding alternative trading partners (Askari et al., 2005).

Special attention has been placed on foreign asset flows with respect to foreign direct investment (FDI). Hufbauer and Oegg (2003) find that on average, sanctions resulting in a 10 percent loss in FDI stock reduce a target country's GDP by approximately 6 percent. FDI receives special attention in sanction research, in relation to foreign aid, for example, because of its interconnectivity with all trade activity. Even without an explicit ban on foreign investment, restrictions on other types of trade might cause additional indirect investment outcomes by creating an environment of political uncertainty. Political uncertainty is found to be a major deterrent of future FDI (Lensink and Morrissey, 2006).

Some research suggests that economic sanctions succeed by causing conflict or political turmoil in the target country (Kaempfer and Lowenberg, 1988; Marinov, 2005; Nossal, 1989). Conflict is defined as creating divisions between the elite and the general population, among the elites, or among both (Olson, 1979). Such divisions assist the sender in destabilizing the regime, resulting in a supposed change in leadership. This is the desired outcome, but is in fact the anomaly in real world outcomes. In most cases, conflict results and creates enough internal instability to encourage the target to bargain with the sender (Marinov, 2005). An argument also exists that even if sanctions do not result in a change in behavior of the target, they can still be considered successful if their main goal is to serve the symbolic function of signaling the sender's disapproval of the target's behavior and policies (Hovi et al., 2005).

Despite the high failure rate, economic sanctions have been successful in some cases. Links have been made between sanctions and the overthrow of Rafael Trujillo in the Dominican Republic in 1961, Salvador Allende in Chile in 1973, Idi Amin in Uganda in 1979, and Jean-Claude Duvalier in Haiti in 1986, and hastening the end of apartheid in South Africa (Carter, 1987). Case studies have illustrated the successful economic impact of sanctions in Nicaragua, South Africa, Iraq, India, and Pakistan that did not necessarily result in the overthrow of dictators, but still contributed to reaching the diplomatic goals of the United States. For example, in 1981 the United States imposed economic sanctions against Nicaragua that blocked trade and suspended foreign aid. The costs of the Contra War in the late 1970s and the economic policies adopted by the Sandinistas had already contributed to the country's poor economic conditions, and the addition of sanctions had a significant effect in causing further economic hardship. LeoGrande (1996) shows that as a result of sanctions in 1985, Nicaragua's GDP had decreased by 5.9 percent and inflation had increased dramatically. By 1988, its GDP had fallen by one-third and the standard of living decreased significantly. In South Africa, Manby (1992) estimates that economic sanctions led to a 7 percent drop in imports between 1985 and 1989. For the period between 1985–1990, sanctions and disinvestment cost the country approximately $20 billion.

Al-Roubaie and Elali (1995) show that sanctions against Iraq resulted in a 9 percent decrease in GDP. The direct impacts were reflected in decreased export earnings, decreased national income, an increase in unemployment, and increases in the price of goods and services. In 1998, the United States imposed economic sanctions on India and Pakistan. Morrow and Carrierre (1999) find that during the first few months following the imposition of sanctions, there was a reduction in capital flows to India. In Pakistan, private inflows ceased almost entirely and the Pakistani rupee depreciated significantly. The authors show that GDP growth decreased by 3 percent and the stock market fell by more than 34 percent when compared to other Asian markets.

As with most diplomatic tools, when it comes to sanctions it is seldom an all or nothing scenario (Hovi et al., 2005; Hufbauer and Oegg, 2003). In a comprehensive study on the effectiveness of economic sanctions, Hufbauer et al. (2009) examine 174 cases of economic sanctions in order to determine when they result in the achievement of foreign policy goals. The authors find sanctions to be at least somewhat successful in 34 percent of the examined cases. The general findings of the literature on sanction success conclude that the likelihood of success depends on country specific conditions such as the economic health and stability of the target, the relationship between sender and target, regime type, and the types of policy goals sought by the sender (Dashti, Davis and Radcliff, 1997; Drury, 1998; Hart, 2000; Miljkovic, 2002; Hufbauer et al., 2009).

Theoretical Gaps From Changing Realities

The period after World War II saw major growth in the development of the academic literature on sanctions. As noted, their increased rate of implementation, particularly after the Cold War, has led to some researchers questioning their newly popular use. The concerns mainly have to do with the effect of unilateral sanctions, that is, sanctions imposed by one nation, given the impacts of globalization. As early as the 1970s, and to this day, arguments are put forth that as a tool of diplomacy, the efficacy of sanctions may be diminishing in an increasingly globalized world because the economic leverage of any one country, even that of the United States—historically the largest economy in the world—has decreased (Doxey, 1971; Pape, 1997). As economies become more interdependent, it becomes easier for nations that are being sanctioned to minimize penalty impact by finding alternative trading partners and investment sources.[2] Such partnerships become viable options to trading with America because of the fairly recent aggregate economic growth in the developing world.

Historically, the world economic balance had been centered in the West with America's power dictating international trade policy and flows. However, since 2002, the impressive growth of the economies of the East and South has changed global economic power dynamics (Anguelov, 2014; Kaplan, 2010, Zakaria, 2011). As a result, increasing numbers of studies have focused on the limitations of sanctions. Many of these studies offer evidence not only of limitations, but also of sanction ineffectiveness (Choi and Luo, 2013; Early, 2009, 2011; Kaempfer, Lowenberg, and Mertens, 2004; Kozhanov, 2011; Peksen, 2009; Whang, 2010; Wood, 2008).

Whang (2010) examines data on sanctions, mostly championed by the United States, imposed between 1903 and 2002 in a multitude of nations, and finds that the overall success rate has been very low. The main reason is, as de Jonge Oudraat (2010) succinctly puts it, sanctions do not cause change in the political behavior of the governments in target nations. For such a change in political behavior to occur, the ruling regimes must feel challenged by local political descent against the policies that have resulted in the sanctions. A clear opposition must develop and that opposition must gain critical mass in popularity. However, because sanctions disproportionately mobilize the political power of the ruling regime, that scenario almost always fails to come to fruition.

An important reason for this failure is that even the most repressive regimes have local support. When sanctions are imposed, those in power feel threatened and respond by augmenting their level of repression in an effort to stabilize their ruling position. Government leaders increase the protection for core supporters who aid in suppressing popular dissent. Wood (2008) explains this dynamic and offers supporting empirical evidence of the proliferation of such behavior in all sanctioned nations in the 1970s, 80s, and 90s. A unifying feature in those examples of sanctioned nations is the presence of a government leader with a strong personality, be that a dictator or a popularly elected figure. Through charismatic rhetoric such leaders can, and as Wood (2008) explains often do, in fact use sanctions as opportunities for self-promotion. Standing up against the sanction, the sender nation is presented as an act of patriotism and bravery. Because of this dynamic, when a leader enjoys established popular support, sanctions simply become tools for strengthening that support. Kaempfer,

Lowenberg and Mertens (2004: 40) describe such support as the "rally around the flag effect."

Taking into account the events of the recent past, including international diplomatic contention as a result of the tragic events of September 11, 2001, Choi and Luo (2013) offer alarming, but very compelling evidence that in the current climate of international terrorism, sanctions actually beget more terrorism. The reason is that the impact of a sanction falls most intensely on the poor, and so often sanctions can lead to increased levels of desperation and a heightened propensity to engage in crime and terrorism. In a related line of analysis concerning rogue political action in sanctioned nations, Peksen (2009) offers evidence that sanctions also negatively impact freedom of the press in targeted nations, which is one of the many liberties they are supposed to improve. The author shows that the stronger and more multilateral the sanctions are, the more negative their impact is on overall freedom of the press. The explanation for this counterintuitive outcome again lies on the ability of local governments to present their contentious policies as patriotic acts of defying foreign imperialism. It is through the means of propaganda and impassioned rhetoric created to justify their policies that targeted governments use the manipulation of the media to control unrest as economic conditions deteriorate. Any opinions or information viewed as divergent from the official local government position is seen as a serious threat and is dealt with forcefully.

As Whang (2010) explains, the overall conclusion that can be drawn from the literature on sanctions is that they are more likely to be successful when the issue at stake is important, when the sender and target are allied, when the target's domestic institutions are more democratic to begin with, and when the target's economy is dependent on the sender's. Increasingly, those assumptions are being challenged. Today the issues that result in sanction deployment—such as the national sovereignty of the Ukraine, the nuclear capabilities of Iran and North Korea, or the genocide in Syria—are very important and yet the imposed sanction measures in all of those cases seem to be frustratingly ineffective. Furthermore, in not a single of these cases are the sender and the target allied in anyway. If anything, just the opposite is happening in the magnitude of ideological discourse and therefore, level of diplomatic alliance. It can also be said that in Russia, Syria, Iran, North Korea, and Cuba the domestic institutions are very much non-democratic. But most importantly, as Whang (2010) states—the importance of economic dependence on the sender nation is challenged. The mitigation of economic dependence on the sender nation is explained by the "black knight" phenomenon. Black knights are nations that offer alternative economic partnerships to targeted nations, and in that way, limit the effect the sanctions have on the targets.

For example, Kozhanov (2011) explains that the main factors undermining American sanction against Iran, are the trade partnerships Iran is cultivating with its regional Islamic partners, Russia, and China. Not only are those two nations undermining the sanctions, but also their defiance serves as a signal to other nations. The reassurance that there are alternative trade options gives such nations impetus to seek tactics to skirt sanctions that can range from outright defiance to less subtle evasive maneuvers. Such maneuvers can take the form of conducting business with firms in sanctioned countries through intermediaries and international affiliates. This ability to shift economic interaction through lengthy and fragmented international production and trading networks even allows firms from the sender nation to circumvent sanctions. In the case of Iran, American conglomerates like Halliburton, Coca-Cola, and General Electric continued to do business with the country through their subsidiaries in other nations despite the sanctions (Kozhanov, 2011).

Today's black knights are an established and powerful force. They are growing the fastest in both economic and political clout, and they are showing increasing defiance towards sender nations. Most importantly, they are strategic in their defiance. Black knights understand that sanctions offer the opportunity to seize valuable market shares, establish preferred production and political platforms, and in that way cartelize entire industries. As an example, Quraeshi, Luqmani, and Yavas (2013) offer detailed description of instances in which sanctions harm American business interests as well their domestic and international partners. That negative impact often has political ramifications, and therefore sanctions cause negative political effects with spillover characteristics. Chapters 2, 3, and 4 track that process and explain its lasting impacts.

Enter the "Black Knights" . . . and the "Gray Knights"

In analyzing black knight behavior, the main focus for Askari et al. (2005) is rooted in transaction costs. Transaction costs are associated with operational difficulties encountered by firms throughout the conduction of business. They increase in cases where firms exert both time and effort on establishing new operations, finding new customers, and convincing these customers to purchase their goods and services. Therefore, transaction costs mainly arise during the expansion of production, innovation initiatives, and market proliferation. The costs are contingent to novelty—be it the novelty of innovation with respect to producing new things, or the novelty of changing market scopes and ranges. During such instances of new production and market activity, at the firm level expenditure of time and effort has a direct link to loss of revenue (Williamson, 1973, 1981). Much like in economic analysis, the explanation of transaction cost in political behavior associated with sanctions focuses on the ability of a target to minimize the transaction costs of finding alternative sources of trade and finance (Askari et al., 2005). A significant decrease in such transaction costs lowers a target nation's vulnerability to economic sanctions.

As already noted, a core factor that can aid in lowering the transaction costs of searching for trade alternatives is the presence of one or more black knights, which are third party nations eager to provide assistance to the target country (Drury, 1998; Hufbauer et al., 2009). Significant research has been devoted to employing the black knight concept as a variable since the seminal work of Hufbauer, Schott and Elliot (1990), in which it is coded (Chan, 2009; Croco and Teo, 2005; Drezner, 1999; Lektzian and Souva, 2007; McLean and Whang, 2010; Nooruddin, 2002; Pape, 1997; Potocki, 2011; Slavov, 2007). The first recorded instances of nations acting as black knights date back as early as the 1950s. Since then, the incidence of black knight behavior has notably increased (Early, 2009, 2011).

Black knights have been defined as fairly significant trade partners that, to some degree, must be considered adversarial to the sender nation. That adversity could be based on the underlying issues behind the sanctions, or it could be based on other existent diplomatic tensions. In the case, that these nations are actively engaged in diplomatic discourse with the sender nation, a black knight will use sanctions as an opportunity for pugilism, looking to augment its subversion against the sender nation.

For instance, during the Cold War it was the Soviet Union that played the role of the black knight leader whose purpose was to counteract American and Western sanctions. However, with its demise, instead of losing support, sanctioned nations have found opportunities to continue defying policies of nonengagement. In certain cases they find opportunities for trade with the sender's supporters. For example, after the dismantling of the Soviet Union, firms in Cuba originating from Canada, Mexico, France, and Spain, moved in to fill the void, bringing with them "western" technology, modernization, and a higher level of efficiency in operations than their previous Russian counterparts had been able to manage (Early, 2009).

These nations also ushered Cuban trade into a free market platform through the establishment of joint ventures and the creation of an internationally compatible financial system. Previously, over 70 percent of Cuban trade had been with the Soviet Union at preferential prices and barters. The USSR conducted the majority of trade in such a way, shielding its

Eastern Bloc partners from global currency pressures and ensuring convenient industrial development that would most closely complement its own industrial needs. For example, it supplied its partners with metals, energy inputs, and industrial equipment. In Cuba, the bulk of barter exchange came in the form of two products—nickel and citrus. The nickel sustained Cuban metallurgic production, which provided essential employment opportunities for the Cuban manufacturing sector. The citrus exported to the USSR supplemented not only direct consumption, but also employment and development in the Soviet prepared foods and chemical industries as its extracts were used for nondurable production (Leogrande and Thomas, 2002). When Russia's economy was redeveloped in the early 1990s, trade with Cuba decreased significantly. During that time, according to Leogrande and Thomas (2002), Cuba adjusted by allowing foreign direct investment joint ventures where up to 49 percent of ownership could be with the foreign investor. This policy change led to the attraction of Spanish, Mexican, Canadian, and Italian MNCs in manufacturing and services. Also, Japanese and Belgian financial firms joined the well established Canadian financial firms that had chosen to set up operations in Cuba during the Cold War. With their support Cuba was able to renegotiate its foreign debt, increase its borrowing, and ramp up the loss of exports to the former USSR. Since then the Cuban economy as managed to continue its trade expansion by reaching out to other Latin American nations with adversarial US attitudes, such as Venezuela, as well as the larger international market. On October 11, 2014, a *New York Times* editorial explained the legacy of Cuban trade augmentation, offering a chronological list of the policy changes toward trade liberalization the Cuban government has taken, as well as data on trade cooperation and partnerships with nations other than the United States. The article uses these policy developments as examples for a call to end sanctions.[3] On December 17, 2014 US president Barack Obama and Cuban president Raul Castro made the announcement that both nations are to normalize relations. The embargo is set to end, and President Obama specifically stated in his speech that economic sanctions against Cuba had been ineffective and it is for that reason that America will pursue alternative paths for diplomatic solutions in its relationship with Cuba.[4]

With respect to black knight nations in the context of Cold War legacies, after the dismantling of the Soviet Union, its trade relationships largely remained. During the transition period of the 1990s, the former Soviet Republics remained tightly linked economically, as did the former members of the entire Eastern Bloc (Aslund, 2002). As their economies restructured, their natural trade partnerships relinked to new sources of commerce, and general economic growth ensued in the recent past, with

Russia emerging as a strong successor to the former USSR, both ideologically and economically. So today the former Soviet Union is back as Russia, acting both as a black knight, and as an extension of its former Soviet adversarial legacy. In recent years, Russia has systematically and predictably opposed many international US initiatives that deal with security and economic issues. It supports Iran and North Korea in their nuclear quests; it supports Syria in its internal dealings with the antitotalitarian opposition; and has applied economic and diplomatic pressure on former Eastern Bloc nations to prevent them from joining NATO (Charap, 2014; Shleifer and Treisman, 2011).

Under presidents Putin and Medvedev, Russia has defined three main policy objectives. First and most importantly is boosting economic growth (Shleifer and Treisman, 2011: 125). The other two objectives are: (1) the fostering of friendly relations with neighboring states that by definition are former communist nations undergoing a period of transition, and (2) improving internal security with respect to minimizing separatist ethnic sentiments that lead to local Islamic acts of terrorism. The first policy objective of achieving economic growth can help in tackling the remaining two goals.

Former communist nations maintain strong trade connections with Russia. In many cases they enjoy preferential trade agreements in commodity exchange that allow for importing Russian energy inputs at subsidized prices (Åslund, 1994, 2002; Moraski and Giurcanu, 2013; Sachs et al., 1994). This fact led to the natural gas disputes with Ukraine that escalated in 2009. As the major tenant of the dispute, Russia demanded that Ukraine stop reselling the natural gas that was purchased under preferential status to West European nations at world market prices (Hubert and Ikonnikova, 2011). Insiders posit however, that Russia did not exactly demand that Ukraine stop the resell. Arguably more strategically, it instead demanded a portion of the profits (Aron, 2013; Schmidt-Felzmann, 2011). The Ukrainian refusal resulted in a standoff. Justification of the Ukrainian position was the explanation that its overall economic well-being depended on that dynamic because it was still a transitioning economy that needed such crutch policies. The West supported Ukraine, hoping to not only demonstrate good will, but to aid toward overtures to have Ukraine join NATO and the European Union—two outcomes that Russia strongly opposes (Charap, 2014).

On the heels of the territorial disputes of 2014, Russia and Ukraine reached a deal on the pricing of natural gas and the repayment of the gas debt in October of that year.[5] The fact that a deal was reached after months of economic sanction activity is worth explaining with respect to sanction effectiveness, particularly when the target is one of the world's most notorious black knights.

In February 2014, internal Ukrainian unrest ousted President Victor Yanukovych—a pro-Russian leader with totalitarian policies on economic, political, and social issues. On the pretext of protecting the well-being of ethnic Russians in the Ukraine, Russia sent military troops to the border region of Crimea. Under criticism of aggression, Russia staged a referendum asking the population of Crimea if it wanted to join Russia. The official results, which the West does not accept as legitimate, indicated that 96 percent of Crimean voters agreed to become federal subjects of Russia.

Both America and the European Union disputed the outcome and threatened to use strong economic sanctions in retaliation, unless Russian forces retreated from Crimea. Stating the American resolve to put economic pressure on Russia, President Barack Obama said at a press conference on July 20, 2014 that if Russia continued its "current path, the costs on Russia will continue to grow."[6] Russia continued in its cause, successfully defying the mostly symbolic at first, then gradually increasing in severity sanctions, while America and the European Union did not follow up with their threat to cause significant economic damage.

When it came to the actual threat of a cold dark winter, after months of sanction muscle flexing, political sanction rhetoric diminished. Russia did not make any concessions in its aggression toward Crimea. America and Europe on the other hand did, by way of abandoning their critical position of the legitimacy of the results of the Crimea separation referendum in favor of efforts to halt the further deterioration of relations with Russia.[7] Emboldened, Russia renewed its military demonstrations, which many caution can mean preparation for a future invasion. On November 12, 2014 NATO officials confirmed allegations by Ukrainian military leaders that Russian tanks and man power were crossing into Ukraine despite international accords. The Ukrainians charged that Russia was preparing for a military offensive.[8]

Put simply, Europe and America agreed to accept the legitimacy of the election results and in turn allow Russia to keep power over Crimea. Europe brokered a deal to directly help insolvent Ukraine with IMF funding to handle its natural gas debt burden to Russia. This deal ensures that gas pipelines going through its territories toward the rest of Europe will keep flowing at current volumes and prices until the end of March 2015.

It is not just natural gas, but gas and oil dependence that give Russia its power over Europe. Since 2007, 67 percent of natural gas consumed in Europe has come from Russia, as has 69 percent of oil (Shleifer and Treisman, 2011). In the fragile and stagnant European economy, such dependence affects not just the consumption through fuel use in heating and transportation, but in all economic activity. Decreasing access to fuel can result in rising energy prices. Rising energy prices mean rising production costs—an outcome Europe cannot bear in the face of modern global competition for its manufacturing exports.

The above mentioned dynamic is an example of how energy exports are the most powerful tool of modern Russian diplomacy. Much of the total energy consumption in the transitional economies of the new European Union is dependent on the preferential price policies and trading platforms that remain unchanged from the time of the Cold War. For example, 48 percent of natural gas consumed in Poland comes from Russian imports. In Bulgaria, the figures average over 97 percent. The total natural gas consumption of the Baltic States comes directly from Russian sources (Shleifer and Treisman, 2011).

Modern Russian economic growth is contingent on the country's ability to expand the number of markets for its natural gas and oil exports (Shleifer and Treisman, 2011). Unsurprisingly, its main overtures are toward ideological allies such as China and India, but they additionally target also the rapidly growing Eastern European nations that have been newly admitted as members of the European Union. By default, Russian and European economies intersect in Eastern Europe, giving Russia considerable diplomatic power. The relationship has grown in reciprocity, as Russia is in turn a major market for EU products. As the Russian economy grows, so does Russian consumption, opening new possibilities for exporting to Russia. For example, over 300,000 tons of dairy products are exported from EU nations to Russia. Overall agricultural exports to Russia totaled $16 billion in 2013,which is 12 times the volume American market options offer.[9] In the recent sanction standoff, the West was made to evaluate the scope and severity of sanctions against Russia for its invasion of Crimea, forcing Europe to face the fact that it could not find alternative markets for its dairy exports and many other products. For such reasons, the sanction dynamic was one of rhetoric and threat, with little actual legislative action. Legislative actions came in the form of targeted sanctions, such as visa bans and asset freezes of certain individuals and their business holdings.

The European Union's main website offers a list of the legislated actions taken against Russia. It includes a "reevaluation" component of bilateral trade summits. In terms of direct economic sanctions, there is a prohibition of exports. However, it only applies to certain sectors, and only if those exports originate in Crimea and Sevastopol without authorization of the Ukrainian government.[10] Overall, Russian exports to the EU continue unrestricted. The visa bans only affect a hundred or so individuals, and there is no clear evidence of any impact of the supposed asset freezes of the counted, but not named, 23 business entities.

As the discussions concerning the sanction stretched from the spring to fall of 2014, the rhetoric of observers, journalists, and analysts focused mostly on the limitations of sanction options. The trivial by comparison implementation of travel bans, suppression of specific investments in Russian state-owned financial enterprises, as well as the seizing of arms sales were accompanied with a great deal of showmanship, especially from the United States. The West spoke in retaliation with these actions, criticizing Russian aggression and vowing to not allow the invasion of sovereign territories, but it did little to act. Economic concerns of European nations took precedence and the diplomatic action became one of "urging" the Russian government to stop its military involvement in Crimea.[11]

With the magnification of globalization, the redevelopment of the Soviet Union into the rapidly growing and increasingly pugilistic Russia, the equally impressive growth of China, and more and more examples of Western allies either not supporting or choosing to support sanctions in name only, are becoming more evident. Such instances of nonsupport can take a direct form, as in the previously mentioned Cuban example, where most notably Canada—the US's largest trading partner and diplomatic supporter—chose not to join in the sanctions. Also, indirect nonsupport can occur when nations exploit sanction loopholes. Governments can officially impose sanctions, but vagueness in legislative language or exemptions can provide opportunities for firms to circumvent actual implementation. In these instances, a new stratum of "knights" emerges—those that are not all black, but rather gray. Gray knights can be allies who outwit or get around sanctions to engage in trade with the receiver nation. Gray knight behavior is evident in the case of Iran.

In 2006, the US imposed sanctions that had to do with the sale of oil, but failed to specify restrictions on the sale of equipment or "investments" in equipment for the Iranian oil and gas industry or petrochemical plants (Khozanov, 2011). The Iran and Libya Sanctions Act (ILSA) of 1996 permitted the US President to take measures against foreign companies that invested more than $20 million during a 12-month period in the development of Iranian oil and gas fields. However, the act excluded the sale of industrial equipment for oil refineries and petro-chemical processing from its provisions. Therefore, companies from Western Europe continued to sell equipment to Iran, rendering the goals of ISLA fruitless. The specific aim of ISLA is stated as to impede the development of the Iranian oil and petrochemical sectors. These two sectors are the backbone of the Iranian economy, and its closest link to the energy sector, which was the official reason for Iran's quest for nuclear technology. According to Khozanov

(2011), who offers a thorough chronology of the Iranian sanction rounds, the United States failed to persuade the Western European nations that had joined the sanctions to stop exploiting the language loopholes and stick to the sanctions by not selling industrial equipment to Iran. Even when Western European nations agreed, their East European counterparts, who often imported the equipment from Western Europe, did not. Equipment sales continued, as did the steady growth of Iranian oil and petroleum exports. In 2011, the US and EU agreed to impose a new round of sanctions with stricter provisions. The sanctions went into effect in early 2012 and according to Van de Graaf (2013) had an immediate impact because oil exports fell by $40 billion by the end of 2013. However, it is unclear if it was the sanctions that led to the drop in revenue or the overall trend of falling global oil sales and prices. According to the Monthly Oil Market Report,[12] from Organization of Petroleum Exporting Countries' (OPEC) between 2012 and 2013, overall oil exports decreased from an average of 32,000 barrels a day to less than 28,000. At the same time, the price of Brent Crude also decreased from an average of $111 per barrel in 2012 to $104 by the end of 2013.[13] Based on those averages, Bloomberg.com estimates that Iranian oil export revenues fell by 30 percent because of lower prices and slowing global demand.[14] The analysis says nothing of a decrease in revenue as a result of tighter sanctions.

The cases of Iran and Russia are just two recent frustrating outcomes of the ineffectiveness of sanctions. More evidence of current day sanction failures comes from areas in which China, America's main modern day economic counterpart, thwarts US sanctions. One of the strongest examples of black knight behavior comes from China's continued support of the military regime in Myanmar during the 20 years of American and Western Europe imposed sanctions. Since the onset of sanctions in 1988, China had been a supporter of the military regime and officially adopted a "good neighbor" policy towards the country (Kudo, 2006). Among that policy's major benefits for China were[15]—the signing of extensive trade and arms agreements, and the securing of exclusive development rights to natural resource projects. In return, China backed Myanmar diplomats in supranational governance disputes at the United Nations by deflecting criticisms of the military regime and its policies (Roy, 2005; Haacke, 2006; Rarick, 2007). In addition, at the time Russia also expressed support for the military government of Myanmar (Rarick, 2007), and since then has increasingly shown an interest in deepening economic and political partnerships with the country. These two major world powers were not the sole perpetrators of such black and gray knight actions, as other Asian nations, including Thailand, India, Singapore, and Japan, continued to strengthen diplomatic and business relations with Myanmar while

American sanctions were in place (Khine, 2008; Steinberg, 2001; Roy, 2005; Seekins, 2007; Egreteau, 2008).

The United States had urged these countries to join the sanctions against the regime, but they defied American pressures and continued to pursue their own economic agendas (Allen, 2008; Egreteau, 2008; Haacke, 2006; Khine, 2008; Kudo, 2006; Steinberg, 2007). In 2007, Myanmar formally reestablished ties with North Korea after signing an agreement to renew diplomatic relations. Former US Secretary of State Hillary Clinton expressed concern over military links between the two countries after evidence emerged that the military junta may be trying to acquire nuclear technology from North Korea.[16] After the lift on sanctions, it is evident that those friendships continue to drive Myanmar's international trade.

The Human Rights Watch offers an examination of the lack of political reform in Myanmar in light of the fact that the 2014 East Asia Summit was held in the country. Leaders of the Association of Southeast Asian Nations (ASEAN) and other Asian countries conducted a series of meetings in October 2014 to discuss regional strategic growth initiatives with respect to economic and political cooperation. The point of the Human Rights Watch story was to urge world leaders to pressure the Myanmar government to follow through with implementing the reforms it had promised, such as revising the 2008 constitution that was passed under the former military regime.[17] The constitution was designed and implemented under Thein Sein, who for more than a decade has been on the world's list of top dictators. He is now the newly elected president of Myanmar who continues to defy local efforts to amend the constitution he created. In 2011, championed by strong complaints from the Indonesian Foreign Ministry, ASEAN delayed its final decision to allow Myanmar to resume the 2014 ASEAN chairmanship. The official statement declared that it would be unwise to give the chairmanship to Myanmar until genuine democratic reforms were implemented.[18] The delay in decision was a symbolic gesture of appeasement mostly for Indonesia's sake. As a signal of disapproval to Thein Sein, it only backfired, showing that he could unscathingly stand up to international pressures.

Myanmar assumed the ASEAN chairmanship without making any signs toward implementing policy reforms. The mere gesture that Rangoon was the chosen site for the summit, despite the fact that its government had not complied with international accords to implement institutional changes, is a telling sign of the efficacy and legacy of sanctions. It indicates international support for the current economic policies and governance of Myanmar. The issue is that those policies, and those that are presently governing the country, are the same as during the sanction years. Members of the old regime hold over 80 percent of parliamentary seats. Since the time the sanctions were lifted and because the Burmese constitution requires 75 percent majority to implement new legislation, no such legislation has officially been passed that would lead to improvements in institutional, business, or human right issues.[19] The Human Rights Watch charges that post sanctions, the regime continues to act in a business as usual manner, consistent with its past policies and unflinching in resolve. Despite these facts, Myanmar was allowed to lead the ASEAN summit, indicating that ASEAN member nations are either compliant with the current lack of progress, or even worse, support it. If indeed the interpretation is that ASEAN nations support existing institutional arrangements in Myanmar, then the question is why? A possible explanation for such, as stated, "support" can be traced to strong direct economic benefits. Twenty years of sanctions have allowed Myanmar's regional partners uniquely protected positions in its resource-rich market. During the US led sanctions much wealth was created in trade with Myanmar, and the benefactors of that wealth seem eager to continue holding on to the benefits sanctions have provided.

Chapter 2

Myanmar—20 Years of Sanctions and Their Lasting Effect

NikolayA nguelov andK ristinB ryant

This chapter examines why US sanctions against Myanmar did not produce results for 20 years and continue to make an impact four years after they were lifted. That impact is political, manifesting in the government's continued unwillingness to comply with international demands, even if those demands were the very conditions for dismantling the sanctions.

Sanctions in a One-Way Power Balance World

Myanmar has been a military dictatorship since 1962, when General Ne Win overthrew the democratically elected prime minister U Nu (Steinberg, 2001). After gaining independence from Britain in 1948, Myanmar, then officially named Burma, started off as a parliamentary democracy. Ethnic divisions and the domination of the ethnic Burmans over the 135 other minorities in the country made a rocky start for the new nation. The largest of those minority groups—the Karen, Shan, and Rakhine—formed a vocal opposition to the domineering Burman policies that discriminated against them in politics, as well as in social and economic opportunities. The strife came to a bloody clash in 1962, when General Win led the first in a series of military coups. The parliamentary government and leaders of ethnic minority political groups were arrested and jailed. For ten years the country was run as a dictatorship with disregard for its constitution and with repression of ethnic peoples, particularly in the border regions.

In 1972, General Win allowed for peace talks with political parties and ethnic rebel groups, but when the talks turned into political action, he unilaterally rejected them to form a multiparty system again. Then, in 1974, he forcefully nationalized all private firms and established the Burma Socialist Programme Party (BSPP).[1] The party became the sole political body in the Burmese parliament, backed by the 1972 draft of the constitution, written by the general himself. Ne Win abolished any democratic features of the extant constitution and his new draft announced the beginning of the "Burmese Way of Socialism," redirecting diplomatic overtures toward the Soviet Union (Ganesan, 2001).

The policies in the new constitution legitimized the absence of free elections, dismissed the need for equal political and social representation of ethnic minorities, and cemented the power of the military by concentrating all legislative and economic activity in its hands. Economically, the policies were isolationist and restrictive to foreign investment, turning Burma into a command state (Maung, 1970). Such policies typically exist in postcolonial governments in the region as a legacy of anti-imperialist sentiments (Ganesan, 1999, 2001; Jewitt, 1995). The sentiment driving this policy direction is best summed up in this quote from the major indictment of the Revolutionary Council:

> The Union was dominated by the feudalists for over a thousand years, by the foreign empirialists for over a hundred years, and by the landlords and capitalists after it had gained independence. (Maung, 1970: 538)

This statement explains the general ideological aversion to capitalism and foreign economic exploitation. Such an ideology is a legacy that defined most socialist transitions in postcolonial nations (Maung, 1970). With the transition to a command economy, foreign ownership was disregarded. However, selling to foreigners was not.

Contrary to the passionate antiforeign rhetoric of the Revolutionary Council, Burmese trade patterns at large did not shift toward the Communist world from their historic Western orientation. Trade was not restricted in terms of exports, and the military regime started amassing significant wealth through the exports of teak, rubies, and rice (Stifel, 1971).[2] Stifel (1971) analyzes export patterns and notes that despite the anti-Western government propaganda, exports to the West did not decrease. Overall trade with Communist nations originally increased, but fell down to pre–1962 levels toward the end of the 1960s.

In the 1970s, Burmese exports continued to grow, increasing significantly with India in particular—another nation that had strengthened its ties with the Soviet Union as a result of its British colonial past. The materials exported were now ores, minerals, and lumber, a change from their historical legacy of rice and tropical fruit (Thein, 2004). Imports also increased, primarily consisting of components and parts used in local assembly to create and grow the centrally planned domestic manufacturing sector. These policies did not bode well for the people of the country, but favored the military regime that managed all trade (Thein, 2004). It gave the regime total control of the economy and, in doing so, isolated its profitability from market competition. As is often the case, such policies led to economic hardship for the general population of Burma. Consequently, significant food shortages and general economic destitution led to massive protests in 1988. Students, intellectuals, and monks led the protests. A visible opposition movement emerged and its enigmatic leader Aung San Suu Kyi captured the attention of the world.

A young, energetic woman embodying democratic progress, Suu Kyi headed the National League for Democracy (NLD) party. In the summer of 1988, mass demonstrations calling for democratic reform brought hundreds of thousands to the streets (Rarick, 2006). The military responded to the protests by killing and arresting thousands of participants. By the end of September 1988 a military junta, the State Law and Order Restoration Council (SLORC), was established to rule over the country (Holliday, 2011). Following these events in early 1989, the new military government changed the country's name to Myanmar.

In effect this regime change constituted another military coup, much like the one in 1962. The leaders of the demonstrations were arrested, and many killed. At this time the already strained relations between the United States and Myanmar began to deteriorate further. After holding general elections in 1990, SLORC refused to hand over power to the winning party, Suu Kyi's National League for Democracy, and Suu Kyi was placed under house arrest (Rarick, 2006). In the summer of 2009, Suu Kyi was put on trial and sentenced to 18 additional months of house arrest after a court found her guilty of violating security laws, when a US national swam to her home.[3] Aung San Suu Kyi remained under house arrest until November 13, 2010.[4]

Following the 1988 military coup, the United States refused to recognize SLORC as a legitimate government. America imposed sanctions in the form of an arms embargo, and terminated it moderate nonhumanitarian economic assistance (Steinburg, 2007). These sanctions did little to effect the repressive Myanmar regime. Mounting evidence of human rights abuses and ethnic cleansing led the United States to implement additional sanctions in the 1990s.[5]

In 1989, the Myanmar government had reached cease-fire agreements with most ethnic insurgents. However, along the borders armed ethnic opposition groups remained active. These groups recruited soldiers from the Myanmar military, and were so successful that they lead to significant desertion rates, particularly of ethnic Karen soldiers. The desertions led the junta to break its cease-fire with the separatist Karenni National Progressive Party (KNPP) in 1995. It launched an on-ground military offensive. South (2011) explains that the military attacks had two main goals. One was to prevent further desertions or other internal army dissent by instilling fear in the army's ranks. The other noted goal was to minimize the support KNPP had in local villages. In 1996, the military began brutal attacks, and reports allege that the military forcibly relocated hundreds of villages and tens of thousands of Karenni civilians, committing atrocities such as public retaliatory killings and mass rapes. As a result of these tragic events, US president Bill Clinton signed Executive Order 13047 under the Foreign Appropriations Act. It banned new investments in Myanmar by US companies or individuals. Round two of sanctions began.

Regardless of the new sanctions, the military dictatorship seemed unfazed. It governed the country with little regard for international human rights codes or any rule of law. For example, The Human Rights Watch reported in 2004 that torture of prisoners, extrajudicial killings, forced labor, child labor, and human trafficking were common in Myanmar, where an estimated 70,000 of the country's 350,000–400,000 soldiers were children. The military forcibly recruited most of them.[6] According to the Assistance Association for Political Prisoners in 2009, there were over 2,100 political prisoners, including monks, students, elected members of parliament, and lawyers, in jails throughout Myanmar.[7] It is also argued that under the military dictatorship Myanmar had become a center for organized crime groups involved in the illegal trafficking of humans, drugs, wildlife, gems, timber, and laundered money (Wyler, 2009). The Trafficking in Persons Report published by the US State Department has repeatedly designated Myanmar a "tier 3" state, indicating that the country does not meet minimum standards for combating human trafficking. Then and now, victims are trafficked both internally and regionally, and junta officials have been directly involved in trafficking, forced labor, and the recruitment of child soldiers.[8] Myanmar is also routinely included in the US government's list of major drug transit and illicit drug-producing countries. It is one of the world's top producers of opium, heroin, and methamphetamines. It accounts for 80 percent of all heroin produced in Southeast Asia and is a leading source of heroin destined for the United States. Myanmar is also the second largest producer of opium in the world, after Afghanistan (Wyler, 2009).

Coping with Sanction Resistance

These facts made Myanmar an international adversary to the West, but not to those nations that during the sanction years, and still today, exhibit anti-Western sentiments. Both in terms of Western definitions of human rights and equitable and fare market behavior, certain nations showed support for the repressive military government through diplomatic and economic cooperation.

As already discussed, China had been a supporter of the military regime during the sanction years. It continues to be the major trading partner with Myanmar today. During the most adversarial period of the sanctions, with the highest evidence of abuse and brutality, China continued to back Myanmar's government in all disputes that resulted in UN resolutions (Roy, 2005; Haacke, 2006; Rarick, 2007). After the collapse of the USSR, its successor Russia continued the historic friendly relations with the Myanmar military regime (Rarick, 2007). As already discussed, other major Asian economic powers—Thailand, India, Singapore, and Japan—maintained their diplomatic and business ties with Myanmar while American sanctions were in place, allowing Myanmar to remain and integrate into the Association of Southeast Asian Nations (ASEAN) (Egreteau, 2008; Khine, 2008; Roy, 2005; Seekins, 2007; Steinberg, 2001). All the while, American calls to those nations to join the sanctions went unanswered (Allen, 2008; Egreteau, 2008; Haacke, 2006; Khine, 2008; Kudo, 2006; Steinberg, 2007).

The above-mentioned studies on countries that evaded the sanctions against Myanmar, explain that there are economic incentives for those countries that cannot be easily discounted. For its close Asian neighbors, richly endowed Myanmar offers natural resource input options without comparable substitutes. The proximity and volumes of trade in valuable inputs make neighboring countries eager to take advantage of this reality, in which there is both ease of access to commodities and relatively low costs. Low-cost transportation using the third world infrastructure of developing Asian nations made movement of goods very slow and inefficient (Bougheas, Demetriades, and Morgenroth, 1999). Furthermore, the willingness of the regime to offer beneficial deals to these Asian countries made sourcing products there cost-effective in relation to other countries. These cost savings were of such magnitude, and so effectively used by the Myanmar government as an incentive to attract business from countries willing to stand up to the West, that they made it hard for the West to gain economic cooperation from key Asian nations (Alamgir, 2008; Ewing-Chow, 2006; Gebert, 2013; Shee, 1997; Wyler, 2009).

Myanmar is resource abundant, boasting extensive natural gas fields, teak forests, and mines containing precious gems (Fujita et al., 2009; McCarthy, 2000; Steinberg, 2001; Turnell, 2008). For example, Burmese rubies are so known for their fine quality that they have earned a special classification—pigeon's blood rubies—because of their deep and dense blood-red color. They are the highest quality rubies, and some of the most famous gems exhibited in museums as pieces of world art are made using rubies and other gems from Myanmar. For centuries, the Mogok valley in the upper part of the country has been the world's main source for rubies. It is known as the "Valley of Rubies" and is noted as both the original source of industrial ruby production as well as the only place in the world where "royal" blue sapphires, again named for their unique color, are available (Walsh, 2011; Shor and Weldon, 2009). To this day, of all the rubies mined and commercially used in the world, 90 percent come from the Mogok valley. Thailand imports most of them (Hilson, 2014; Hose and Genser, 2007; Wyler, 2009).

Such natural resources and their large volumes available for commercial development have made access to Burmese commodities important in the manufacturing-intensive regional Asian economy. As Southeast Asia, in particular, moves up in terms of industrialization, the main export categories in Myanmar have changed. Agricultural exports, which traditionally dominated export volumes, have gradually diminished in favor of commodities and energy exports. For example, Turnell (2008) estimates that Myanmar's natural gas fields hold over 500 billion cubic meters of reserves, assessed to bring in over $2 billion annually for the next 40 years. The author posits that because of the sanctions, only one American firm has had any stake in the numerous pipeline projects, which have been divvied up among the French, Thai, Japanese, Malay, Chinese, Korean, and Indian firms. China is said to be the biggest benefactor signing exclusive development rights for natural gas and other natural resource projects.

As China's economic power grew in the 2000s, its role in the region became progressively more important. As an increasing number of countries chose to do business with China and its trade partners, arguments against the wisdom of economic sanctions against Myanmar amplified. The main argument expressed that continuing the sanctions had hurt US business and strategic interests (Rarick, 2007). Decades of prohibiting US firms from entering and/or expanding in the Myanmar market allowed nonamerican companies to take advantage of local trade and investment opportunities. Roberts (1997)[9] warned that leading economists have argued that the sanctions only disadvantage US oil companies and benefit their French and British competitors. Furthermore, Khine (2008) argued that the sanctions minimize American diplomatic influence in the region, potentially harming US strategic interests by weakening ties with ASEAN nations and tipping the regional balance of power toward China.

The Unintended Consequences of Sanctioning From Protecting Business Interests

Niksch and Weiss (2009) show that US sanctions against Myanmar had gone from slight to very strong, from 1988 to their end in 2010. During the first decade of the sanctions, their severity was minimal. They only impacted military sales. It was not until 1997, that the first round of sanctions really restricting economic activity was put in place because that round affected private American firms.

Prior to 1997, when President Clinton prohibited US entities from further investing in trade with Myanmar, sanctions only affected Myanmar's business interests with respect to the American government. The 1988 sanctions prohibited the sale of military equipment to Myanmar[10] and ended nonessential humanitarian aid, but legally allowed private US businesses to continue engagement with Myanmar. Of course, those businesses had to follow the rules of the military controlled local economy, which had serious restrictions on foreign property rights. Still, business was possible through local intermediaries and joint venture partnerships, as long as business operations were acceptable to the Myanmar regime. It is no wonder then that, for ten years those sanctions did not put any pressure on the regime to change its policies. As already discussed, all business entities were owned by the regime because in 1962 the Revolutionary Government of the Union of Burma (RGUB) nationalized all private trade. It established the Government Trade Council through which all trade was conducted (Stifel, 1971). Therefore, as business with the Trade Council continued, so did the regime's repressive rule until the atrocities against the border tribes in 1996. Then, the second round of sanctions came into effect, but the regime still continued its defiance, eventually leading to more American sanctions.

Niksch and Weiss (2009) chronologically track three distinct rounds of gradually magnifying sanctions. They are:

1. Period 1 of no, or symbolic, sanctions, affecting only military sales and fairly low amounts of foreign aid from 1987 to 1997;

2. Period 2 of sanctions prohibiting further investment but providing a platform for the maintaining of existing operations and assets from 1998 to 2003; and
3. Period 3 of prohibiting most trade and investment, old or new, from 2003t o2 007.

To examine why sanctions needed to be tightened gradually, one should focus on how the regime absorbed their economic impact. The most common way to assess the overall national economic performance is through analyzing changes in Gross Domestic Product (GDP). Prior research on sanctions has used GDP as a measure, and studies have found that effective sanctions result in a significant decrease of GDP (Dashti et al., 1997; Drury, 1998; Hart, 2000). In order to judge effectiveness of economic pressures from the sender government, the decrease needs to be contingent to the loss of trade. For that reason, the following regression tests are offered as examples of how GDP values can be influenced by sanctions. In the case of the Myanmar Official Exchange Rate (OER), it is examined during the sanction rounds with respect to how general trade metrics affected it. OER GDP is a good measure to employ when studying overall economic performance during sanctions because its value is derived from the price of the local currency. Fluctuations of demand for the currency affect the valuation of OER GDP and therefore, OER measures would capture trade impacts directly because their value is tied to international demand and volume of trade in Burmese products. A query into what factors influenced the amount of OER GDP in Myanmar during the sanction rounds is offered here, based on data from the United Nations Conference on Trade and Development (UNCTAD) database.[11] The following explanatory variables of trade intensity are evaluated with respect to OER GDP:

1. Total net exports—the value of total exports less total imports for Myanmar in a given calendar year. Growth in exports has been linked to industrial development in developing nations and growth in GDP (Baharum and Ataharul, 2010; Chow, 1987).
2. Total net exports to the US—value of total US exports leaving Myanmar less the value of total US imports entering Myanmar.
3. Total FDI net inflows—the value of foreign yearly purchases of productive assets such as factories, mines, and land. FDI inflows data is presented on a net basis, with a negative sign indicating disinvestment. Prior research on the relationship between economic growth and foreign direct investment has found a positive relationship between FDI inflows and overall economic growth (Dritsaki, et al., 2004; Chowdhury and Mavrotas, 2006; Ozturk and Kalyoncu, 2007).

4. Total official net financial flows—the value of total net disbursements by the official financial sector at large in Myanmar. Total official financial flows include grants, loans, and other transactions such as official export credits, official sector equity and portfolio investment, and debt reorganization. Overall foreign financial flows are associated with positive economic growth by complimenting domestic financial resources and enhancing existing production capabilities (Chenery and Strout, 1966; Papanek 1972; Asteriou, 2009). Additional research has found that when aid is separated into loans and grants, loans significantly increase GDP growth, while grants do not (Quazi, 2005).
5. Total long-term debt—amount of debt that has an original or extended maturity of more than one year, is owed to nonresidents, and is repayable in foreign currency, goods, or services. Long-term debt includes public debt, privately guaranteed debt, and private nonguaranteed debt. Prior studies have found a statistically significant negative relationship between debt and economic growth (Fosu, 1996; Geiger, 1990).

Data on total net exports, total FDI net inflows, total official net financial flows, and total long-term debt come from the UNCTAD. Data on total net US exports come from the International Monetary Fund Direction of Trade Statistics database (DOTS).[12] All dollar amounts are reported in millions of current US dollars.

First, to examine the relationship between trade and investment with the US and Myanmar's economy, the explanatory variables are regressed against Myanmar GDP in two time series analyses. Due to limited data, the regression results are presented as diagnostics on which further analyses of variance are based. Degrees of freedom problems arise in multiple regression tests where the parameter estimates are high in relation to individual observations, and therefore the coefficients need to be shrunk (Tibshirani, 1996).[13] However, Derksen and Keselman (1992) show that increasing the sample size does not affect the results, therefore the results are offered here as an example of an investigative method to seek the presence of statistical relationships rather than to interpret the coefficients, as regression analysis is aimed to do.

The first linear regression test allows for observing the impact of time. The approach is based on the methodology of Greene (2008, Chapter 21) and Wooldridge (2009, Part Two). When studying time series data of economic indicators, the individual observations are expected to show similarities across time, which is particularly the case with metrics such as GDP and exports because their fluctuations on yearly bases are incremental. This fact is due to capacity constraints and platforms of economic activity that vary little from year to year because they are based on economic states that are most reliant on each previous year. In other words, annual decreases or increases of GDP, exports, imports or debt, are based on the success of economic activity in the prior year. If business was profitable, economic activity is expected to increase. If business was not, a decrease is feasible. Therefore, a time effect can be useful to observe because it can indicate how yearly operations impact growth through time. Furthermore, the capacity constraint limits the possibility of variability on yearly bases. Therefore, the numbers of individual observations tend to exhibit high level of similarity, and therefore, low level of change from year to year.

Some statisticians argue that when examining change over time, time effects are factors that are sometimes necessary to observe in order to study trends and their change (de Boef and Keele, 2008; Greene, 2008; Wooldridge, 2009). In the case of FDI, observing time effects might be useful because the decision to invest is contingent on existing assets in the target market. Amounts are also subject to prior investments, as there are natural and political impediments to operational expansion. FDI net inflows denote the balance of annual assets to liabilities, schedules of foreign acquisitions, and their levels depend on the decision of expansion and divestment based on assets accumulated in previous years. A similar argument can be made for exports because their amounts depend on market share, which is also contingent on existing market presence, and decisions and/or possibilities of market expansion. Table 2.1 shows the results of an

Table 2.1 OLS regression, OER GDP, 1987–2007

Variables	Coefficient	Standard error
Total net exports	2.38	0.50***
Total net exports to the US	0.37	1.20
Total FDI net inflows	5.00	1.59**
Total official net financial flows	2.93	3.81
Total long-term debt	0.84	0.49
Constant	–8227.86	3528.19*
Prob. >F	<0.000	
R-squared	0.95	
Observations	20	

Dependent Variable: Official Exchange Rate GDP represents the market value of all final goods and services produced within the nation in a given year. Level of significance is represented by the following symbol: $p < 0.1$^, $p < 0.05$*, $p < 0.01$**, $p < 0.001$***

ordinary least-square (OLS) regressing without implementing a time effect control.

The results suggest that total net exports and total FDI net inflows significantly contributed to the annual growth of Myanmar's GDP. Total net exports to the United States does not seem to have been a contributing factor, which implies that despite dropping exports to America, Myanmar was able to increase its GDP by finding alternative export markets. Furthermore, the positive and statistically significant relationship between GDP and total FDI net inflows suggests that despite the sanctions Myanmar was able to attract foreign investment from nations other than the United States in such amounts as to contribute to notable economic growth.

Table 2.2 provides results for the same analysis while controlling for time effect. King (1986) argues that a time effect violates the independence assumption of linear regression and therefore should always be controlled. The control method is the addition of a lagged dependent variable. This approach allows for more conservative estimates by assuming that each observation is independent (King, 1986). In other words, the mathematical calculations treat each individual observation as independent of the preceding value in the prior time increment.

The results here also suggest that total exports were the most important predictor of Myanmar's annual GDP growth from 1987 to 2007. The

Table 2.2 OLS regression, OER GDP, 1987–2007, controlling for time effect

Variables	Coefficient	Standard error
Total net exports	2.22	0.62**
Total net exports to the United States	2.52	1.22^
Total FDI net inflows	3.67	1.99^
Total official net financial flows	–2.62	6.31
Total long-term debt	0.88	0.57
Lagged GDP	0.48	0.83
Constant	–1023.93	1883.79
Prob. >F	<0.000	
R-squared	0.95	
Observations	19	

Dependent Variable: Official Exchange Rate GDP represents the market value of all final goods and services produced within the nation in a given year. Level of significance is represented by the following symbol: $p < 0.1$^, $p < 0.05$*, $p < 0.01$**, $p < 0.001$***

major difference is that net exports to the United States now show statistical significance at the 0.1 level. The relationship is positive and to explore it further an analysis of variance technique is employed. Compared are the means of each variable over three separate time periods. Time period 1 represents the symbolic sanction years from 1988 to 1996; period 2 represents tighter sanctions, restricting market expansion from 1997 to 2003; and period 3 represents trade prohibition from 2004 to 2007. Although the sanctions did not end until 2010, 2007 is the last year with available data.

The analysis of variance shows that counterintuitively the second round of sanctions increased both total exports and export to the United States—the very thing they were supposed to decrease. The contribution to GDP growth with respect to both those export categories also significantly increased. To understand why gradually increasing in severity sanctions produced exactly the opposite of their intended effect, it is important to put each sanction round in the context of the different economic interests iti mpacted.

Chapter 3

Myanmar's Sanction Legacy: The Results of Nonengagement

NikolayA nguelov and KristinB ryant

This chapter tracks the three sanction rounds against the military regime of Myanmar through longitudinal analyses of variance of trade metrics. The discussion focuses on why despite tightening sanctions Myanmar experienced economic growth and what specific sectors grew the most. Due to improving trade and diplomatic relations with its rapidly-developing Asian neighbors, Myanmar was able to mitigate sanction effects to the point of running an impressive trade surplus. These facts built significant wealth for the ruling regime and lowered the incentives for the government to comply with sanction demands.

Pressuring Myanmar

As already noted, American legislative action restricting trade with private US firms in Myanmar started with the 1997 Executive Order 13047 issued by President Clinton under the Foreign Appropriations Act. It banned new investments in Myanmar by American companies and citizens. Existing US operations in Myanmar were allowed to continue to do business as long as they did not expand. Seeing no impact, in 2003, President Bush signed the Burmese Freedom and Democracy Act, which banned the importation of most products from Myanmar into the United States. This addition mandated all firms, American or otherwise, to cease bringing any product into the United States that had Burmese origins. However, exceptions existed for certain commodities, such as jade and others, for which a US entity could benefit as long as the Myanmar exporter did not show evidence of ties to the State Peace and Development Council (SPDC). The Burmese Freedom and Democracy Act also authorized the president to freeze the funds or assets of government officials or individuals holding senior positions within the Myanmar government, as well as deny visas and entry into the United States to former or current leaders of the Myanmar government or the Union Solidarity Development Association (USDA). The association de facto acted as a political party whose members were involved in local government. Through its 320 township associations, its membership had grown to over 20 million by the time the Burmese Freedom and Democracy Act was signed.[1] In addition, the act required the US government to vote against the extension of any financial assistance to Myanmar by international financial institutions. President Bush also signed Executive Order 13310, which banned the export or reexport of financial services to Myanmar by US entities and prohibited US citizens and companies from approving, aiding, or supporting a foreign party's investment in Myanmar and purchasing shares in a third-country company, if that company's profits result mainly from the development of resources in Myanmar.

Possibly because of those sanctions, or a combination of their effect and bad central management, in 2007 Myanmar faced a serious fuel shortage. The military junta dramatically increased fuel prices in August,2007. The increase led to protests and the CIA reported that thousands of citizens rallied in peaceful demonstrations against the regime. Again, the military brutally suppressed the protestors, killing at least 13 people and arresting thousands.[2] As a result, President Bush signed Executive Order 13448, which granted the Treasury Department the authority to impose specific targeted sanctions on persons responsible for human rights abuses or public corruption within Myanmar—a broad classification under which arguably all government officials fell. In addition, Executive Order 13448 allowed for the levying of sanctions on individuals who provided material and financial backing to those persons directly responsible for human rights abuses.[3] A year later, in 2008, President Bush signed the Burmese Jade Act, which prohibited the importation of all Burmese jade into the UnitedS tates.[4]

To track exactly how trade was restricted Niksch and Weiss (2009) argue that each round of sanctions must be examined in magnitude, in terms of exactly what economic activity was sanctioned and in what way. Following that call, analyses of variance are employed here to see how under each sanction round the main economic sectors of Myanmar performed with respect to their contribution to GDP.

Economic Growth Despite Increasing Sanctions

During the sanction years GDP in Myanmar increased. Figure 3.1 offers a graphical representation of that increase.

The time period coinciding with the military actions against the ethnic tribes across the border in 1996–1997 interrupts the overall rise. It appears that the beginning of the second round of sanctions in 1997 caused GDP to decrease sharply, but that decrease only lasted for one year. GDP started to rise again in 1998 and its growth rate spiked in 2001. In 2002, GDP declined for a year, then in 2003 it showed a slight growth rate. However, it escalated in 2004 as the final and most restrictive round of sanctions took effect. It is interesting to note that at the beginning of each round of sanctions GDP decreases for a year, but then it recovers and its growth rate escalates. To examine the reasons for such rapid recovery a comparison of net exports and net exports to the United States only is offered in figure 3.2. When sanctions restrict trade in the export-dependent local economy, they cause the government to find alternative partners. Therefore, the aggregate amount of exports would be denoted if (a) such partners indeed were found and (b) if they offered significant purchasing alternatives for Myanmar inputs to limit sanction impact. Net exports refer to the balance of exports

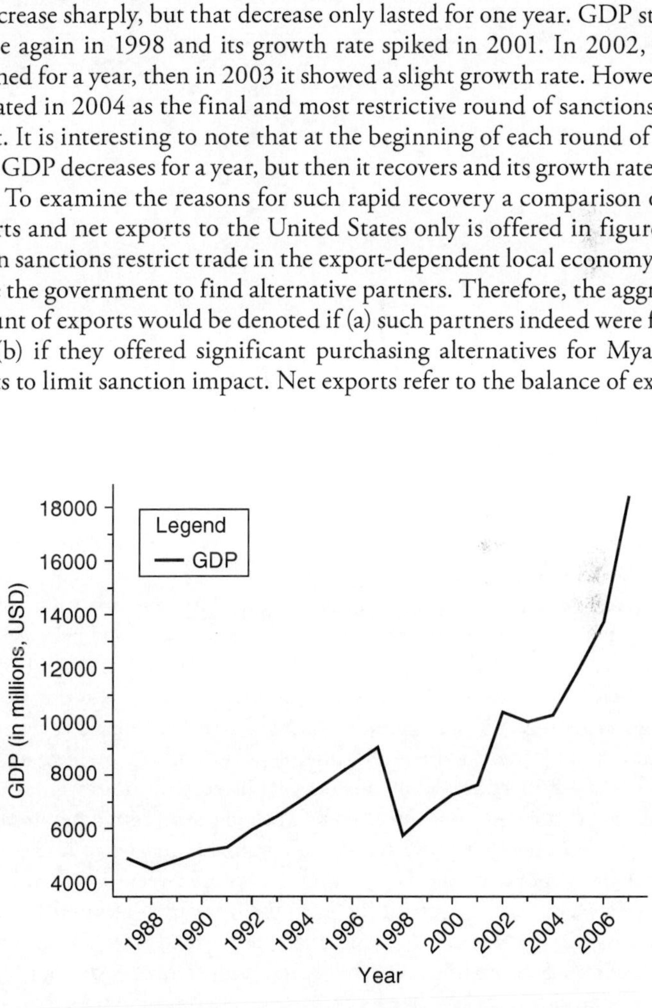

Figure 3.1 GDP, 1987–2007. Change in the value of GDP over time.

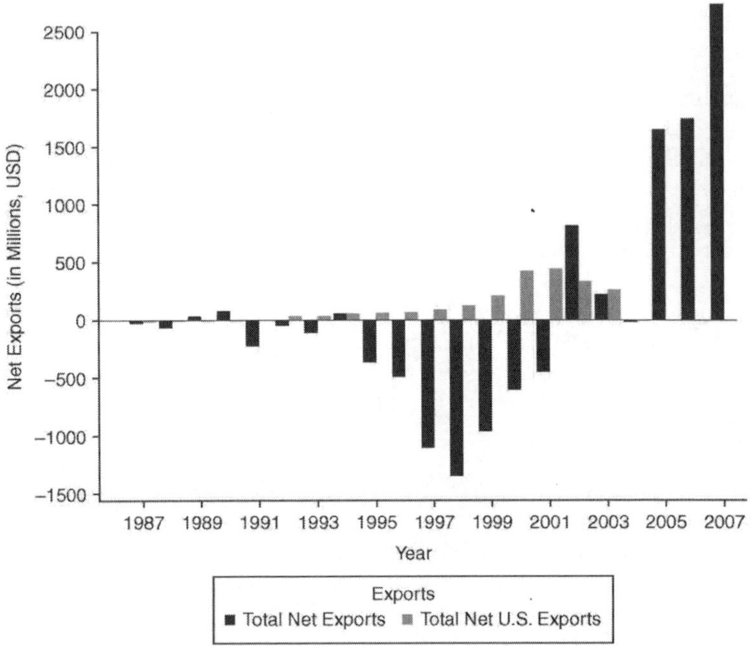

Figure 3.2 Total and US net exports, 1987–2007.

minus imports. Figure 3.2 denotes imports below the 0 level on the x-axis asd ownwardp ointingb ars.

In the beginning of the first round of sanctions, exports and imports remain fairly close to each other and in negligible amounts. Then, as instability increases in 1995, imports increase significantly. This could be due to the increasing import of military equipment as well as food, as local food production would have been impacted by the military clashes in the agrarian countryside. At the same time, exports to the United States also start a period of increase. As the rate of that increase escalates, so does the decrease of imports in the context of a trade balance. From a net importer, Myanmar becomes a net exporter as the sanctions increase in intensity.

Total net exports to the Unites States grew between 1992 and 2001 with the largest increases coinciding with the implementation of sanctions in 1997. As already discussed, these sanctions banned new investments in Myanmar by US companies or individuals. However, they did not impact existing operations, and it appears that exporters to the Unites States may have responded to the sanctions by increasing export volumes. Then, in effect, the second round of sanctions caused the opposite outcome of economic pressure—substantial economic growth.

A possible implication is that sanctions affecting future operations may be perceived as a signal to local and foreign businesses in the target nation that the future may bring further business uncertainty. Then, a conceivable response by producers would be to ramp up production, if capacity permits it, to maximize profits in order to prevent any further political action fromaffecting their business interests. In this case, the sender nation erroneously assumes that FDI inflows, that is, additional investment, will produce the desired economic pressure in the target nation because of loss of the possibility to expand business. Inability to expand business operations is not necessarily a loss. This is the case in developing nations because market entry for new firms, and/or expansion of existing operations and facilities for firms already on the ground, carries high transaction costs (Buckley and Ghauri, 2004; Jung and Marshall, 1985; Ozturk and Kalyoncu, 2007). Businesses carefully weigh decisions of additional investment (Chowdhury and Mavrotas, 2006). Often expansions are sporadic and, in certain underdeveloped nations, even rare because of local capacity constraints. Even, if a business is willing to invest further in a market, it may not be able to do so due to limitations of inputs, infrastructure, supply chains, local supply networks, and manpower.

Matters of efficiency concern firms in high-transaction cost economic environments because of uncertainty. Possible future difficulties create incentives to optimize operational capacity for each entity to maximum levels in order to maximize profitability while business opportunities allow. In that context, the first round of sanctions would not have impacted US business partnerships in Myanmar at all since it allowed those businesses to carry on operations with existing assets. Then, sanctions would have affected American firms in Myanmar by not altering incentives to scale down existing business volumes. A normal reaction from firm management would have been to continue doing business as usual, just not expand further. It is reasonable to assume that most of those businesses operated at sufficient profit margins. If anything, the sanctions might have stimulated better management to improve short-term profitability. To illustrate the magnitude of trade with the United States at the time, figure 3.3 shows how important exports to America were in relation to other nations.

Exports to the United States comprised 17 percent of total Myanmar exports, second only to trade with Thailand, and closely followed by exports to India. With all the evidence of Chinese support, up until 1997 China accounted for only 11 percent of Myanmar's export market. The data shows that during the first round of sanctions Myanmar's export composition had a mostly Western orientation. Additionally, the main

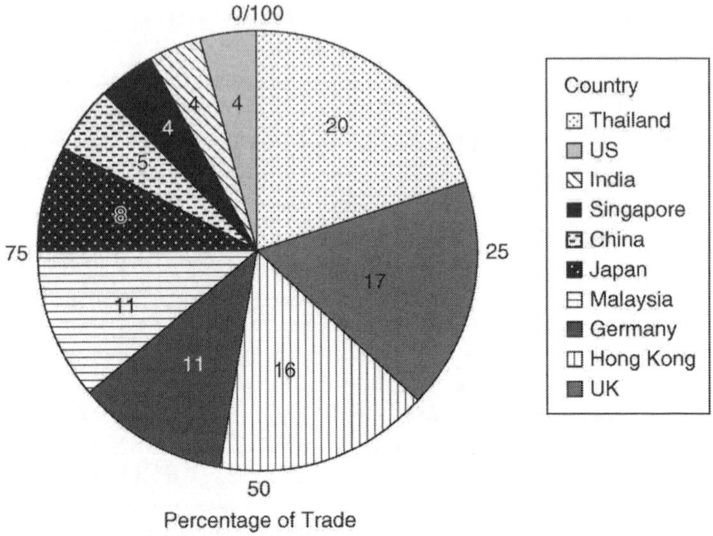

Figure 3.3 Major trading partners, 1987–1997. The percentage of net exports to each of Myanmar's top ten trading partners for the years 1987–1997 (IMF, Direction of Trade Statistics database).

Asian export markets were also liberal democracies with open-market economic structures.

When the second round of sanctions took effect, exports to the United States decreased from 2002 to 2004 as President Bush banned the importation of products ofBurmese origin into the US.[5] These sanctions affected American firms in Myanmar that exported directly to the United States. However, they still did not affect those firms' exports to other nations. A US entity could still export products completely or partially made in Myanmar, and/or from Burmese inputs, to anywhere but the United States. Furthermore, profits from those operations could be repatriated back to America. The outright prohibition of such repatriation did not come into effect until 2007, which is after the time frame examined here.

As figure 3.2 shows, exports from Myanmar to the United States cease in 2005, while exports to the rest of the world increase dramatically, resulting in an impressive surplus, in fact the first such surplus in Myanmar's postcolonial history. The surplus and a significant, positive relationship between total net exports and GDP, noted in Chapter 2, show that Myanmar was able to decrease its vulnerability to American sanctions by finding viable alternative export options. This fact not only supports earlier arguments that in many cases third party "black knights" weaken sanctions (Askari et al., 2005; Hufbauer et al., 2009), but also indicates how powerful such black knight support can be. As already noted, China was Myanmar's strongest ally and trading partner. Figure 3.4 shows the market share of other trade partnerships by nation and how it changed duringt hes anctiony ears.

Interestingly, China remains Myanmar's third largest export market, but its share of all exports decreases from 11 percent to 9 percent. Figure 3.4 indicates the most important black knights were Thailand and India. Additionally, a significant amount of trade was directed toward other nations that supported sanctions in the United Nations Security Council, such as Germany and the United Kingdom, but exports to those nations do not cease. Their exports decrease, but it is unclear whether the decrease is due to sanctions or due to more attractive options available in the growing regional economies.

In addition to exports, much of the literature points to the importance of foreign investment in generating economic growth (Dritsaki, et al.,

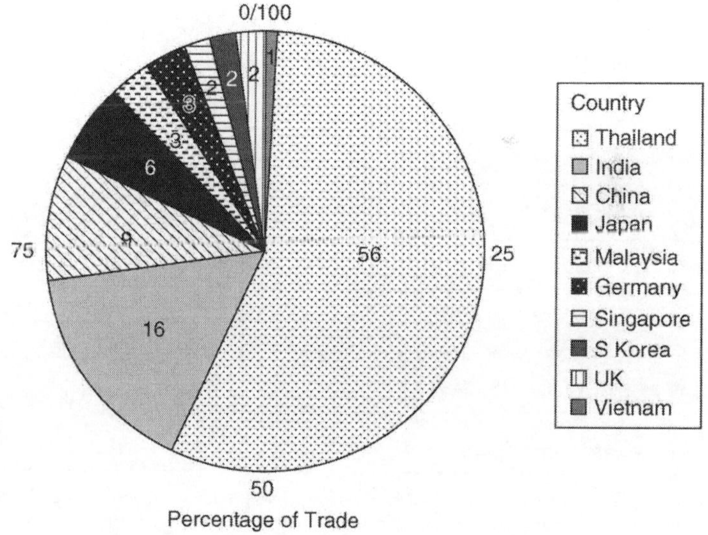

Figure 3.4 Major trading partners, 1998–2008. The percentage of net exports to each of Myanmar's top ten trading partners for the years 2004–2008 (IMF, Direction of Trade Statistics database).

2004; Chowdhury and Mavrotas, 2006; Ozturk and Kalyoncu, 2007). With respect to sanctions, the most compelling empirical evidence comes from the panel data analysis by Hufbauer and Oegg (2003), which found that sanctions prohibiting FDI have a significant, negative effect on the economy of the target country. Table 3.1 shows the difference in means among the three sanction periods in net FDI for Myanmar. The graphical representation is a plot of a Tukey Kramer analysis of variance test. The x-axis is separated into three segments, each representing the individual sanction rounds. The y-axis shows the amount of FDI net inflows in millions of US dollars. The width of the diamonds spans the length of each sanction period. The height of the diamonds indicates the 95 percent confidence interval around the mean value of FDI net inflows. To the right,

Table 3.1 Myanmar FDI net inflows in the three sanction periods

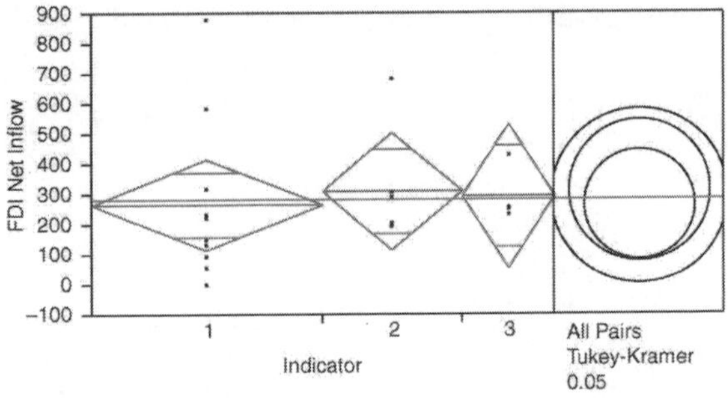

Analysis of variance

Source	DF	Sum of squares	Mean square	F ratio	Prob > F
Indicator	2	7845.27	3922.6	0.0775	0.9258
Error	17	860591.68	50623.0		
C. Total	19	868436.95			

Mean comparisons for all pairs using Tukey-Kramer Hsd

Level	– Level	Difference	Std Err Dif	Lower CL	Upper CL	p–Value
2	1	44.86667	116.1873	−253.195	342.9285	0.9215
3	1	26.45000	133.1092	−315.023	367.9227	0.9785
2	3	18.41667	145.2341	−354.161	390.9939	0.9912

the circles indicate dispersion of range around the mean for the combined periods. Each circle represents an individual round of sanctions.

The data indicates that the mean FDI amounts remained around $300 million through each sanction period. The variability of amounts received changed. In period 1, FDI ranged from insignificant to close to $900 million. In period 2, the lowest amount was $200 million and the highest $720 million. In period 3, the upper bound decreased as the most FDI received in a calendar year was $490 million.

Although, mean total FDI net inflows decreased following the implementation of US sanctions in 1997, this decrease was not significant. The same is true for total official net financial flows. Table 3.2 shows their impact during the sanction periods:

Table 3.2 Myanmar total official net financial flows

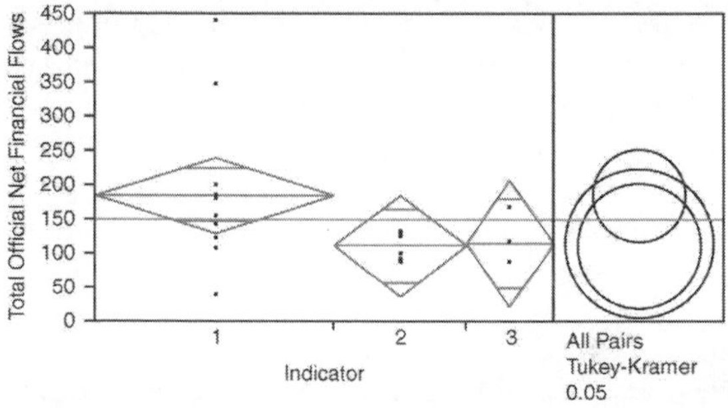

Analysis of variance

Source	DF	Sum of squares	Mean square	F ratio	Prob > F
Indicator	2	27751.75	13875.9	1.8297	0.1891
Error	18	136506.06	7583.7		
C. Total	20	164257.81			

Mean comparisions for all pairs using Tukey-Kramer hsd

Level	–Level	Difference	Std Err Dif	Lower CL	Upper CL	p–Value
1	2	74.21212	44.19694	–38.586	187.0099	0.2401
1	3	70.54545	50.84626	–59.223	200.3134	0.3681
3	2	3.66667	56.21265	–139.797	147.1305	0.9977

Total official net financial flows differ from FDI net inflows accounting for foreign aid, loans, grants, export credits, and other monetary yearly gains. They are examined because the second sanction round stopped most direct foreign aid from the United States to Myanmar. The implications of the fact that official net financial flows did not significantly change through the sanction periods suggests that foreign aid benefits were either not that important or easily replaced with alternative sources of finance. Therefore, in relation to total net financial flows, more importance lies in focusing on FDI, because it indicates willingness of both the Myanmar government and its international trading partners to enter into investment arrangements despite the transaction costs of sanctions. Such costs include possible loss of favorable trading platforms with the sender nations, if they choose to implement punitive trade policies in response to noncompliance with sanctions. Another form of such transaction costs can be the fact that FDI by definition is dependent on the unpredictability of the military regime. Its restrictive property right granting policies, with respect to majority ownership of enterprise, mandates that majority stakes remain with the Burmese portion of the business. Even with such impediments, FDI inflows increased slightly from 2004 to 2007, mainly due to large Thai investments in hydropower projects in Myanmar in 2005 (Zhao, 2012).

It must be stressed that the estimates analyzed here are relatively conservative because total FDI net inflows into Myanmar might be underreported. McCarthy (2000) explains that FDI inflow data reported by the Myanmar government do not include flows resulting from substantial Chinese investments in manufacturing, mining, and infrastructure projects in the northern part of the country, near the Chinese border. Khine (2008) analyzes FDI flows in Myanmar and shows that by 2008, 89 percent of all inward FDI came from Thailand, 4 percent came from China (on paper), 4 percent from the UK, and the rest from India, South Korea, and Singapore, each responsible for 1 percent of total inflows.

Based on such evidence an attempt is merited to disaggregate investment intensity by industrial sectors. The goal is to gain insight about which economic activities grew during the sanction years and how their growth contributed to the overall economic prosperity of Myanmar. Because of the general underdevelopment of the country, as noted by the literature on the local economy examined in Chapter 2, it is reasonable to posit that any industrial growth would be contingent on international trade partnerships. Seeing which sectors grew most with respect to the overall economy would offer insight into which product sectors were most valuable to the black knight trading partners that were behind the strong growth of exports.

Understanding structural dynamics of the time can help see the creation of the economic foundations that sustain the regime's continued commercial control today. To that effect, analyses of variance for each of the three sanction periods are conducted with a focus on value added to GDP by industry for the five largest industrial sectors of the Myanmar economy: (1) agriculture, hunting, forestry, and fishing; (2) wholesale, retail trade, restaurants, and hotels; (3) mining, manufacturing, and utilities; (4) transport, storage, and communications; and (5) other industrial activities. The categories are ranked in descending order based on the monetary value added to overall GDP. In addition, the construction sector is analyzed because of its importance to infrastructure development. Definitions for each category come from the International Standard Industrial Classification of All Economic Activities, Rev. 3.1.[6] Data for value added to GDP by industry comes from the United Nations National Accounts Main Aggregate database.[7]

As a category, agriculture, hunting, forestry, and fishing comprises the commodity export legacy of Myanmar. As already noted, rice, tropical fruit products, and teak are among Myanmar's most valuable commodities. Table 3.3 combines the graphical representation and summary statistics of change in that category for the three rounds of sanctions with respect to its contribution to GDP.

The results indicate a strong and increasing contribution of growth in that sector to overall GDP. The interpretation is that since most of the population remained poor, and previously examined evidence suggests high incidence of famine and increase in food prices, agricultural production contributed to GDP with respect to exports not through impact in local consumption. This fact suggests that the Myanmar government chose to starve its people and create food shortages in the country while continuing to increase agricultural exports.

The analysis of the second largest industrial sector—wholesale, retail trade, restaurants, and hotels—indicates that services as a whole became more important to overall GDP growth, particularly in the last period of sanctions. Table 3.4 illustrates how the sanction rounds impacted the service sector's contribution to overall economic growth.

The fact that services became an increasingly important contributor to GDP in the third round of sanctions can best be explained in conjuncture with the results of the third-largest sector of the economy—manufacturing, mining, and utilities.

Table 3.3 Value added to GDP by agriculture, hunting, forestry, and fishing

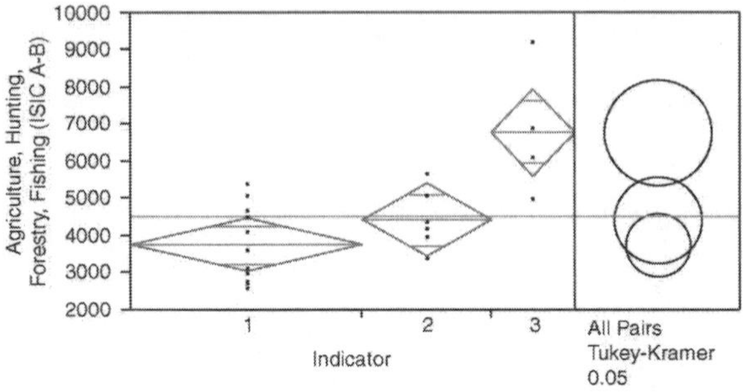

Analysis of variance

Source	Df	Sum of squares	Mean square	F ratio	Prob > F
Indicator	2	26783296	13391648	10.4234	0.0010*
Error	18	23125801	1284766.7		
C. Total	20	49909097			

Mean comparisons for all pairs using Tukey-Kramer hsd

Level	– Level	Difference	Std Err Dif	Lower Cl	Upper Cl	p–Value
3	1	3016.773	661.8071	1327.73	4705.813	0.0007*
3	2	2355.000	731.6553	487.70	4222.304	0.0126*
2	1	661.773	575.2606	–806.39	2129.932	0.4968

* statisticallys ignificant.

Table 3.5 illustrates its change and contribution to GDP. The analysis indicates that both sectors contributed significantly more to GDP in the third round of sanctions when the United States prohibited trade. Both sectors are examined together because of their interdependence. The contributions of manufacturing, mining, and utilities to GDP growth can only be observed when efficient wholesale and trade platforms exist. They are at the core of all trade. Without such efficient platforms, output cannot be moved profitably and its increase would not result in overall economic growth, but rather in waste from direct and transaction costs, which would result in economic decline. The fact that both the service intensive and the manufacturing and extraction intensive sectors performed in a similar manner is an example of how contingent they are to each other for growth in Myanmar. Additionally, the fourthlargest sector—the transportation

Table 3.4 Value added to GDP by wholesale, retail trade, restaurants, and hotels

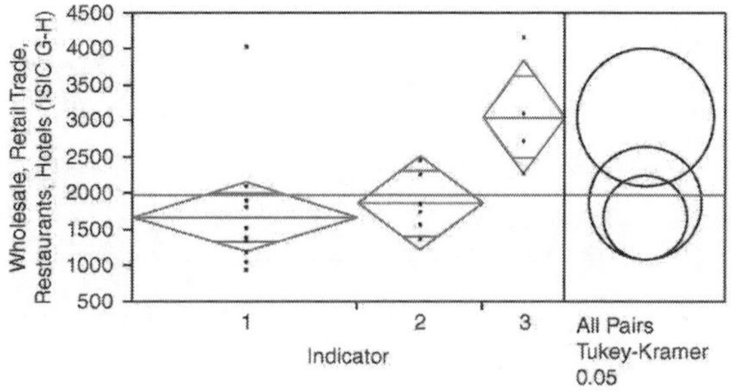

Analysis of variance

Source	Df	Sum of squares	Mean square	F Ratio	Prob > F
Indicator	2	5768594	2884297	5.0737	0.0179*
Error	18	10232572	568476		
C. Total	20	16001167			

Mean comparisons for all pairs using Tukey-Kramer Hsd

Level	–Level	Difference	Std Err Dif	Lower Cl	Upper Cl	p–Value
3	1	1386.341	440.2258	262.813	2509.869	0.0146*
3	2	1191.417	486.6879	–50.690	2433.524	0.0614
2	1	194.924	382.6561	–781.677	1171.525	0.8677

* statistically significant.

sector—showed a similar pattern. Table 3.6 shows how the transportation, storage, and communications sector impacted the GDP growth of Myanmar during the sanction years.

The increase in contribution to GDP is strongest in this sector. In each round the contribution increased significantly. Like the other sectors, the third round caused the highest jump in sector value. The reason being that the growth of all other sectors is contingent on efficient transportation. The results suggest that during the sanction years the Myanmar government invested in transportation infrastructure, supported the overall operations management and supply chain management segments of the economy, and had efficient logistics management policies. The aggregate dollar numbers suggest such efficiency. In sanction period 1, the sector added negligible value to GDP. In sanction period 2, the value had grown

Table 3.5 Value added to GDP by mining, manufacturing, and utilities

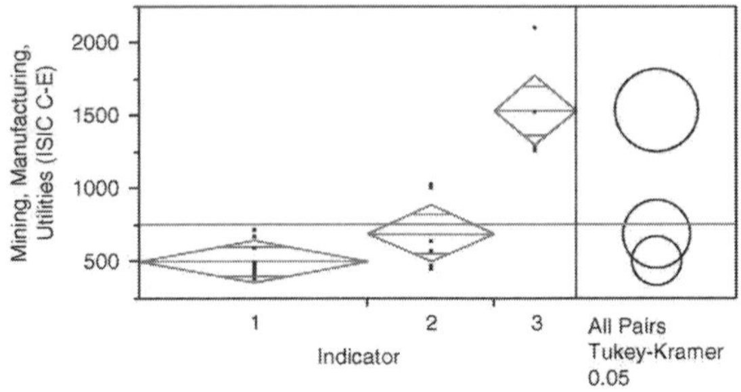

Analysis of variance

Source	Df	Sum of squares	Mean square	F ratio	Prob > F
Indicator	2	3175263.4	1587632	31.2479	<.0001*
Error	18	914536.6	50808		
C. Total	20	4089800.0			

Mean comparisons for all pairs using Tukey-Kramer Hsd

Level	–Level	Difference	Std Err Dif	Lower Cl	Upper Cl	p–Value
3	1	1034.886	131.6084	699.000	1370.772	<.0001*
3	2	847.583	145.4986	476.247	1218.919	<.0001*
2	1	187.303	114.3976	–104.658	479.264	0.2562

* statistically significant.

to half a billion dollars. In period 3, it averaged just under a billion and a half, on equal par with the mining, manufacturing, and utilities sector. Another important implication is that during the period Myanmar's economy diversified and changed in nature from labor-intensive closed format to service-intensive and relatively more open format. Logistic services and the other service sectors, comprising the wholesale, retail trade, restaurants, and hotels category—the second largest value contributor to the overall economy after agriculture, husbandry, and forestry—indicate movement of goods and people beyond Myanmar's borders. The average income levels of the local population could not sustain local purchasing power in numbers strong enough to result in capital formation in billions of dollars. According to the World Bank's database, World Development Indicators, Myanmar's gross national income per capita, the metric most

Table 3.6 Value added to GDP by transport, storage, and communication

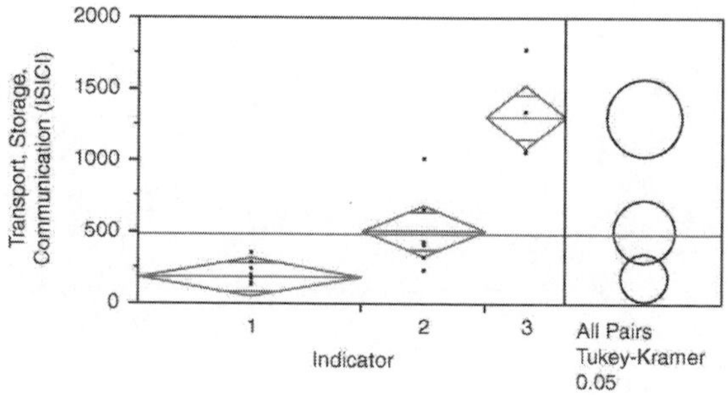

Analysis of variance

Source	DF	Sum of squares	Mean square	F ratio	Prob > F
Indicator	2	3682076.0	1841038	41.1002	<.0001*
Error	18	806289.8	44794		
C. Total	20	4488365.8			

Mean comparisions for all pairs using Tukey-Kramer Hsd

Level	–Level	Difference	Std Err Dif	Lower CL	Upper CL	p–Value
3	1	1120.023	123.5744	804.6406	1435.405	<.0001*
3	2	797.917	136.6167	449.2486	1146.585	<.0001*
2	1	322.106	107.4142	47.9674	596.245	0.0201*

* statisticallys ignificant.

often employed to indicate purchasing power of the average citizen, ranged from $400 a year in the 1990s to $910 a year in 2008. According to the Central Intelligence Agency (CIA), over 37 percent of the people in the country live below the official poverty line, which Gentilini and Sumner (2012) estimate to be below $1.25 a day, suggesting even lower levels during the sanction years. Those numbers make it among the poorest countries in the world in terms of its ability to internally generate economic growth. For those reasons the above examined value added to GDP metrics can only be as high as they are if their value comes from the purchasing power of the external economic exchange, that is foreign trade. Those metrics also depend on overall infrastructure expansion in critical as well as hard infrastructure, such as roads, dams, and power plants. All of those

Table 3.7 Value added to GDP by construction

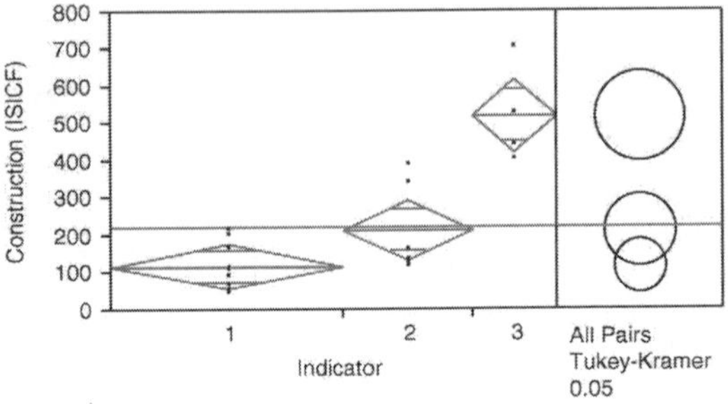

Analysis of variance

Source	DF	Sum of squares	Mean square	F ratio	Prob > F
Indicator	2	479771.25	239886	27.2844	<.0001*
Error	18	158256.75	8792		
C. Total	20	638028.00			

Mean comparisions for all pairs using Tukey-Kramer Hsd

Level	–Level	Difference	Std Err Dif	Lower CL	Upper CL	p-Value
3	1	404.2500	54.74748	264.525	543.9745	<.0001*
3	2	306.2500	60.52562	151.779	460.7213	0.0002*
2	1	98.0000	47.58799	–23.452	219.4523	0.1269

* statisticallys ignificant.

assets by definition need to be constructed and therefore, table 3.7 offers an analysis of the construction sector.

The construction sector shows a similar but stronger gradual pattern of change. During each round its contribution to GDP grew significantly. In the other sectors in the majority of cases the growth between periods 1 and 2 was insignificant, while the growth in period 3 was the main contributor to the changing averages. The fact that in construction in each round the growth rate is strong and the number amounts are at a particular level, also indicate that the centrally planned economic policies of the military regime prioritized infrastructure development. In most free market cases growth in the construction sector does not necessarily indicate government policy support for the creation of infrastructure. It is generally correlated with the growth of the housing market. However, in a closed underdeveloped economy where the average citizen has neither diverse needs nor financial options to make purchases in housing, a growth in construction suggests government direction in building structures other than housing.

In a free market economy the largest contributor to the construction sector growth is new home construction or private commercial building. Infrastructure development still has importance, but displays incremental annual growth. In managed economies, particularly underdeveloped ones such as Myanmar's during the sanction years, growth in construction by definition is not reliant on private homes or private commercial real estate development. Therefore, it is mostly contingent on government-created capital projects such as roads, ports, damns, railroads, or government-owned factories and other production facilities. Construction growth can also come from projects owned by foreign companies, but because at the time FDI did not significantly increase, a link cannot be established between construction growth and foreign firms building new facilities in Myanmar. These facts suggest a carefully managed government support for infrastructure development for aiding trade platforms.

Another particular aspect of the underdeveloped Myanmar economy is that a significant portion of economic activity does not clearly fall into the defined industrial sectors. In many poor subsistence agriculture reliant economies, that is, where most of the population lives off the land and does not engage in employment measured by wages, barters account for the majority of trade transactions. Eventually those barter arrangements can produce monetary profits. Such profits can be noted in overall economic intensity of demand for such goods as commodities, fuels, and foodstuffs that can be purchased with money generated through the trade of barter outputs further in the trade chains of formal and informal market exchanges. For example, a rice farmer can exchange a portion of the rice crop for citrus fruit, then use the fruit to make alcohol that can be sold for money. Any portion of self-generated agricultural output can be traded for cash equivalency, but it is unclear at which stage of exchange,making difficult to break down direct monetary contributions to GDP from individual industries. Therefore, it is no wonder that the fifth largest economic sector in Myanmar is "other industrial activities." This sector is huge because it is by and large nonwage earning and as noted, the majority of the population in the country then and now consists of subsistence farmers. Table 3.8 shows the sector's response to sanctions.

This fifth largest sector shows a starkly different pattern than the wage-based sectors. Its amount decreased significantly during round two, coinciding with the military actions against villagers and the government's attempt to cut off the support for the minority rebels in the countryside.

Table 3.8 Value added to GDP by other activities

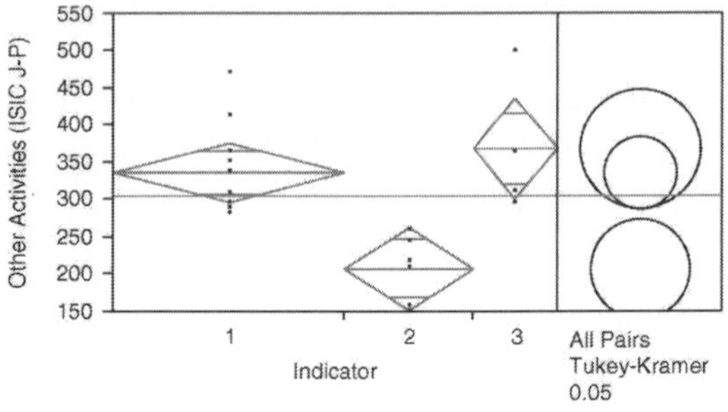

Analysis of variance

Source	DF	Sum of squares	Mean square	F Ratio	Prob > F
Indicator	2	83384.79	41692.4	10.1498	0.0011*
Error	18	73939.02	4107.7		
C. Total	20	157323.81			

Mean comparisions for all pairs using Tukey-Kramer Hsd

Level	–Level	Difference	Std Err Dif	Lower CL	Upper CL	p–Value
3	2	160.8333	41.37090	55.2480	266.4186	0.0029*
1	2	128.1061	32.52768	45.0901	211.1220	0.0026*
3	1	32.7273	37.42139	–62.7782	128.2328	0.6627

* statisticallys ignificant

The end of the systematic pogroms in which much of the evidence suggests that the destruction of farms and crops was the main goal, in order to starve the rebels and the ethnic villagers that supported them, shows an increase in the importance of the sector to overall economic growth. Its average contribution to GDP in round three becomes slightly higher than it was before the civil unrest, but that increase is not significant. The interpretation is that the economic hardships the central government could, and potentially can still, inflict on its people can most directly be seen in the informal sector. In the case of Myanmar, the poorest segments of the population—the repressed rural ethnic minorities who live off the land—comprise that sector. In that context, the third round of sanctions might have helped them indirectly. As the government focus shifted toward increasing exports, its attention from rural insurrection might have diminished, or its repressive actions during the pogroms might have worked to the point of minimizing rebel activity. In either scenario, little evidence exists to prove that the rural ethnic poor persons' plight produced economic benefits for them. After the military offensives ended, the poor went back to being poor, living on less than $1.25 a day, and did not move to a higher industrial bracket of wage earners, as one would expect, given the strong growth in GDP contribution from the other industrial sectors.

Because of the unique nature of Myanmar's economy, that is, centrally controlled, relatively poor in local economic diversity and activity, and defined by export-oriented policies, a link can be made between the significant growth in those sectors and foreign trade. The link is that for the capital-intensive sectors, in other words, those reliant on wage-based labor inputs—mining, manufacturing, forestry, services, tourism, transportation, utilities, construction, whole sale, retail, and trade—revenue generation in the analyzed dollar amounts could not have happened through local economic activity. The fact that all sectors, excluding the informal nonwage based "other activities" sector, experienced concomitant significant growth in their importance to GDP while American sanctions increased indicates that for the Myanmar government the alternatives to trading with the United States proved to be viable and valuable. Figure 3.5 indicates exactly how valuable those alternatives became. It shows the above-examined industrial sector in relation to overall GDP and each other and visualizes their growth rates when America suspended trade.

During round three of the sanctions, when the United States suspended all trade with Myanmar, both the service and manufacturing sectors grew significantly. The development of mining and natural gas extraction with foreign assistance and for export to Asian markets displays the increased economic contribution of the sector. It provides evidence of how Myanmar's Asian partners were much more important in terms of volume trade options as compared to their American counterparts. This finding has implications for the overall importance of the United States as an economic partner. If that importance diminishes, then the American sanction impact also decreases. This implies that when allowed, exports of mined commodities and energy outputs for the United States either operated at capacity or had reached finite levels that did not have the same contribution to Myanmar's GDP growth that their Asian counterparts offered. Therefore, trade in manufactured goods, energy, and mined products with the nations that replaced the United States proved to be much more valuable and lucrative. That value fueled the local regime, generated significant profits when compared to American and Western alternatives, and more importantly, established the new institutional arrangements for doing business in Myanmar. Because of the restrictive totalitarian nature

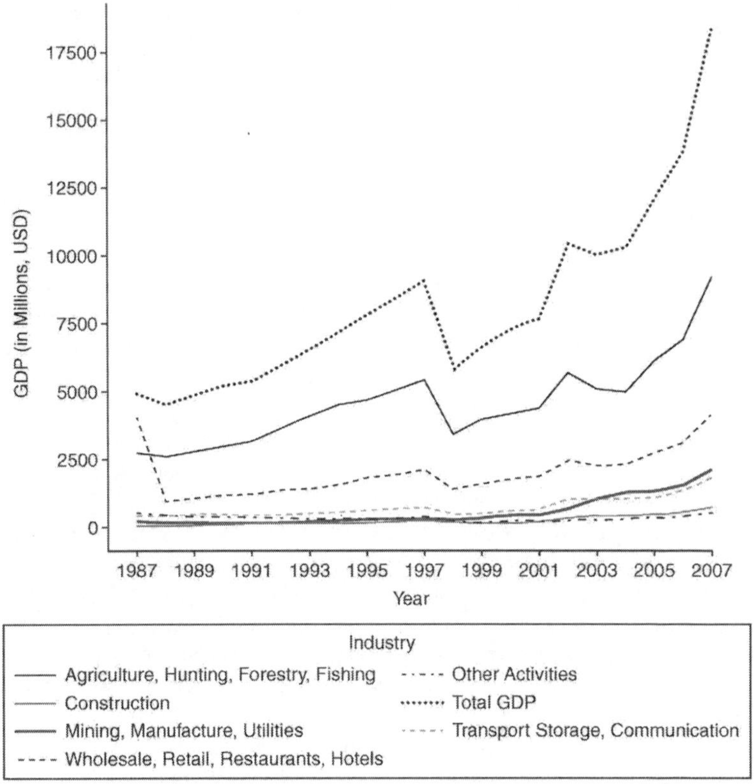

Figure 3.5 Change in value added to GDP by industry, 1987–2007.

of the regime, it is reasonable to assume that these institutional arrangements would offer the best terms of trade for the regime. It would set the rules in terms of majority enterprise ownership, division of profits and operational standards with respect to health and occupational labor conditions, environmental safeguards, and quality controls. When a regime has a track record of human rights violations, it cannot be assumed that its business platforms would differ. Therefore, for its trade partners the implications suggest that doing business in Myanmar would offer savings through lower than international standards costs on labor, environmental mitigation technology, that is, clean up or investing in pollution-lessening technologies, which are expensive, or quality control safety inspections for toxicity of final product, particularly if those products are directed toward other nations with developing institutions in such respects.

The lack of impact of sanctions denotes impunity to international common business practice management. Traditional interpretation of business efficiency in trade would suggest that trade would increase if the trading parties both benefited from the marginal increases. The terms of trade can be set by the trading parties to optimize such marginal benefits. Because one of the trading parties is a repressive, property right constricting and a nonregulatory nor legally compliant government, the implication is that the terms of trade would be such as to strengthen its nature. Therefore, by definition those nations eager to trade with Myanmar at the time fueled the regime's institutions in terms of validating its abuses and disregard for international law. The problem is that once the sanctions ended, the then-established ways of doing business became institutionalized as the accepted platforms of doing so in the country. This fact indicates that in Myanmar, sanctions led to the creation of powerful economic and institutional rents that continue to have an impact after the end of sanctions.

Rent Seeking, Rent Extracting, and Rent Protecting: Solidifying Existing Elites and Creating New Ones

After the official lift of US economic sanctions against Myanmar in 2010, an argument has been made that the concessions made by the military government are so perfunctory that the sanctions de facto remain in place (Harris, 2012). The dynamics of economic sanctions and trade presented earlier indicate why that would be the case. The local government faces incentives to continue the same pattern of behavior it followed during the sanction years because that behavior maximized its monetary gains. The absence of any signs of policy change implementation is so strong that in response on May 14, 2014, President Barack Obama extended the National Emergency Act, which prohibits US businesses and individuals to invest in Myanmar. The justification is that not enough progress is evident, and the country continues to pose "unusual and extraordinary" threats to US national security.[8] Even though the Myanmar government has agreed to make changes to its human rights, democracy, and property right policies it is concluded that so far the changes have been insignificant.

Harris (2012) observed that two years after the lift of sanctions, US investors shied away from entering the Myanmar market because of uncertainty and institutional instability. Two years later, on January 4, 2014,

The Economist magazine offered a report based on World Bank data on the negative economic reality in the country since little has changed after the lifting of sanctions.[9] Most Western investors face strong deterrents for expansion based on the same institutional problems of human rights violations, business uncertainty, and legal protection that defined the sanction years. Attention is drawn to the point that American and other Western investors are disadvantaged. Hence, Myanmar trade with its long-standing non-Western partners seems to be expanding.[10]

The problem is that this current trepidation, which is undoubtedly the legacy of decades of sanctions, continues to impact mainly US interests rather than the policies of the Myanmar government. American businesses continue to lose market share to their Thai, Indian, Chinese, Malay, and other competitors. For example, as reported by *USA Today*, it took until June 2014 for GAP, as the first Western clothing conglomerate, to decide to manufacture clothes in Myanmar.[11] The article notes that GAP is late in entering the local garment industry in relation to Asian producers that have built a strong presence there.

Such information helps explain why the local government's ability to resist US pressures during the sanction years defines its current continued resistance to implementing the institutional and political changes advocated by the United States.[12] No incentives exist for the local government to change its policies. If anything, disincentives might pervade. During the sanction years, the same political members of the military regime in power today made decisions on how to handle the increasing severity of sanctions. They found that their mitigation policies—reaching out to America's regional adversaries (e.g., China and North Korea) and economic competitors (India, Thailand, China again, Malaysia, Singapore, and Japan) and offering them preferential trade conditions—resulted in much more wealth generation for the Burmese economy than when trade with the United States was legal. Furthermore, evidence suggests that there is an increasing complacence and placation from the United States for the current lack of progress in Myanmar.

On April 1, 2014, the Office of Foreign Assets Control at the US Department of the Treasure published a list of the most frequently posed questions on legal American action against Myanmar. The list clearly states that the Department of State has concluded that the SPDC—State Peace and Development Council—no longer exists. Therefore, the sanction provisions in the Jade Act of 2008 impacting SPDC holdings are no longer applicable.

The SPDC may in effect have been dismantled, but the SPDC structure very much remains the same and is owned by the same individuals.[13] Its former acting president is now the "democratically" elected president of the country. He is the man who under SPDC rewrote the Myanmar constitution in 2008 to include provisions to define the guidelines for the interpretation of democracy. The most important of those provisions is the need for a 75 percent parliamentary majority for any constitutional changes to be legislated. As already discussed, the *Economist* magazine reported that as of 2014 over 80 percent of the members of parliament are former SPDC officers.

The main implication of all of these facts is that it was economic rents extracted during the sanction years that have led to this disturbing current reality. Trade during the period was defined by the regime in terms of enterprise ownership. Currently, the owners of those enterprises comprise the vast majority of the local political elite. Therefore, it is the augmentation of the then established economic relationships that fuels the current political resilience of the regime. The policy implications are that sanctions can have unintended consequences in political rent extracting and protecting, years after they have been lifted.

As early as the 1990s, scholars raised arguments that as economies become more interdependent, it becomes easier for target nations to minimize sanctions' impact by finding alternative trading partners and investment sources (Schott, 1998).[14] Even when sanctions succeed in restricting the flow of goods and services to the target country, the governing regime can often control access to remaining resources within the country. This outcome is the definition of rent-seeking behavior. Rents accrue to the regime because local populations become more dependent on the government in order to gain access to essential goods and services (Gibbons, 1999; Peksen and Drury, 2009; Rowe, 2000). Then, incentive structures develop that can fuel increasing the local political support for the regime. When rent seeking leads to rent extracting, sanctions can cause disproportionate harm to average citizens and disadvantaged groups that are outside the support base of the ruling regime (Peksen and Drury, 2009). Rent extracting is the process of increasing wealth through the special arrangements the regime offers its supporters. Since political activism depends on financial support, increasing the wealth of the regime loyalists can lead to increasing their ability to amass political power. In this way, sanctions can impede the development of a strong opposition to the ruling regime, which is essential for a successful political change.

Oppositions can be thwarted with respect to gaining a critical number of supporters. With poverty and oppression a certain opportunity to improve material well-being by siding with the regime is more attractive than uncertain future promises of change. In support of that logic, Choi and Luo (2013) analyze sanctions in 152 nations in three decades and find evidence that sanctions intensify hardship on the poor of the targeted countries, as already summarized by the previous noted studies, but a consequence of that hardship is an increased propensity for the poor to seek alternative regress for their state of despair. Their heightened level of grievance, as Choi and Luo put it, causes them to engage in international terrorism and criminal activity.

In summary, as Askari et al. (2005) state, the uniqueness of the target's exports, the level of global demand for the target's goods and services and the target's ability to evade sanctions define the target's transaction costs of finding alternative trading partners. The above analyzed data and examples suggest that Myanmar falls into the outlined classifications. Its strong growth then suggests that it was not hard for the regime to find alternative trading partners, that is, the transaction costs of sanction mitigation were low.

Its natural endowments make the case of Myanmar unique. Based on the fact that during the sanction years Myanmar's biggest trading partners became its relatively poor and ambitiously industrializing neighbors, one could conclude that for them access to the country's precious commodities outweighed the possible displeasure of the American government, or other international repercussions from supporting the oppressive military regime. Their support provided not only wealth for the regime, but also validation. As a result, instead of seeing evidence of the regime changing its human rights legacy, its diplomatic pugilism continues. Alarmingly, not only is retaliation to such pugilism not evident, save for the United States' decision to keep certain sanctions in place, there is evidence that nations have subsided the strength of their demands for the implementation of meaningful democratic and human rights policy changes in Myanmar. The best example is a smiling, victorious Thein Sein on the ASEAN website as the face of the new ASEAN 2014 chairmanship. The same man was among the leaders of the 1996 pogroms against the Karen in his role as commander in the Triangle Regional Military Command (TRMC). For his service during the military unrest, he was appointed officially as a member of the State Peace and Development Council (SPDC) in 1997. Military leaders committed to even stronger repressive policies in order to prevent further ethnic uprisings created the SPDC that year to replace SLORC. Only the most powerful regional military commanders, who were members of SLORC, were promoted to new positions in SPDC. This was the same SPDC against which the US State Department concluded on April 1, 2014, that no evidence of its operation or existence remained. The evidence is that its former Secretary 1 (acting president, appointed in 2004 after holding a Secretary 2 position since 1997) is now the country's president. The same person rewrote the constitution in 2008, including provisions in its draft that would make real democratic changes unlikely, as the 75 percent majoritarian rule. The fact that currently over 80 percent of former military regime leaders are the "democratically elected" members of the Myanmar parliament explains why little evidence exists of any legislative change. It also points to the power the former regime holds over current political mobilization. Even with the strong possibility of election fraud, gaining an 80 percent parliamentary majority is not to be discounted easily as mainly reliant on fraud. It suggests strong local support from the electorate. The fact is a compelling testament of the legitimate continued rule of the military regime. This is a very dangerous result. The smiling, defiant Thien, who should be prosecuted for crimes against humanity, is now the face of Asia's new capitalism. For America, making an official proclamation that there is no longer evidence of the old military dictatorship is tantamount to admitting defeat and offering an olive branch of compliance to the man directly responsible for the deteriorating conditions in Myanmar, which led to gradual increase in sanction severity. The severity did not produce results, and now America quietly just goes away and lets things stay as they have been in Myanmar. And so do its West European allies. As the leader in the sanction actions, this reality lowers American credibility. It also undermines international strides toward defining and defending a coherent set of human rights principles. It shows that even if such a set is generally agreed upon, its interpretation and enforcement are for sale. The sale depends on the economic importance of local factor endowments of sanctioned nations. Because of this argument, a similar possible scenario could be at play in North Korea. The North Korean economy is growing at levels similar to Myanmar's during the sanction years. Recent discoveries of precious earth deposits have made it the world's third largest source of the commodity most important in the production of modern day technologies.

Chapter 4

Absorb and Control: How North Korea Responds to Economic Sanctions

Bradley J.H ornback andN ikolayA nguelov

This chapter examines the internal and external factors that contribute to the North Korean economic growth despite the United States and United Nation's imposed sanctions. The specifics indicate a possible repeat of Myanmar's current reality if the present course of sanction ineffectiveness continues. The adjustments of the North Korean economic policy in the past 25 years suggest a calculated ideological government response to sanctions by focussing on the growth of the economic sectors closely associated with the revered Korean cultural virtues of "self-reliance" and "military first." The growth has allowed the regime to show enough progress to its citizens and provide enough marginal quality-of-life improvements to maintain critical citizen support.

60 Years of Sanctions and No Change: Defiance and Resilience

The United States and its allies have imposed various forms of economic sanctions on the Democratic People's Republic of Korea (DPRK) since the outbreak of the Korean War on June 25, 1950. In spite of these sanctions, the ruling regime has shown resilience in its ability to remain in power and maintain control over the people of the country. To date, the DPRK has not complied with any of America's demands among which are to end the pursuit of nuclear weapons, to limit the DPRK's overall weapons arsenal, to loosen the grip of totalitarian communism on the country, and to improve the welfare of the nation's citizens (Noland, 2009).[1]

North Korea, along with Cuba, is the nation in which the United States has the longest-standing history of sanctions with the least success of achieving their goals. During the 55 years of sanctions, diplomatic relations with the DPRK have not improved because the government has been able to defy American demands (Kimura, 1999). In fact, arguments suggest that relations have deteriorated in recent years because of the increasing intensity in the government's defiance to sanction demands with respect to North Korean pursuits in the development of nuclear weapons.[2] Current discussions state that because of its nuclear ambition the DPRK poses direct and indirect threats to American national security. North Korea's fairly recent continued testing of ballistic missiles with increasing range, in addition to nuclear proliferation, magnifies such dangers. In light of its proximity to vital American military bases in South Korea and Japan, analysts have argued that such a threat poses a greater and more immediate danger to peace and stability than the nation's nuclear agenda (Cha and Kang, 2013; Hughes, 2013; Noland, 2009). Presumably, increasing ballistic missile range capabilities has the potential to reach a level that would allow North Korea to successfully launch a missile that could target areas in Alaska.

At one time the United States officially considered the DPRK a state sponsor of terrorism. The American government has also raised concerns that the DPRK receives revenue from illicit black market dealings, many of which involve weapons and weapon components (Rothman, 2007). While no direct links have been found between the DPRK and any recent terrorist attacks, a future possibility does exist. The likelihood of the DPRK launching a nuclear attack is low, but the real danger lies in the potential for its nuclear development and materials to be leaked, stolen, or sold. Therefore, the United States sees the possibility of terrorists or hostile nations obtaining nuclear information and materials from the DPRK, whether directly or indirectly, as a serious threat.[3]

North Korea's behavior and increasing pugilism of late has been puzzling diplomats because it appears irrational. However, the question remains whether this sentiment is valid or whether there is an economic rationale behind the defiance of international political pressures. Evidence suggests that the government employs carefully placed pugilism as a propaganda tactic in strategic time periods of international adversarialism to mobilize support from the population. It cements its power by demonstrating military might through its nuclear tests, while showing the clear economic connection between the nuclear power agenda and internal economics.

Much has been written about the government oppression and abuse of its population. However, evidence suggests that it is not all despotic, nor all abusive. Cumings (2013) explains that recent evidence released by the United States Central Intelligence Agency (CIA) indicates that the DPRK does genuinely provide free housing and health care to all its citizens, has made major progress toward the societal position of women, and has a compassionate and well-executed national policy for the care and education of children. As a result, the latest data show that welfare indicators such as life expectancy and infant mortality are comparable to advanced Western nations (Cumings, 2013: 1; Lankov, 2008).[4] Not all agree. The 2013 Human Rights Watch report posits a much bleaker picture with no mention of notable improvements.[5]

As other totalitarian governments of past and present, the regime relies on a certain level of support from its people. It achieves this support in many ways, chief among which are notable economic improvements. Improving economic conditions visibly, albeit to the average Westerner, not sufficiently, does help a regime garner support. For this reason one must examine how economic activity is developing in North Korea, who are the beneficiaries of the internal and external economic growth, and how the defiance of the government in international politics is connected to those who benefit from it.

Historically, the United States has been the primary supporter of economic sanctions against the DPRK. Kim and Chang (2007) state that the three most important types of sanctions America unilaterally imposed are the revocation of Most Favored Nation trade status in 1951, the addition of the DPRK to the list of state sponsors of terrorism in 1988, and the private financial sanctions put in place in 2005 in the wake of the DPRK being linked to a significant counterfeiting scheme of US dollars. The financial sanctions imposed in 2005 targeted Banco Delta Asia—a private international financial MNC headquartered in Macao, China. Banco Delta Asia was charged as being the primary source of money laundering for the DPRK. The pressure placed on this private bank, in turn, made it difficult for the DPRK to find other international banks that would be willing to deal with any financial business of North Korean sources. Loeffler (2009), former deputy director of global affairs at the US Treasury Department, argues that economic sanctions of this type, implemented in partnership with private banking firms, can be extremely effective.

Cho and Woo (2007) argue that economic pressures, particularly from such targeted sanctions, have forced North Korea to consider changes over the past twenty years. Kim and Chang (2007) state that an example of such considerations could be seen in the late 1990s when the Clinton administration engaged the North Korean government in "significant" diplomatic discussions. These discussions resulted in the DPRK agreeing to cease nuclear development and, in exchange, the United States dropped a large number of economic sanctions.

VanWagenen (2000) states that economic sanctions are an effective "bargaining chip" for the United States in dealings with the DPRK. Stradiotto and Guo (2007) agree, contending that the DPRK began a series of economic reforms in 2002 primarily due to the economic pressures that preceded them. These reforms were modeled after the economic reforms that had occurred in China andVietnam in an attempt to test the waters of market socialism. While McKay (2005) agrees with Stradiotto and Guo (2007) on the impetus for the reforms, he states that the reforms ultimately had no effect on the real problems of the troubled North Korean economy or on the international concerns about the nation. The explanation is that the regime was unwilling to fully commit to the changes and there was not a sufficient level of direct international economic support for the reforms.

Marinov (2005) explains that while economic sanctions are often successful in "destabilizing" rulers of targeted countries, in North Korea that has not been the case. The author defines the DPRK, Cuba, and Iraq (before the 2003 US led invasion) as "atypical" cases because an all-controlling dictator rules each country. A point less often made is that all-controlling or not, dictators do not rule in isolation. They rely on some level of local support and gain it through adding effective propaganda tactics to their repressive policies.

Absorb, Control, and Withstand

North Korea's government has masterfully adopted and maybe even perfected the control tactics of former Communist regimes by adding a few cultural components in the way it uses propaganda on its people. Henriksen (2001) points to the fact that throughout the nation's existence, the ruling regime has been able to preach the ideas of *juche* (self-reliance) and *songun* (military first), adopted from traditional virtues revered by the Korean people throughout history. This indoctrination tactic has allowed the DPRK to keep its citizens under control while in the midst of the direst of hardships, such as the 1990s' famine (Haggard and Noland, 2007).[6] Jin (2003), Frank (2005), Kimura (1999), and McKay (2005) all conclude that the regime has used the sanctions to only serve its purpose further, because they give it a platform from which to continue to indoctrinate the principles of *juche* and *songun* by pointing to the evils of the uncaring outside world. Hufbauer et al. (2007: 106) state that economic sanctions against the DPRK are a "powerful incentive for evasion," which has in turn created more potential danger through increasing the militancy of the population and its support for military aggression. Mazarr (1995) explains that the government uses that platform to reject almost all international options for cooperation if they are confronted with the threat of sanctions of any kind. Interestingly, Dingli (2008) argues that so far sanctions have not been severe enough, nor have they had enough support, to have a major effect on North Korea. Noland (2004) comes to the same conclusion, stating that the only way for sanctions to be successful is for the world to engage in a true international embargo in which it completely cuts off the NPRK from any and all trade. However, it is virtually impossible to achieve such a mass agreement among the nations of the world. Much like in Myanmar, in the case of North Korea, varying interests exist, particularly within the region of Southeast Asia. Niemann (2005) points out that South Korea has increasingly distanced itself from supporting sanctions and active vocal participation in UN resolutions against the regime. Concomitantly, South Korea has also become the DPRK's second-largest trading partner.

China remains the DPRK's largest trading partner. Like Myanmar, North Korea has been able to maintain, and even grow, its economic platforms in the face of economic sanctions primarily because of Chinese support. According to Lee (2007), over 90 percent of all of the DPRK's oil comes from China, as does most of its imported food. Beyond trade, Noland (2004) and Wrobel (2007) point out that both South Korea and China worry about the potential influx of refugees into their respective countries from the DPRK, in the event that the ruling regime should fall or implement a greater degree of freedom. For that reason both nations continue to engage the North Korean government in economic partnerships.

Economic sanctions remain in place mainly because of the poor human rights record in the DPRK. However, as already noted, some researchers caution that imposing economic sanctions is often a counterproductive measure in attempting to address human rights issues. Sidel (1999: 1498) states that sanctions have "frequently been associated with severe deterioration of the health and welfare of the populations affected."[7] This holds true in the case of North Korea. Haggard and Noland (2007) state that the ruling regime of the DPRK would rather subject its citizens to abject poverty, disease, famine, and death than to give into the demands of economic sanctions. These acts exhibit a demonstration of communal sacrifice in the face of foreign attempts at domination.

According to Manyin and Nikitin (2009) of the United States Congressional Research Service, in recent years the American government has attempted to separate the strategic interests of sanctions from humanitarian aid when it comes to the DPRK.[8] The North Korean Human Rights Act (H.R. 4011), which President George W. Bush signed into law in 2004, serves as an example. The law allows for humanitarian aid to be disbursed in North Korea with the stipulation that all financial incentives offered, including incremental increases in the amount of humanitarian aid, would be based upon improving humanitarian conditions. The act was reauthorized in 2008.

Other acts of revising sanctions against the DPRK include an increasing amount of recently passed legislation that promulgates targeted sanctions. Sanctions imposed by the United Nation's Security Council as a response to North Korean military tests serve as examples. The UN adopted Resolution 1540 unanimously on April 28, 2004, in response to the DPRK test firing a long-range missile. The resolution prohibits UN member states from engaging in any transactions with the DPRK that are in any way related to arms.[9] On October 14, 2006, the UN passed Resolution 1718 in response to the DPRK's nuclear test conducted on October 9, 2006.[10] This resolution required UN member states to freeze all financial assets of North Korean origin with any links to illicit activities. Additionally, the UN placed sanctions on luxury items and directed member nations to inspect any suspicious cargo en route from or to the DPRK. These two particular resolutions point to the fact that, as Noland (2004) and Dingli (2008) suggest, sanctions against North Korea may not have been sufficiently strong. The fact that prior to 2004 arms sales to the DPRK were legal and North Korean financial assets, which by definition mean coming from government sources, were allowed to be integrated into international financial platforms, suggests that nations at large other than the United States continued to engage in trade with the North Korean government despite sanctions.

UN Resolution 1874 includes more recent augmentations of the actions taken by the previously noted resolutions in response to further nuclear tests conducted on May 25, 2009. The mandate essentially reiterates the provisions of Resolutions 1540 and 1718, but adds the provisions that UN member nations and international financial institutions are not to engage in any financial agreements or funding of any sort with the DPRK outside of humanitarian and developmental purposes.[11]

Marks (1999), Sidel (1999), and Hufbauer, Clyde, and Oegg (2000) all agree that "targeted sanctions" are a way of applying economic pressure in an attempt to avoid as much humanitarian collateral damage as possible. The justification is that targeted sanctions are directed toward the ruling regime and the elite within the country who have the capacity to carry out the changes desired by the imposing nations. Therefore, UN Resolution 1718 specifically placed restrictions on the luxury goods trade.

The assumption is that only the ruling elite can afford luxury items and the hope is that the impact of such targeted measures will be directly felt by the regime. For such reasons, targeted sanctions have grown in popularity when imposed not only in North Korea, but in general across other nations against when there are sanctions as well. As discussed in Chapter 1, at present, they are the only type of sanctions in effect against Russia.

Targeted sanctions leave room for trade that could directly benefit the citizens of the receiving nation. However, in the case of North Korea that argument does not necessarily stand. If there is no private sector that could engage in trade outside of the scope of the local repressive government, then by definition, all profits from any trade accrue to government-owned and managed entities.

Delving deeper into the particular economic structure of the North Korean model, Kimura (1999) notes that the economy is based on a ruling structure that has unique cultural features, which define its command-style nature in an exceptional way. It has a strong collectivist foundation built on a combination of communism, Confucianism, Korean heritage, Asian cultural emphasis on the family, and nationalism born from pride against successful resistance to Japanese imperialism. Therefore, the previously discussed principles of *juche* (self-reliance) and *songun* (military first) define economic activity in whole because they reinforce the virtues of unity.

No residual trade or other economic engagement occurs in North Korea without a heavy dose of regime rhetoric of how its particular implementation builds *juche* and *songun*. The exaltation of these virtues has allowed the government to maintain its influence and control over the people by building its economic policy around the ideals and making the people active ideological participants. Possibly for those reasons, the economy of the DPRK has managed to increasingly develop. The recent past has shown a very rapid growth. As reported by the *Financial Times* on February 20, 2014, the nation has tripled its trade volume in the past six years with exports to China, its largest trading partner, increasing fivefold.[12] The economy of North Korea revolves around several main industrial activities where defense and construction lead in volume in relation to GDP—a testament to *songun*" militaryf irst."[13]

Communist nations have often focused on construction in an attempt to prove to their citizens and to the world both their stability and growth. As examined in Chapter 3, the construction sector is also the foundation of trade capabilities because in poorer nations trade volumes can be negatively impacted by an insufficient transportation, storage, and inventory management infrastructure. Therefore, construction of such an infrastructure is needed as trade grows. For these reasons, in Myanmar, the growth of the construction sector was concomitant with the growth of exports and the trade and services intensive sectors.

Construction is a fairly easy sector to manage in a planned economy because it is not subject to clear market demand, if the government does not price its output. However, it is subject to economic hardship. Lack of public funds and disruption of trade with respect to inputs can cause investment in construction to decline. In North Korea, both have occurred and this is worth analyzing because we can gain insights into sanction impacts and their mitigation by the government. Figure 4.1 illustrates fluctuation in construction expenditures in North Korea between 1989 and 2008.[14]

Construction spending notably decreased in the aftermath of the collapse of the Soviet Union and during the famine of the 1990s. However, in around 1999, a strong and sustained growth followed, indicating general economic expansion. Construction is the main subcategory that benefits from infrastructure developments, investment in energy and natural resource extraction, expansion of military and civil research and development, not to mention quality of contingent enterprises such as building hospitals, schools, and recreation centers. All of the above have been mentioned as growing in the recent past under the careful management of the North Korean government (Byman and Lind, 2010; Cumings, 2013; Lankov, 2008).[15]

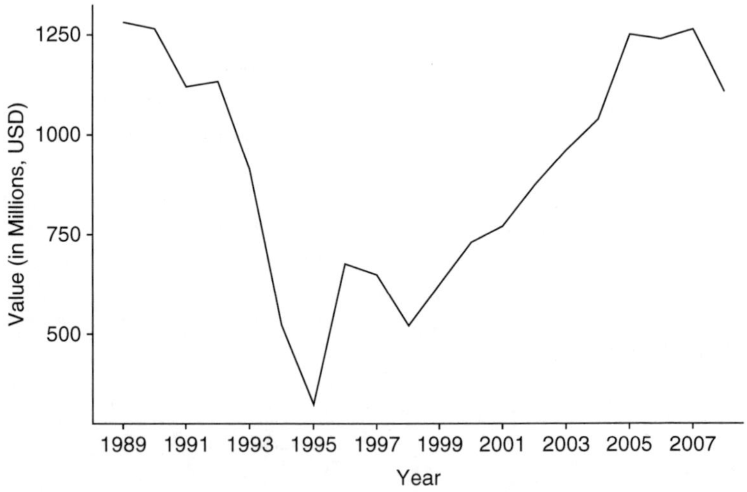

Figure 4.1 Value added to GDP by construction spending.

Another indicator of economic growth despite sanctions is the change in exports illustrated by figure 4.2.[16]

For many years, North Korea imported far more than it exported. Although continuing to run a trade deficit, the DPRK has seen a steady rise in exports since recovering from the famine of the 1990s. Yoon and Lee (2013) track the developments that have led to such a growth and explain that China and South Korea are the leading export markets for North Korea, particularly in minerals, metallurgical products, and military equipment. For example, Haggard and Noland (2012) examine 250 Chinese firms that do business in North Korea and conclude that the majority are involved in direct export of North Korean raw materials and minerals. In addition, North Korea uses Chinese intermediary firms to procure inputs from nations that sanction it.[17]

It has been well-established that China is a supporter of the DPRK (Jeffries, 2012; Nanto and Manyin, 2011), but the more recent and growing economic cooperation between North and South Korea is less

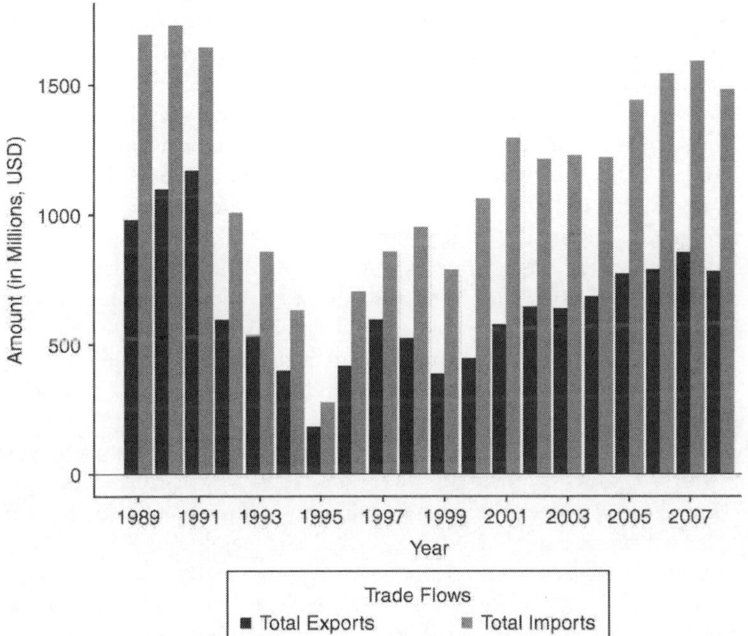

Figure 4.2 DPRK imports and exports.

discussed. Cha and Kang (2013) offer a thorough explanation of this dynamic and conclude that the economic incentives for both North and South Korean leadership drive this somewhat silent relationship. A major recent development is the expansion of free-trade zones with the support of China and South Korea. The expansion started in 2007 under the liberal South Korean leadership, but stalled in 2010 when a conservative government change occurred in South Korea, and all intra-Korean trade was halted with the exception of that done through the largest of free-trade zones—the Kaesong Industrial Complex (Manyin, 2012). Still, the zone generated over $2 US billion in 2012.[18] North Korea is pursuing further expansion of free-trade zones, and is getting economic support, despite official diplomatic admonitions of its nuclear policy.[19] According to the CIA World Fact Book, Country Profile of North Korea, in 2013 the government announced the creation of 14 new Special Economic Zones open for foreign investors.[20] And foreign investors have exploited opportunities already. *Businessweek* reports that as of 2012 many foreign firms had established strong presences in North Korea, but none of those firms are from the United States or Canada. The examples offered are Egypt's Orascom Telecom that builds a 3G mobile-phone network and DHL drivers in Pyongyang. Tourism has grown to such an extent that not one but two Hong Kong–listed companies operate casinos for tourists who mostly come from China and South Korea. Also mentioned are French utility giant Lafarge, German Nosotek—an outsourcer of programming services—and Swedish Noko Jean.[21] Cha and Kang (2013) offer a thorough breakdown of international industrial partnerships and their growth in North Korea and note that among the leading initiatives are a German partnership for the development of utility projects and communications infrastructure, an Australian partnership in mining and education, and the much-discussed Russian Trans-Siberian expansion.[22] But chief among all those examples of why North Korea is becoming more attractive to international partners is the government's role in developing and supporting the extraction of rare earth elements (REE). Recent information on that dynamic became the point of discussion, when in 2013 it was announced that the largest rare earth deposits on the planet were located in North Korea. It was to be mined in a joint venture partnership between privately held, but run by North Korean government officials, SRE Minerals and British Virgin Island MNC Pacific Century Rare Earth Minerals Ltd.[23] Multiple sources estimate that North Korea now holds two-thirds of global rare earth deposits, surpassing China as the leader.[24] By the summer of 2014, most of the newly excavated elements were exported to China.[25]

Rare earth elements are becoming increasingly valuable in the technology age because they are the core components in the manufacturing of modern technology. The proliferation of personal electronic products, the growth of sales of those products in the developing world, and the increasing innovation in their production, all rely on rapidly improving their information processing capabilities. Rare earth elements define information processing and performance capabilities (Massari and Ruberti, 2013). For example, indium is critical to all flat panel, high-resolution displays in televisions, computers, tablets, and cell phone screens. Platinum is at the core of hybrid automobile technology development because it is used in both pollution control devices in cars and in fuel cells (de Bruijn, 2005). The presence of significant rare earth deposits in DPRK, the current international operations of extracting and trading them, and the possibility to grow the North Korean rare earth sector into a leading world supplier, change the strategic market importance of the country. Based on their governments' economic policies, we now understand the similarities in market features between North Korea and Myanmar.

The examples of North Korea's economic growth follow the scenario of Myanmar. In both cases, China, Russia and other regional partners augment their trade despite sanctions. An important fact to remember is that the increase of trade creates wealth for the governments, since in both nations all industrial activity is controlled and owned by the authoritarian regimes. Such evidence suggests that in Myanmar and North Korea international MNCs are finding ways to deal with the sanctions and the unpredictability of the governments. But, are both regimes behaving unpredictably in terms of business savvy? The noted impressive wealth creation suggests that the business process in both national markets had and still have levels of efficiency that allow for the formation of a strong and rising growth rate over time. Such a rise is dependent upon market stability. Lack of stability would result in fluctuations of averages, which in both nations have not been observed since the early 2000s—the time period for the onset of the current unprecedented economic growth in the developing world. Therefore, it appears that despite sanctions, these repressive regimes exploited and continue to exploit new business opportunities well. Their success is based on incentives target nations face in garnering support from black knight partners. It can be deduced that the governments provide a critical level of business stability and other attractive features to augment trade options and grow their wealth. It can be seen in the case of Myanmar and to some degree in the examples of those who argue that there are improvements in the human conditions inside North Korea, that the governments are using their new wealth to grow their political clout.

Repressive regimes face two main incentives to be good business partners to those that support them in the face of sanctions. One is to provide favorable business opportunities to them so that when faced with pressure from their Western trading partners, the governments of the black knights can discount economic repercussions from such pressures, if the benefits from doing business in or with the sanction nations are significant. The other is self-serving—to make as much profit for the owners of the local industries as possible. A way to grow such profits is through increasing trade, particularly in resource-dependent sectors such as natural gas, teak, precious gems, and ores (as in Myanmar), and rare earth elements (as in North Korea). Therefore, scholars such as Hajzler (2014) observe a paradox in foreign trade and government structure. The paradox is that, as Hajzler's data indicate, high-risk countries—those with least favorable environments for doing business according to world standards—have a high concentration of foreign direct investment in the resource sector. There are two reasons for this paradox to exist. One is that, most FDI has a developing nation's MNCs or government as its source. In nations such as Myanmar and North Korea, it is MNCs from Asia that channel the FDI toward these two nations. Furthermore, as the results of Myanmar and North Korea foreign investment flows suggest, the investors themselves may prefer local platforms for doing business.

One must not take for granted the historical legacy of FDI originating mostly in the developed world. As developing nations grow, so do their world investments, which means that today's aggregate world FDI contains a significant and growing portion, which has a developing nation as its source. The other reason is that today's climate of global competitiveness makes it necessary for MNCs to bear the increasing transaction costs of local institutional instability in order to gain preferential positions in the development of resource-rich markets. The examples of Western firm engagement in North Korea, as well as the Iranian oil equipment sale evidence examined in Chapter 1, suggest a willingness of global firms to bear the high risks of unfavorable business environments if the pay off is access to valuable commodities.

In light of these findings, it is confounding that economic sanctions are so widely employed today. It is understood that as alternatives to military action, sanctions and related diplomatic threats are preferable, but if their impact is understood to be easily counteracted, then what alternatives can be explored? Possible options are diplomatic alternatives aimed not at the regimes of repressive or adversarial states, but at the general population in target nations.

Chapter 5

Alternatives to Sanctions

TiffanyK aschel andN ikolayA nguelov

This chapter offers an evaluation of the effectiveness of soft power—the direct alternative to sanctions. Metrics for quantifying soft power are explored and their results are evaluated in the context of Middle Eastern diplomacy, post 9/11. The Middle East is examined because soft power efforts have been strongly developed there during the War on Terror.

Soft Power

The *raison d'être* of sanctions is to create significant economic hardships that would lead to political unrest. The unrest is said to originate in segments of the population decidedly different from the ruling elites. To that effect, among the many criticisms of sanctions explored so far, one stands out—that economic sanctions are detrimental to human rights. Peksen (2009) shows that economic sanctions are a counterproductive policy tool when enacted with the goal of improving human rights because they lead to a decrease in the flow of free information. With that finding in mind, it is worth exploring how information proliferation impacts government action in rogue or nondemocratic (according to Western definitions) nations. It must be understood that all repressive governments consider themselves democratic in their own right. Communist nation leaders base their legitimacy on Marxist and Leninist dogma, claiming that they represent the people, and that their version of a united proletariat democracy was, and is, the real definition of equitable representation. Elections and resistance to that platform are condemned as challenges to the nature of democracy, because they supposedly lower the ability of the people to be represented equitably in government. The possibility of voting against the government is seen as an opportunity to vote against the people, and therefore, against democracy. Such rhetoric is at the heart of propaganda that fueled the ideological divisions of the Cold War. It was so successful for so long because the Eastern Bloc nation governments were able to limit alternative information from reaching their people. Today, such expropriation of information is becoming harder to execute. Information technology has advanced and with it opportunities for knowledge exchange have increased manifold. With respect to political information, such exchange has fueled the modern growth of transnational civic activism.

With respect to information proliferation and its impact on transnational civil society formation, Smith and Wiest (2005) show that technology has stimulated an explosion of transnational social networking, movements, and activism. In both developed and developing countries, social activism increases with the degree of global economic exposure. In developing countries this exposure is particularly dependent on the role of the state because intergovernmental cooperation increases contact with global institutions. Smith and Wiest (2005) offer empirical evidence that in low-income countries, improving ties to global governance structures leads to an increase in global activity network action with respect to individual nations. The result is an increase in local social activism. These patterns are especially important in light of the previously examined impacts of policies, such as sanctions, that limit international exposure. As the case of Myanmar shows, during sanctions, the repressive policies of the regime increased with respect to retaliation against local political opposition. The result is that significant political opposition groups are unable to develop and participate in political action, even after the end of sanctions. Therefore, because sanctions not only impact economic activity, but also decrease nongovernmental social activism, they can prevent local political challengers from getting much-needed international support. This support can be directly monetary, but most importantly, it can come through amassing knowledge on political mobilization. Because of such dynamics, the findings of Smith and Wiest (2005) are important. They provide evidence that local government engagement with the international community, rather than isolation, leads to beneficial civil social transformation. This is because social media technologies connect networks of local social movement actors, who are looking to change domestic politics, to supporters outside their national borders.

In this dynamic, local governments play an important role in the structures of governance in nations with underdeveloped institutions. Local government has two main forms—the central regime and its regional arms. When it comes to policy implementation in developing nations, the central regimes face difficulties in overseeing implementation because of direct and indirect costs of distance. It is this vacuum that gives regional government officials significant discretion. Research has found that regional officials engage increasingly in international diplomatic exchanges that fall outside the scope of their central governments. This dynamic occurs because of the growth of international civic activism. Today it is international non-governmental organizations (INGOs) that serve as central actors in the implementation of diplomatic exchange initiatives, such as education programs, forums, community development work, public health, and poverty alleviation, or environmental and natural resource conservation (Ahmed, 2011; Dryzek, 2012; Edwards and Gaventa, 2014; Schroeder, 2008; Xie, 2011). When local governments allow for such initiatives to take place, local political activism increases. Since the initiatives are executed at the community level, the central government is somewhat removed. Therefore, official government structures are a weaker counterpart to transformative civic engagement, and in effect, opposing political structures can develop more easily at the local level because of community isolation problems. In developing nations, where most sanctions and political unrest occur, infrastructure and underdevelopment problems raise the transaction costs for centrally mandated governance at the local level. Local government officials are usually appointed by the central government but operate in relative isolation (Bardhan, 2002; Bratton, 1989; Kanbur and Zhang, 2005). Because most INGO initiatives operate at the regional level, they represent major sources of new information, resources, and knowledge coming into a community. Often the benefits of these resources raise local population welfare, increase community awareness of issues, and provide impetus for political mobilization (Dobbin, Simmons, and Garrett, 2007; Fisher, 1997; Kamat, 2003). Therefore, the more opportunities for international interaction there are, the higher the probability of local institutional transformation becomes. The probability increases because a significant portion of international civil action information exchange is of a political nature (Chesters, 2004; Colas, 2013; Schroeder, 2008).

International political information exchange falls under the scope of soft power. Soft power is a phenomenon fairly recently explored in diplomacy as an alternative to "hard power"—military actions, threats, and economic sanctions. It is the art of using cultural charm, appeal of ideals, and influential means of attraction to condition a positive relationship that tempers hostility (Nye, 1990). Soft power aims to cultivate mutual understanding in a positive manner. It is based on information transmission from sender to receiver nation. Today, such information comes in many forms, from radio broadcasts, to television programs, to discussions in social media outlets. Soft power information embodies the ideals behind the official political position of the sender nation.

The measurement of soft power and its effectiveness is an issue previously approached in a variety of ways by researchers. Soft power has many forms and, without a clear definition, can come to encompass anything outside of hard power from television, radio, social media, product branding, and advertising, to exchange student programs and local government partnerships such as sister city programs (Atkinson, 2010; Fan, 2008; Hayden, 2012; Nye, 1990, 2002; 2004; 2008; 2010). According to the US Department of State's 2014 Fiscal Year Executive Budget Summary,[1] the United States spends millions of dollars on programs to support such initiatives with the hope that they help promote a positive opinion of the United States, its people, and its foreign policies. Consequently, soft power is employed and funded in its various forms by the American government, which makes it an official foreign policy tool. However, the specific definitions of soft power incarnations are subject to academic debate.

The literature on the topic comes in many forms as researchers attempt to quantify the elusive concept. As noted by Hayden (2012), the ambiguity of soft power manifests itself when analyzed, whereby the measurement of soft power is reduced to measuring resources or looking at it through a lens of case-based assessments of circumstantial situations. Hayden argues that neither is representative of the way soft power translates into policy outcomes. The issue is that, in concepts such as policy outcomes, their own definitions are case specific. For example, in a post 9/11 world, one of the goals of soft power is to reduce the threat of terrorism. It is subjective to quantify soft power impacts on such a threat and to measure what the threat of terrorism would have been in the absence of soft power.

In attempting to quantify soft power some researchers have elected to use qualitative methods of interviews and polling (El-Nawawy, 2006; Telhami, 2006; Nisbet et al., 2004; Rugh, 2006). Qualitative research is useful when secondary data or defined numeric metrics are not easily accessible as proxies for studying social phenomena. The problem with qualitative research with respect to soft power is that it is prone to information asymmetry problems. If the research community has a hard time defining soft power, then the implication is that explaining the concept to those being interviewed and polled would be subject to the researchers' discretion. Framing issues can arise with respect to questions being posed in a leading fashion, suggesting the "right" answer to those being surveyed. Because of such reasons some social scientists prefer quantitative approaches to studying soft power outcomes (Atkinson, 2010; Golan and Yang, 2013; Knack, 2004; Smith, 2007). Some examples include assessments of government programs, such as education exchange programs executed through the US Bureau of Educational and Cultural Affairs (Telhami, 2006), while others rely on information coded through surveys taken by think tanks (Yun and Kim, 2008). All offer snapshots of insight into soft power effectiveness and their collective findings indicate that soft power has limited benefits.

Examining soft power in a global context, Yun and Kim (2008) outline the relative importance of three main resources in the formation of soft power—ethnicity, relationship, and reputation. They conclude that there is a significant link between ethnicity and national attraction. Additionally, the authors argue that reputation precedes countries. If a country has a bad reputation among an ethnic group, it is unlikely soft power methods would be very fruitful. Therefore, context and environment are both important.

What works in one country may not work in another, even if the countries are similar in demographics and culture. To that effect, Fan (2008) points out that the perception of the target country is the determinant of soft power effectiveness, because local populations define what is attractive to them and what is not. The overall implication is that soft power tools must be tailored to the specific peoples and places of deployment. What may work in South America may not work in the Middle East. The existing relationship, religion, ethnicity, and perceptions of the people dictate the potential effectiveness of soft power tools. Examining perception in that context, Goldsmith and Yusaku (2012) analyze 58 multinational surveys and the respective countries' foreign policy decisions. The authors conclude that public opinion of US foreign policy legacies influences foreign leaders' decision making as it pertains to the formation of their own local foreign policies. The implication is that soft power can be used as a rhetorical tool for leaders and media. It seems soft power can have a top-down as well as bottom-up effect because soft power can influence governments indirectly by the effects it can have on citizens.

One of the most discussed ways of applying soft power is through education. Atkinson (2010) found evidence that greater participation in educational exchanges is associated with new perceptions of America in the recipient country, which ultimately translates into improved local human right records. The United States utilizes a variety of exchange programs both through private and public organizations as a form of diplomacy. As Snow (2008) points out, however, it is not merely enough to say exchanges work. There must be quantitative research on how people in other nations view the West, specifically the United States, that is a direct result of such exchanges. For example, according to multiple sources[2] Kim Jon-un, North Korea's "Dear Leader" was educated in Switzerland, like his brothers and his mother, and yet Western education does not seem to have influenced his views of the West, human rights, nor has it improved his attitude toward the United States. The paradox of authoritarian and anti-US leaders being educated themselves, and sending their own offspring for Western, often American education, is much discussed in the literature on local elites in undemocratic nations (Acemoglu et al., 2005; Bu, 2003; Rizvi, 2011; Spilimbergo, 2009). In 2014, *Business Insider* covered a story on the world's top 16 despots and their wives, and explained that most of the wives, as well as the authoritarian leaders, were educated in the West.[3] To that effect, Spilimbergo (2009) argues that there is no relationship between Western education and local democracy building. Ultimately, building democracy through soft power is the goal. However, quantifying democracy itself can be problematic, albeit it being the most studied concept of political action. Considering the challenges of quantifying the various forms of soft power, the relationship between democracy and soft power is subject to empirical contention.

Another soft power method that has been studied, because it lends itself to empirical analysis, is foreign aid. Its amounts, as well as aim, have been examined with respect to building democracy. For example, using various democracy indices in combination with socio-economic metrics such as GDP, aid, change in income, illiteracy, and infant mortality rates, Knack (2004) estimates that foreign aid has been largely ineffectual in promoting democracy in recipient nations. Bjørnskov (2010) delves deeper into reasons for its ineffectiveness and explains that local elites in nations that receive aid are able to basically usurp aid funds. The conclusion is that it is not aid itself, but the presence of accountability structures around aid disbursement that can increase democracy levels. However, Savun and Tirone (2011) find aid to be highly beneficial in preventing civil conflict and thus aiding democracy. More recently, Van de Walle (2012) argues that, in the case of Mali, aid can be credited with strengthening accountability measures that are critical for democracy. Scott and Steele (2011) find a positive relationship between specific aid packages and progress toward democracy building. Smith (2007) shows a relationship between declining American public diplomatic efforts, which encompass certain forms of foreign aid, and rising anti-Americanism. The overall implication from these studies is that monetary aid without diplomacy may be counterproductive.

In addition to Knack (2004) and Smith's (2007) admonitions of placing attention on money as it relates to soft power, Nye (2008) argues that soft power cannot be measured in dollars; it is measured by the number of changed minds. Nye states that soft power is about people, not money; therefore, it is imperative to understand the target audiences, their thoughts, values, and desires. Such a recommendation is commendable, but it does not imply that this understanding can cause a direct government response. Understanding the thoughts, values, and desires of the people will do little because it is not the people, but their governments that are the problem. By definition, the aid and diplomacy efforts to build and strengthen democracy stem from the fact that target local governments are undemocratic and do not represent the thoughts, values, and desires of their people. Understanding their change, as Nye states, is not only defeatist in terms of measurement, as it is contentious to try and estimate a change of mind,[4] but also, in impact. Shifting the attention in that direction removes the focus from studying outcomes of government action that are direct and time specific.

Smith (2007) rightfully points to the multifaceted nature of soft power, noting that soft power, in combination with other factors, shapes public opinion about a foreign nation. Other factors include the foreign policy legacies of each country, official diplomacy, and individual interactions among citizens. The strongest of these, Smith argues, are the policies of one government toward another and therefore, its people. In other words, if people believe that the policies of US government are against them or their interests, they will not respond to soft power methods. Again, the question arises of the separation between "peoples" beliefs and the actions of their governments. It was previously discussed that in adversarial nations, where economic sanctions have been deployed, evidence of rent-seeking behavior denotes that the governments had some degree of local support. The question is how to employ soft power to minimize such support for repressive governments. A look at the Middle East helps explain why this question must be addressed.

The Middle East is the region where America is most engaged in economic and diplomatic discourse through its War on Terror. Much has been said about the dynamic with little agreement on successful policy options. In a speech at the National Press Club in Washington, DC on September 23, 2014, former Virginia senator Jim Webb—who served as an assistant secretary of defense as well as the secretary of the navy, and among his many accolades, won an Emmy award for his documentary on US Marines in Beirut—argued that the Middle East is a core problem for America's international credibility. Webb's exact words are:

> Once the Cold War ended we lost our way. We continued to be trapped in the never-ending entanglements in the Middle East beginning with the invasion of Iraq, to the Arab Spring, to Libya, to Syria, to now ISIS and Turkey.

The explanation is that the continued Middle Eastern engagement has become "a tangled mess of situational ethics" with no improvement, nor end in sight. The continued increased engagement is due to unique strategic and economic factors.

The Middle East Example: Strategic and Economic Importance

The relationship between the United States and the Middle East has been notoriously strained (Little, 2008; Tillman, 1982; McAlister, 2005). Much has been written on the reasons for the difficulties, from the historical legacies of Christian versus Muslim values, to current policy-specific reasons centered around American support for Israel. Tracking the post-colonial rise of Islamic conservatism and anti-Western sentiments in the Middle East, Lewis (1990), in his much discussed and strongly titled essay "The Roots of Muslim Rage," concludes that the "rage" is based on frustrations from failures in Western policies. Lewis writes:

> For vast numbers of Middle Easterners, Western-style economic methods brought poverty, Western-style political institutions brought tyranny, even Western-style warfare brought defeat. It is hardly surprising that so many were willing to listen to voices telling them that the old Islamic ways were best and that their only salvation was to throw aside the pagan innovations of the reformers and return to the True Path that God had prescribed for his people. (Lewis, 1990: 55)

In support, in his seminal work "The Clash of Civilizations?" Samuel Huntington (1993) argues that Islamic civilizations, by the very nature of their religion and cultural beliefs, clash and will continue to clash with Western civilizations, just as they have for over 1300 years. Fundamental differences between Islam and Christianity serve as the basis for the differences in political values. Huntington (1993) lists numerous instances in which these political differences manifested themselves in violence. These two works have generated much interest in a post-9/11 world because of their prophetic implications. As a direct response, Norris and Inglehart (2002) tested Huntington's thesis by examining cultural values of 75 predominantly Muslim countries using the World Values Study 1995–2001.[5] The authors concluded that although culture does indeed matter, claims of a "clash of civilizations," especially with respect to fundamentally different political values held by Western and Islamic societies, represent an oversimplification of the issues. This argument is consistent with Lewis (1990) who offers examples of Muslim political systems that have adopted Western values and policies such as voting, even through strife. The general conclusion is that in many political dimensions Islamic and Western societies are similar in their positive orientation toward democratic ideals. Therefore, Norris and Inglehart (2002) argue, any black-and-white "Islam versus the

West" interpretation of a "culture clash" is far too simplistic. There are policy reasons at play that fuel the discourse. Fareed Zakaria summed the main policy reasons for American resentment in the Middle East in his much discussed 2001 opinion piece, "The Politics of Rage: Why Do They Hate Us," published in *Newsweek* magazine.[6] Zakaria states that there is no need to look back centuries for the root of Arab hostility toward the United States.[7] The main reasons can be explained through American politics of the past 70 years. Namely, Zakaria points to the creation of Israel in 1948 as the source of the Arab World's disillusionment with America. He explains that there is a perception in the Arab World that Israel, composed mainly of foreign outsiders, was created at a time when the region believed it was finally gaining its freedom from the West. Zakaria published a follow up piece in the *Washington Post* in 2014, titled "Why Do They Still Hate Us, 13 Years Later."[8] In it, he expands on the previous points and relates them to the Arab Spring, the failure of the nation-building policies in Iraq, the rebellion in Syria, and the rise of ISIS/ISOL. Zakaria concludes that it is the lack of civil society that fuels hate and division in the Arab World. He remarks that the problem is not Muslim, but Arabic, and is due to the low degree of governance in the region. Civic engagement is low and has been so historically. Most nations in the region were artificially drafted during and after colonialism in tribal cultures that lacked a coherent civil national identity. Such an identity failed to develop, and tribal sentiments continue to fuel Arab politics.

One common thread in the Arabic political rhetoric has become the fight against Western intrusion. When the British and French colonialists left, America counterintuitively inherited their legacies of Western imperialism. The United States became the representation of the entire West, and Israel became the personification of continued oppression, infiltration, and interference. This hostility only increased as the United States continued to support Israel with the Arab-Israeli wars in 1967 and 1973, and its continued support then established the view that America was against the Muslim Palestinians. Understanding the legacy of the Arab-Israeli wars in building the lasting public sentiment that fuels anti-Israeli and anti-American feelings in the general population in the region has been the focus of extensive discussion. Telhemi (2006) explains that the relationship between Israel and the United States is a key source of resentment for the Arab World and posits that it may be the single most important issue. Israel's occupation of Palestinian lands is interpreted as the West's general support of the aggression. In relation, Furia and Lucas (2006), analyzing the sources of contention between Middle East and North African (MENA) nations (specifically Egypt, Jordan, Kuwait, Lebanon, Morocco, Saudi Arabia, and the United Arab Emirates) and the Western World (this includes but is not limited to the United States), find that the issue of Palestine is so important to Arabs that it serves as a "litmus test" for their evaluation of Western countries. The conclusion is that due to America's staunch military, diplomatic, and economic support for Israel, the United States inevitably fails this test. However, Furia and Lucas (2006) argue that the support for Israel is only one aspect and that there are significant confluence factors that must be accounted for in explaining the negative perception of America and the West. Peterson (2002) offers examples of such factors that include trade and environmental policies, as well as agricultural subsidies, and the general American "unilateral" behavior in international power wielding. The author analyzes those factors as results of policy legacies and links them to emotional causation of hostile attitudes. A conclusion offered is that while perceptions about the United States are not monolithic, the stereotypes that Americans are arrogant, hypocritical, and culturally ignorant are quite pervasive, due to the "contradictory" behavior of the US government. It is American government action, judged through the overall direction, and execution of American foreign policy in the region, that has cultivated a deep-seated source of mistrust. Among the specific policies, identified as causes for this mistrust, are economic sanctions. As an example, Tessler (2003) posits that there is a "perceived lackadaisical" attitude of the United States on the suffering of the Iraqi people as a result of American sanctions. The author states that the perception is a result of such outcomes as the fact that, according to official estimates, in the first five years of sanctions in the 1990s, more than 500,000 children died as a direct result of their imposition. Tessler further posits that the sanctions did not deter anything but the overall economic and human development of the country, and eventually their ineffectiveness resulted in the United States going to war with the defiant Saddam Hussein.

With respect to US sanctions in the region, Murtaza Hussain (2012)[9] explains that the pervading attitude of Arab populations is that sanctions disproportionately affect the average citizen, causing mass human suffering, and do little to the regimes they are supposed to penalize. Citizens take them personally, Hussain argues, because they feel their direct impact. This is the case in the Middle East because of specific inequities. Local structures facilitate repressive governments' wealth accumulation, which is disproportionately high in relation to the average person, leading to a very high degree of economic isolation and absorption of restrictive economic activity. Oskarsson (2012) explains the structural dynamics and their use by Saddam Hussein to remain in power. The conclusion is that damage caused by sanctions to Iraq's financial, healthcare, and socioeconomic structures helped the dictator remain in power.

The Zogby International annual "Arab Attitudes" polling series, started in 2002, pays special attention to Middle Eastern attitudes toward sanctions. The 2002 polls indicated US favorability would increase by nearly 50 percent in the region if sanctions against Iraq were lifted. In explaining the sentiment, ten years after the aforementioned results, Greenwald (2012)[10] claims that Arabs consider American sanctions to be the main reason for the massive human suffering in their homelands. The author argues that this fact is largely ignored by American policy makers, as Tessler (2003) argued a decade earlier. The implications are that the lack of acknowledgment depicts the American government as unsympathetic, uncaring, and hostile to the Arab people.

Sanctions are only one aspect of the factors that are behind the strained relationship between America and the Arab World. Another factor is the continued US presence in the region. According to a 2008 report by the Pew Research group,[11] the dual wars in Iraq and Afghanistan had driven American favorability "into the ground," as a majority of people in most surveyed Muslim nations believed America's War on Terrorism is merely a smokescreen to both control Mideast oil and "dominate the world." Those are pretty strong words that denote a high level of contention. It is understandable that such passion can develop around foreign military presence, given the legacy of colonial occupation in the region. Although formal military operations have ceased in both Iraq and Afghanistan, the 2014 Zogby poll[12] indicates the majority of respondents (in all but the United Arab Emirates) cited the "continuing occupation of Palestinian lands" as the biggest obstacle toward peace and stability in the Middle East. The second biggest was "US interference in the Arab world." Again, the notion of physical presence in the region is noted, not just military action. However, one cannot ignore the legacy of 9/11, and its role in the intensifying American regional "interference," as Zogby International puts it.

Much has been said about the transformative legacy of the terrorist attacks in increasing the role the United States plays in the region. As a result, the Islamic world sees America as the face of the West. In a world where media defines intercultural communication, America has made strides toward policies of employing media channels as tools of diplomacy. To that effect, the United States has increased ways to utilize soft power methods in the Middle East (Rugh, 2006).

American Soft Power in The Middle East

There are several targeted American programs for the Middle East that were developed post 9/11 with the goal to debunk local extremist ideological rhetoric. It is the belief that this type of rhetoric employed by radical factions is the seed of ideological disparity that leads to violence (Esposito, 2002).

The most prolific of these soft power programs are the Middle East Partnership Initiative (MEPI)[13] or Radio Sawa.[14] They can be seen as extensions of the well-established practice of using media, which the United States employed during the Cold War. Then, radio programming delivered by the Voice of America, Radio Liberty, and Radio Free Europe broadcasted news-heavy anticommunism content into the Eastern Bloc (Mickelson, 1983). The Voice of America was established as the official broadcast institution of the American government in 1942, mainly to deliver news to the American troops fighting in WWII. At that time, radio transmission offered easy penetration of borders, and that ease of communication was embraced fully during the Cold War as more powerful transmission technology allowed for more and more varied content to be delivered deep behind the Iron Curtain. Puddington (2003) explains that gradually the content veered from news-based to entertainment-based, with American music becoming its focus, and the promotion of American culture its goal.

Following the same structure as The Voice of America, Radio Sawa (which means "together" in Arabic) was set up under the Broadcasting Board of Governors (BBG) and funded by Congress to provide a positive image of America through popular culture (Schneider, 2003). Radio Sawa broadcasts in Morocco, Lebanon, Iraq, Jordan, the Palestinian territories, Kuwait, Bahrain, Qatar, the United Arab Emirates (UAE), Djibouti, Egypt, Yemen, Saudi Arabia, and Sudan. But unlike the Voice of America, Radio Sawa employs a mix of local cultural programming as well as American pop culture content. During the Cold War, local programming was not part of radio content, except for the historical references to national cultures before the arrival of Communism. Today, Radio Sawa strategically alternates between contemporary Arab and Western music (popular with the youth), with periodic news spots that are broadcast in various languages and dialects of the region. The Voice of America has relied exclusively on English language content with minimal news segments in local languages, usually limited to ten minute increments broadcasted twice a day—morning and afternoon. The new strategy of radio programming for the Middle East shows respect for local culture, rather than criticism of the local government, which was the core mission of the Voice of America and Radio Liberty.

Schneider (2003) explains that Radio Sawa enjoys popularity because people in the Middle East are surprised by its unexpected objectivity. The legacy of American international political programming is one of presenting a single political position—that of the American government. This mission was mandated into law by President Gerald Ford in 1976, who set up its charter to proclaim that the Voice of America is to be the official news source for the American government. It is entrusted with providing reliable news consistent with official American policy to the rest of the world. Radio Sawa's mandate is decidedly different because it reports stories that depict the United States positively and negatively (Schneider, 2003). The goal is to implicitly illustrate free speech. Radio Sawa is a clever addition to the Voice of America because the Voice of America is still very much active and operates around the globe. It continues to follow its historic mandate—to glorify American international policy through justifying the official actions of the American government.

Because of its unique role and nature, Radio Sawa has generated interest among researchers of political communication. El-Nawawy (2006) conducted an opinion study of Arab students in five Arab countries on Radio Sawa, and its TV counterpart—Television Alhurra. The students were asked if they perceive the media outlets as credible news sources. The results reveal that students who had listened to Radio Sawa actually had a worse opinion of the United States in part because they believed to have been manipulated by the broadcasts. Another key finding, which El-Nawawy (2006) states is contrary to much of the literature, is that there was no significant relationship between the frequency with which one listened to Radio Sawa and positive views of American foreign policy. However, the author finds a positive relationship between Television Alhurra's credibility and US foreign policy favorability. Surprisingly, the results also suggest that students' opinions of American foreign policy actions had declined slightly since they had started listening to Radio Sawa.

Although used extensively in the West, as a research tool polling has many limitations. The general literature on the drawbacks of polling methods indicates that they suffer from a high degree of selection bias. The selection bias is hardest to avoid with respect to respondents. In regions such as MENA with remote locales, high rates of poverty, and low rates of literacy, polling students by definition is conducting a biased study. Only the children of political elites or fairly affluent citizens go to school. Also, they are mostly male. For those reasons, as Melissen and Sook's (2011) caution, the use of polling data is very subjective and often unreliable. In light of such caution, El-Nawawy's (2006) findings merit further exploration because they offer key observations that have to do with information processing. One of the conclusions is that awareness of manipulation may impact the credibility of a soft power source. This observation is interesting because it juxtaposes soft power messages with the knowledge base created by the local regimes. It suggests that soft power information is questioned.

Its credibility is put in the context of local counterinformation. The conclusion that opinion about American foreign policy in the region did not improve based on frequency of listening to Radio Sawa programs because of the general belief that the content is not reliable suggests that soft power tools face high scrutiny for foreign propaganda. Other researchers also suggest that citizens are sensitive to media sources that are believed to have been created and financed for propaganda purposes (Kamalipour & Snow, 2004; Shaw, 1996; Taylor, 1992).

Radio and other media programs that are heavy in news content are the tried and tested venues of soft power. But in the age of global commercialism, the tools of advertising are also employed by the American government to create a favorable image of the nation and its values. An additional media venue for such a purpose is the US government sponsored program the Shared Values Initiative (SVI). SVI was organized by advertising guru Charlotte Beers post 9/11, while she served as the undersecretary for public diplomacy with the US State Department.[15] This program televised commercials in predominantly Muslim countries of the lives of happy Muslims who lived in America (Fullerton & Kendrick, 2006).

The SVI program received enormous criticism from the media, politicians, and pundits, and was pulled almost as soon as it launched, lasting only two months (Plaisance, 2005). It was criticized for being condescending, patronizing, and culturally insensitive. However, Fullerton and Kendrick's (2006) book "Advertising's War on Terrorism" presents research that suggests the campaign ads may have been effective in their goal of improving attitudes toward America among international Muslim audiences. The authors gathered data from 500 international students across 39 countries and found that the commercials did improve the way students perceived American life.

In addition to polls, survey techniques have been employed for measuring soft power impacts in the Middle East. One such survey by Nisbet et al. (2004) was conducted in nine predominantly Muslim countries and it includes participants who are not all Muslim. The approach to survey citizens in the Muslim world who are not followers of Islam is important because anti-Americanism is mainly connected to the legacy of Muslim versus Christian cultures. However, the variety of religions and religious sects should not be ignored when studying anti-American and anti-Western sentiments in the region. Reducing the dislike of American policies to equalization with its Christian values would be misleading, as argued by Nisbet et al. (2004). The authors find that Muslims and non-Muslims living in Islamic countries had an "anti-American perceptual screen." That screen was deeper than just issues of religious division. It only allowed those messages that fit within people's preconceived notions to pass through.

Those that did not were dismissed. Such preconceived notions are based on local culture, historical knowledge and tradition, and patriotic pride. The overall conclusion of Nisbet et al. (2004) is that there are no discernible benefits from deploying diplomatic media programs. Additionally, there is evidence to suggest that US-sponsored news was selected based on ideological positions and therefore had only a slight buffering effect. The recommendation is to utilize a trusted media source in the region, namely Al Jazeera and other emerging pan-Arab television news station, as a purveyor of American ideals. Much of the surveying and polling research on anti-Western attitudes in the Middle East comes from studies and initiatives that closely followed the events of September 11, 2001. An example is the Zogby International "Impressions of America" series. In June 2004 Zogby International, a polling arm of Zogby Analytics,[16] surveyed 3,300 Arabs living in Morocco, Saudi Arabia, Jordan, Lebanon, the United Arab Emirates, and Egypt. The poll was commissioned by the Arab American Institute as a follow-up to the 2002 "Impressions of America" study. Questions in the 2004 poll focused on how Arabs view America and how Arabs learn about America.[17] With the exception of Jordan, in all countries surveyed, watching US television programs created a favorable impression of America. In Saudi Arabia, the positive influence of watching these programs even surpassed knowing Americans or having visited America. However, this positive outlook of America and Americans does not extend to a favorable outlook of US foreign policy.

With respect to the difference of opinion based on soft power venues such as watching American television program and actually having been to the United States, the general results in the Zogby polls since 2004 reveal that people who had visited the United States have an overall favorable rating of the country itself. It is important to discuss the fact that those who had been to the United States personally liked American people, American values, including democracy, and American products. The same holds true for people who have personally known Americans but have not visited America. In both cases personal experiences are associated with higher favorability rating of the United States. An actual visit is the strongest contributor to having a positive opinion of America.

There seems to be a link between witnessing examples of American life and favorability. Both watching American television and/or having been to America emerge as the leading factors in building a positive view of the United States. This fact speaks to the power of seeing versus hearing. Nisbet et al. (2004), Fullerton and Kendrick (2006), and the Zogby polls all discuss the strong impact of television programs. An implication is that viewing American life provides an emotional connection. Personal visits are unparalleled for establishing such a connection, but the fact that television programs come second is important. Popular culture products, such as television shows, popular music, and Hollywood films are said to be "America's main exports" because they put American products in a marketable context that increases their desirability (Craig and King, 2002; Kraidy, 2005). From movies to television programs to music and Internet website platforms, America is singularly the main global culture that permeates every other country's national culture (Crothers, 2012; Pells, 2011). Discussing the features of American soft power options in the age of mass communication, Melissen (2005) states that for those reasons American soft power capabilities are unmatched by any other nation.

Visual access to seeing America in real-world situations is important, but with respect to policy recommendations one must tread with caution in interpreting causality. In the Zogby polls much is said about the strong relationship between actually visiting the United States and positives views of America. However, one must remember that average Middle Easterners cannot afford to make such visits. Even a short trip can cost more than a year's worth of income in Libya, Morocco, Egypt, Syria, Iran, Iraq, and Djibouti—the poorest and most prone to Islamic extremist activity nations. By definition then, those that have visited America were the relatively wealthy and possibly better educated Arab citizens. It is not among those segments of the population that anti-Western sentiment is a serious problem or is associated with terrorist activity. As discussed, terrorism has been found to take hold among the poorest and most desperate strata of the population. Therefore, soft power options of easing travel may not bring about a strong amelioration effect, if they mostly benefit those who are already predisposed to have a favorable opinion of America.

In relation, a key insight is the fact that favour ability resulting from visiting America and watching American programs does not extend to foreign policy. In the Zogby polls, all participants—those who favor America and those who do not—rated US policy in Iraq and Palestine very poorly. Offering a thorough analysis of the early polls—those closest to 9/11—Jreisat (2006) juxtaposes this important fact with the general political and media rhetoric at the time, that Arabs hate Americans for their way of life. The numbers of the Zogby surveys do not show that Arabs and Muslims hate America for its freedom or democracy, rather, they deplore the American policies in the region. The implication is that the policies of the American government and their legacies are not easily mitigated by seductive images of high-quality life styles or entertainment. In relation, Golan and Yang (2013) examine the influence of American political leadership on perception. The study tracks the actions of President Barack Obama with a focus on the decided gesture of reaching out to the Middle East in his 2009 Cairo speech. The authors examine whether Obama's informal policy toward the region had altered perceptions or opinions of the United States. Their data was gathered from the 25-Nation Survey conducted for the Pew Research Center's (2009) Global Attitudes Project[18] by Princeton Survey Research Associates International. The research focuses specifically on the Pakistani sample (1,254)[19] to examine effects of assessments of President Obama in mitigating anti-American sentiment. Published in 2013, the study shows that since the beginning of the Obama presidency, there has been a significant increase in positive sentiment toward both the United States and Americans. Of note is the conclusion that such positivity had translated into an increase of favorability toward the War on Terror. The confidence in President Obama's leadership appears to be the cause of this increased favorability and approval of international policies (Golan and Yang, 2013).

The Pew Research Center has also undertaken a global attitudes project that has offered great insight across many related topics. A wider scope examines people's perception of America in 60 nations. The Global Attitudes Project has conducted over 330,000 interviews in 60 countries in the past 13 years. In 2012, Pew Research Center conducted a widespread survey regarding soft power and Arab public opinion. Similar to the Zogby results, Pew's analysis concludes that in many nations where overall ratings for the US remain low, certain aspects of American "soft power" are often well regarded. For instance, over half of the population in Lebanon, Tunisia, Jordan, and Egypt favor the American way of doing business. It is discussed that American business practices have become more popular since President Obama took office, which coincides with Golan and Yang's (2013) conclusion that American leaders and their policies have a significant impact on opinions around the world and can be used to cultivate soft power.[20] The Pew Research Center US Image Report (2012)[21] also provides an important demographic clarification on what segments of the population are most likely to respond well to American popular culture, and therefore American soft power platforms. The findings indicate that American ideas about democracy are more popular among people under the age of 30. The significance of this finding lies in the fact that in the Middle East more than half the population is under the age of 30. Assaad and Roudi-Fahimi (2007) describe the growth of youth as a chief proportion of the population as a "youth bulge." The 2012 Pew Report also notes that local youth, just like their older compatriot generations, is uneasy about the proliferation of American culture in the region. The report terms it as "fear of American ideals drowning local culture." The opinion of the respondents in 17 of the 20 surveyed countries is that it is a bad thing that US ideas and customs are being spread to their homelands. The overall lowest approval comes from predominantly Muslim nations.

Less than 20 percent of those in Egypt, Turkey, Pakistan, and Jordan hold positive views about the United States.

The findings on youth bulges, and the positive attitude of Arab young people toward the West, point to a soft power connection to education. Because such a large percent of Middle Easterners are young and they show a more positive outlook toward the United States, it is understandable that the American government heavily invests in educational exchanges. The Bureau of Educational and Cultural Affairs (ECA), part of the United States Department of State, is responsible for US sponsored exchange programs. Their Office of Policy and Evaluation conducts evaluations of current exchange programs. With respect to the Middle East, the Youth and Exchange Study (YES) program[22] was established post 9/11. It is specific to 15–17-year olds from countries with significant Muslim populations. Participating countries include Turkey, Saudi Arabia, Jordan, Kuwait, Pakistan, Syria, Yemen, Iraq, Palestine, Oman, and Qatar. As most other exchange programs, the students come to the United States and attend American schools while staying with American families for a typical term of one academic year. How it differs from YES is that it is fully funded by the Department of State with contributions from nonprofit organizations that have presence in the host nations. Students get all of their travel expenses covered and receive a monthly stipend. These facts undoubtedly help with the previously mentioned relatively high costs for Arab citizens to travel to the United States. However, the scholarships are based on merit. The merit criteria include significant English language proficiency. But by definition the merit-based requirement would disproportionately benefit certain students, since factors related to socioeconomic inequality with respect to education imply that only those with access to such educational options that provide high quality foreign language education would be eligible. Those options are mostly private, that is expensive primary and secondary schools in the Middle East. Additionally, students who excel in English proficiency in their early years would also be students coming from families where studying English would be a priority. The implication is that they would come from families where pro-Western sentiments were likely held. Therefore, the typical student accepted in the YES program would come from the same segment of the population that most likely would have had an opportunity to travel to the United States regardless of the presence of a student exchange program. Furthermore, the benefits of such highly expensive programs do not clearly show a strong return on investment. For example, the evaluation report of the 2009 YES program finds that the initial strong positive effect of the experience on the participants immediately following the exchange had worn off "slightly" after becoming acclimated again in their home society. The

YES 2009 evaluation examined the program's four stated goals—satisfaction with the exchange program, learning and understanding, behavioral changes, and personal linkages. It was administered through surveys and focus groups comprising program participants immediately after completing the exchange and one year after having been back in their respective countries. The results indicate that initially the participants not only took away a better understanding of the United States, but also of their own countries. The interpretation is based on responses to questions about the definition of individual rights, improved leadership capabilities, a sense of empowerment, and tolerance for another culture. Often programs such as YES offer self-lauding evaluations and the general indication from the overall tone of the report suggests that to be the case. However, through the optimistic tone a limitation is evident in the fact that the improved attitudes toward America decreased upon returning home. Although the decrease is said to be slight, what constitutes "slightness" is unclear. This fact is important because it shows that young people are equally susceptible to external information coming from soft power sources as well as internal anti-American rhetoric, even in light of having had a very positive personal experience in the United States. Possibly for that reason there is the contradiction noted by the Pew Global Attitudes Toward America 2012 report, that on one hand Arab youth had a favorable attitude toward American culture, but on the other hand, there was a fear of this culture's spread in the region.

With all forms of increasing international information exchange, message distortion occurs in the fact that individuals interpret the essence of the message through their own perceptional prisms. With respect to that fact, Rugh (2006) provides ten recorded anecdotal examples of soft power and diplomatic efforts in effectually altering and improving negative American perceptions of Arab individuals. One example explains the personal transformation of a 2004 Fulbright participant from Iraq, who, while in the United States, internalized his political and social observations there, which were very different from that of his home-nation. His understanding of human right issues, tolerance, multiculturalism, and pluralism had such a profound effect on him that he became an active peace advocate after returning to Iraq. Another example is a 1997 retreat for 30 Israeli and Palestinian youth in which they participated in challenging training sessions. Surmounting the challenges led to a joint declaration of peace, in spite of being initially hesitant. Interestingly following the experience, both groups of youth were threatened when they returned home for their activities. Rugh (2006) explains that through the adversary many of the students maintained their pacifist positions. Eventually the group traveled to the United States together and developed an action group based on the

American Council of Young Political Leaders (ACYPL) model that helped them in their retreat.

Testimonies, interviews, and other qualitative measures are valuable to assess soft power effectiveness, as Rugh's study shows. The problem is that access to average citizens in the remote realities of unstable nations in large enough numbers is difficult. Still, the feedback received from people in their own words can be a powerful tool in the attempt to understand how soft power works, and efforts should continue to gather information of personal nature.

It is this approach that the World Bank employs in creating the variables in the Worldwide Governance Indicators (WGI) Project that measure government effectiveness and political stability. The project draws on four different types of data sources to compile scale metrics for grading government performance.[23] Mostly based on polls, interviews, and surveys, the WGI methodology is vested in understanding average persons' perceptions of their governments' actions. Therefore, as Joseph Nye puts it, it has a "measuring the hearts and minds of people" component.

The body of work on soft power stresses there is no one right way of quantifying soft power, as there is no one form of soft power. Therefore, there is quite a bit of interest in soft power methodology. There have been studies, polls, surveys, and papers focused on the vast and various aspects of the phenomenon. As the literature examined here shows, those that try to quantify it have found it to be effective, ineffective, and even counterproductive. However, does that mean that, as Nye's (2008) arguments would suggest, that the concept is unquantifiable? A way to quantify it is to explore the conductive properties, so to speak, of its venues. In other words, if it is understood that information channels are used for deploying soft power, examining the structures of those information channels can aid in understanding soft power transmission.

Soft power lends itself to asking basic questions such as: Do exchange programs work in improving America's image? Does increased media exposure help or hurt? Does leadership matter? Jonathan McClory has been attempting to develop a soft power index through his series of "New Persuaders" papers.[24] His attempt to rank soft power resources is based on fundamentals of cultural and trade openness. As a follow-up to that approach, one can focus soft power measurement efforts on studying the relationship between government action and metrics that record openness to foreign information. Such metrics are concrete numbers of trade volume, foreign investment, and telecommunication connectivity because they are the channels through which soft power ideas can be disseminated. Fewer studies have looked at such metrics, and those that have employed older data (Busse and Hefeker, 2007; Chan and Gemayel, 2004).[25]

Quantifying Soft Power: A Methodological Query

As an example of studying soft power with respect to improving democracy, the following exercise offers ideas of methods that can be developed. Today more and more data is available from a variety of indices put forth by governmental and nongovernmental organizations that are developed to measure the effectiveness and impact of governance. Among the most comprehensive datasets with respect to country inclusiveness and availability of data points throughout time, the World Banks's World Development Indicators (WDI) and Worldwide Governance Indicators (WGI) databases stand out. From these databases, the following indicators can be chosen to study soft power effectiveness:

1. *Government effectiveness.* It is defined by the World Bank as "perceptions of the quality of public services, the quality of the civil service, and the degree of its independence from political pressures, the quality of policy formulation and implementation, and the credibility of the government's commitment to such policies."[26] Kaufmann et al. (1999) note the strong causal relationships between good governance and high per capita income, higher literacy, and increased overall prosperity, and security. Brown et al. (2008) note the negative impact poor governance has on economic growth. In addition, Lee and Whitford (2009) show that countries with unstable economies are unable to staff or maintain quality government infrastructure. Soft power is created partly by governments and partly in spite of them (Nye, 2002). Therefore, government effectiveness could be viewed as a measure of responsiveness to soft power from either direction. A country's government is a conduit for soft power, being in the position to both give and receive the lessons of soft power. Nye (2004) notes that an aspect of soft power is the skill to achieve a purpose by affecting behavior. Government behavior is manifested through policies and services and may either be influenced by diplomatic means from other governments, or through constituency pressures, as a result of soft power exposure.
2. *Political stability and absence of violence and terrorism.* It involves "capturing perceptions of the likelihood that the government will be destabilized or overthrown by unconstitutional or violent means, including politically-motivated violence and terrorism."[27] Albeit the causes of terrorism are diverse, Tujan et al. (2004) correlate instability and terrorism, as terrorism capitalizes on the difficult circumstances found in unstable, underdeveloped countries to mobilize disaffected citizens that have no other means of protest or participation in the local political system. In fact,

terrorists may actively seek out these unstable, or failed, states as the lack of law enforcement and other government structure creates a power vacuum whereby terrorist organizations can recruit more people and acquire more territory (Gvosdev and Takeyk, 2002). The best way to combat terrorism is to use soft power tools such as education and free market investment (Wunderle et al., 2007).

One can employ these two variables as both dependent and independent to evaluate their fit as predictors and outcomes of soft power. The following tests offer interpretations of both instances. Depending on the nature of inquiry, the causality direction of the relationship may be reversible. Technically, such circular relationships, as they are referred to, are questioned by researchers because of the statistical problems of reverse causality. Put in terms of temporal precedence of cause and effect, reverse causality problems arise when temporal precedence is not clearly observed. In everyday language, this problem is referred to as the chicken or the egg problem. In social science, many relationships are circular because they are products of cultural factors. Cultural factor development is a complex and long-time frame-dependent process. Therefore, isolating its components in terms of temporal precedence is challenging. However, it is a challenge one must face when evaluating soft power effectiveness. It is an important quest because investment decisions for future expansion or cuts of funding for soft power programs depend on benefit-cost analyses of their impact. To help such evaluation efforts, as noted, concrete metrics of monetary variables that channel soft power should be examined. Such metrics employed in this methodological query are:

3. *Foreign Direct Investment (FDI) Assets.* FDI is widely studied in the globalization field as the international investment of mostly private firms. It is the combination of equity capital, reinvestment of earnings, other long-term capital, and short-term capital as shown in the balance of payments.[28] It has been shown that government effectiveness and overall good governance, including respect for human rights, have an impact on FDI inflows (Kaufmann and Zoido-Lobatón, 1999; Globerman and Shapiro, 2002), as these conditions indicate a politically stable environment conducive to investment. Blanton and Blanton (2007) find that respect for human rights signals enhanced political stability, which is the core attractor of FDI. FDI is also a vehicle through which new products penetrate markets, and with them, advertising campaigns and marketing tools that often show different lifestyles (Anguelov, 2014; Luo and Tung, 2007). Based on that argument, it is reasonable to examine whether FDI, as a soft power tool, is both a predictor and an outcome of soft power effectiveness.

In relation, empirical evidence suggests that FDI leads to an increase in the income earnings of recipient nations (Pournarakis and Varsakelis,

2004; Tanoos, 2014). For this reason variable number 2 is gross national income per capita.

4. *Gross National Income (GNI) per capita (formerly GNP per capita)*. It is the gross national income, converted to US dollars using the World Bank Atlas method, divided by the midyear population. GNI is the sum of the values added by all resident producers plus any product taxes (less subsidies) not included in the valuation of output, plus net receipts of primary income (compensation of employees and property income) from abroad.[29] Although GNI indicates the average level of income per person, it does not indicate the distribution of income. Nincic and Russett (1979) use GNI as a socioeconomic variable and note its normative impact on both political and economic governance as it relates to a nation's soft power. Husted (1999) finds a high correlation between GNP (also known as GNI) and corruption in a country, as corruption not only preserves or deepens inequality, but also can be the source of increasing inequality. With respect to income and government service problems such as corruption, foreign assistance numbers can also help study the relationship between external funding, local income levels as indicators of poverty and need, and international funding for the creation of local governance institutions. For these reasons, a good option to include in soft power models is the variable Net Official Development Assistance (ODA) and Foreign Aid.

5. *Net Official Development Assistance (ODA) and Foreign Aid.*This metric comprises disbursements of loans made on concessional terms (net of repayments of principal) and grants by official agencies of the members of the Development Assistance Committee (DAC), by multilateral institutions, and by non-DAC countries to promote economic development and welfare in countries and territories in the DAC list of ODA recipients.[30] ODA and foreign aid are used to win the goodwill of developing countries and are a direct soft power output (Lam, 2007; Radelet, 2003). Unlike foreign direct investment, foreign aid and ODA come from public entities, not private sources. A metric that embodies foreign sources that are both public and private is imports. Imports can take many forms, including services, and their sources can be viewed as truly global. With respect to soft power, imports can reveal additional to FDI and foreign aid sources of foreign information.

6. *Imports*. As a percent of a country's GDP, they denote the value of all goods and market services purchased by a nation from the rest of the world. They include the value of merchandise, freight, insurance, transport, travel, royalties, license fees, and other services, such as communication, construction, financial, information, business, personal, and government services that are paid for by local private and public entities. It is in the concepts of these services that the connection to soft power lies.[31] Miller

and Thorr (2003) explain that products imported by MNCs rely on marketing techniques that often have political and, therefore, policy overtones. In their example, the policies of the World Press Freedom Committee (WPFC) in India yielded free television content rife with advertisement. As a result of marketing new ways of product consumption, the number of soap brands in India, which was in the single digits, grew to hundreds. Additionally, Ahmed et al., (2011) find evidence of the existence of a positive causal long-run impact of exports, imports, and FDI on income, where import growth causes FDI as well as GNI growth.

The impact of imports and FDI on local consumption is contingent on the ability to reach local consumers. The promotion of foreign goods and services is based on information channel connectivity. Therefore, direct metrics of information transmission infrastructure can also be examined.

7. *Internet usage per 100 people.*This variable indicates the number of people with access to the World Wide Web.[32]

8. *Mobile phone subscriptions (per 100 people).* They are subscriptions to a public mobile telephone service using cellular technology, which provides access to the public switched telephone network. Postpaid and prepaid subscriptions are included.[33] Mobile phone usage should be examined in light of recent findings from analyses of international communication proliferation. One finding is that transaction costs of mobile service dissemination are much lower than the traditional infrastructure needed for land-line connectivity, and therefore are rapidly and more easily adopted (Agar, 2013). Aker and Mbiti (2010) show that fact to be true with respect to Northern Africa and the Middle East. Examining the impact of mobile phone technology proliferation on political outcomes, Khamis and Vaugh (2011) argue that mobile phones were the primary tool of civic engagement during the Egyptian uprisings of 2011. Similarly, Newsom and Lengel (2012) examine Arab feminist cyberactivism and offer examples of how social media utilization—via both the Internet and smart phones—was an important component of political mobilization during the Arab Spring.

Internet and mobile phone usage are important to examine, as connectivity to the West lends itself to openness of ideas and allows the spread of soft power. Mattern (2005) notes that soft power is rooted in communication, as the most fundamental way to harness it is through spreading social knowledge. Mobile phones and the Internet certainly permit this activity, allowing people access to alternate news sources and social media like Facebook and Twitter, and a wide variety of Western popular culture venues. Additionally, such technology facilitates communication between citizens and government, which may affect government responsiveness. It is not simply the availability of the tools that may carry soft power messages, but the ability of people to employ those tools toward achieving notable policy changes. Therefore, the above-mentioned cases of social media deployment in Egypt are important because they provide a specific example of how technology enabled the launch of a successful political movement via social media. This case offers an applied illustration of soft power's magnitude and its potential to affect change in government structures.

Access to mobile phones in Egypt was undoubtedly one of the most valuable tools in the arsenal to mobilize Arab Spring activists (Dunn, 2011). Analyses of who those prodemocracy activists were noted, showing the link between social networks and women. Historically, gender inequality, from education to options for political engagement, have been a core cultural difference in terms of developmental paths between the West and conservative Islamic nations (Roudi-Fahimi and Moghadam, 2003; Sidani, 2005). Because of this divergence, a lot of research is focused on how soft power can improve social gender equality (Moghadam, 2003). For example, social activism to increase educational opportunities for women is one of the core external soft power tools for applying pressure on both governments and families to support female education.[34] Educating girls is one of the most contentious social issues in Muslim nations (Cooray and Potrafke, 2011; Keddie, 2011). Because of this dynamic, a metric for equitable gender education can offer insights into soft power's capacity to affect established traditional norms. One such suitable metric is the ratio of female to male secondary school enrollment described next.

One could employ the metric as an independent and a dependent variable. As an independent variable, that is a predictor of soft power impact, it can be employed to examine how more educated females may be a voice of political activism. With respect to answering that question, any model which includes the secondary school gender enrollment ratio must be longitudinal. This is because enough time must pass in order to examine how educating minors can impact their political actions as adults. The hope is that more educated adults can put significant political pressures on governance structures that can result in improved government effectiveness. Therefore, much like basic soft power questions, the question of educating Middle Eastern girls, and therefore breaking with tradition, are often discussed (Cooray and Potrafke, 2011; Kelly and Breslin, 2010). Consequently, attempts to improve quantification methods are warranted. For those reasons the World Bank and other organizations record the variable. Its change across time is of interest here to see how soft power platforms affect issues of gender equality. As a dependent variable, the secondary school enrollment ratio can be viewed as a possible outcome of soft power—a product of the cultural and political change that occurs as a result of external value penetration.

9. *Ratio of female to male secondary school enrollment.* It is the percentage of girls to boys enrolled at secondary level in both public and private schools.[35] Both the conservative culture and economic structure of the MENA region contribute to generally lower levels of women's education (Roudi-Fahimi and Moghadam, 2003). A change in the percent of females enrolled in school would indicate the adoption of education equality policies. Although the education of women in this region has improved over the past three decades, educational development has varied wildly in the MENA region (Sidani, 2005).

The Middle East does not have a definitive geographic or political area (Davison, 1960). Based on approaches in previous studies of the MENA region, one can see that different geographic units of analysis can be formed. For this query, all 20 MENA nations in the Middle East, southwest Asia, and northeast Africa are included. They are: Afghanistan, Algeria, Bahrain, Djibouti, Egypt, Iran, Iraq, Jordan, Kuwait, Lebanon, Oman, Pakistan, Qatar, Saudi Arabia, Syria, Tunisia, Turkey, United Arab Emirates, West Bank/Gaza, and Yemen.

This exercise also notes the importance of time. The years of choice are 2004 to 2012. The goal is to examine most current data. Of particular interest is the effect of soft power during the Iraqi, Egyptian, and Syrian unrests.

The main difficulty researchers face is access to data. With the above-mentioned benefits of the World Bank data collection methods and access to metrics, missing values are often an issue when employing longitudinal methods in nations such as the MENA countries. Therefore, researchers should examine all other options such as the UNESCO data bases, United Nations Conference on Trade and Development (UNCTAD)—the research arm of the United Nations, as well as specific economic activity databases that focus on particular data that may be applicable for certain research initiatives. Building a comprehensive dataset for analyzing the complicated relationships between soft power, international commerce, and government action can be challenging in regions where data reliability is an issue, such as in the Middle East. In such cases it may be necessary that several data sources be consulted, cross-examined for validity, and used for obtaining missing values. A list of those databanks can serve as an example of data sources for future related international relations inquiries.[36]

Longitudinal cross-country comparison studies that evaluate change in indicators from year to year are subject to data similarity issues that stem from consistent patterns of closely related numeric values. For example, FDI in Iraq in 2005 would be very similar to FDI in Iraq in 2004. Such similarity can be a problem in calculating accurate coefficients that measure the strength of relationships among the individual countries and note how those relationships increase or decrease across time. For those reasons a fixed versus random effect goodness of fit test should be employed. In this query, as per Baltagi (2008), Baltagi, Egger, and Pfaffermayr (2008), and Greene (2008), a Houseman test is employed to determine the appropriate method for analyzing each of the panels. In addition, variance inflation factor (VIF) tests are performed to control for multicollinearity. Multicollinearity problems may arise when independent variables are close in value to each other with respect to both number and change of number from year to year. It is unclear from the scales of government effectiveness and political stability if the noted similarity in values would pose a multicollinearity problem. For example the political stability score in Iran in 2004 is –0.78 and the government effectiveness score is –0.17. Those numbers decrease significantly in 2005, but the magnitude of decrease between the two categories is similar. In 2005, the political stability score of Iran dropped to –2.72 and the government effectiveness score dropped to –1.66.

The VIF test revealed that multicollinearity is not a problem in this case, but imports posed a problem. Imports showed no statistical value in the regressions discussed here, and for that reason were omitted from each test. The lack of relationship counters the hypothesized link between imports and soft power, based on the works of Miller and Thorr (2003) and Ahmed and Messinis (2011), which explain that products imported by MNCs rely on marketing techniques that often have political and, therefore, policy overtones. In the case of the Middle East, the link between imports and MNCs is not clear. A possible explanation could be the centrally controlled economic structures of the nations in the sample. Much of their imports are government purchases. The MENA nations mostly import food (Breisinger et al., 2012) and military and industrial equipment (Ali, 2013). Private firms do not make those purchases; mostly government-owned enterprises do (Abdelfatta et al., 2014; Ali, 2013; Shahbaz, Shabbir, and Butt, 2013). In that case, imports would not be significant soft power mechanisms because their aggregate amount would constitute a small portion of private firm goods for personal consumption. Because the connection between imports and soft power relies on the promotion of such goods with respect to advertising, their use in introducing aspects of the importer nation lifestyle with possible cultural change implications is uncertain. Because of this specific feature of the nature of imports in MENA nations, a clear link is not evident between the dollar amounts of imports and ideological information transmission. In fact, the opposite might be occurring as a link has been discussed between military spending and deteriorating government effectiveness (Michaels, 2012; Shahbaz, Shabbir, and Butt, 2013). Therefore, the interpretation of the diluting effect of imports on the general model here is that in the MENA countries imports did not significantly influence any of the institutions of governance of interest in this query. For this reason, they are left out of each regression. The analytical aim of this study is to focus on the direct contributors to policy change that can have stronger links to soft power platforms.

The first regression uses government effectiveness as a dependent variable and the Houseman results suggest a fixed effects approach is best suited. The results are presented in table 5.1.

As noted previously, the relationships in this methodological exercise may not necessarily be unidirectional. In this particular regression test a reverse causality problem, also referred to as an endogeneity problem, can occur when employing political stability as an independent variable to be regressed against government effectiveness. One could make the argument that it could be government effectiveness that causes political

Table 5.1 Fixed effects cross-sectional time series regression analysis, government effectiveness[a]

Variables		Coefficient	Standard error	Significance
Internet subscribers (per 100)		0.0048597	0.0017762	**
Mobile subscribers (per 100)		−0.0012613	0.0008479	^
Political stability$_{it-1}$		0.0363932	0.0198017	*
FDI		1.23e−11	1.23e−11	***
ODA and foreign aid		−6.18e−12	5.45e−12	NS
Female to male ratio secondary school enrollment		5.45e−12	0.0024986	NS
Constant		−1.319343	0.137882	***
Prob. > F	< 0.0000			
R-squared	0.96			
Observations	179			

[a] Dependent variable: government effectiveness—perceptions of the quality of policies and public services provided. Level of significance on a two-tailed test denoted by the following symbols: NS—not significant, ^p<0.10, *p<0.05, **p<0.01, ***p<0.001.
An explanation of the methodology behind building the score can be found at: http://info.worldbank.org/governance/wgi/index.aspx#doc.

stability, not necessarily that political stability increases government effectiveness. Notwithstanding the possibility of a circular relationship, it is worth exploring the connection. It is important because insights can be gained into the applicability merits of the scores developed by the World Bank in terms of representativeness. Questions arise intuitively if one tries to interpret the meaning of political stability and absence of terrorism. During the Arab Spring, it was political destabilization that was lauded as the positive outcome because the demonstrations and general social unrest were hailed as a step forth in building democracy in the region (Campante and Chor, 2012; Gause III, 2011; Goodwin, 2011). By definition then, the nature of the Arab Spring uprisings denotes political instability. However, in this case, political instability is a positive step toward building better governance. Therefore, combined with the absence of terrorism, although seemingly related, instability analysis can lead to counterintuitive interpretations. In light of such issues, both metrics—political stability and absence of terrorism, as well as government effectiveness—should be examined as causes and effects. A way to control for temporal precedence in their relationship is to employ a lagging technique. Using that approach, the individual country or year scores for political stability in this regression are lagged by one year. With that control mechanism in place, the results in table 5.1 indicate that political stability and the absence of terrorism, do indeed increase government effectiveness. Following the Arab Spring's example that political destabilization itself led to improvements in government effectiveness, the relationship here reveals that a higher level of stability causes a higher degree of effectiveness in the region overall. Then, in actuality, the term "stability" is overshadowed by the follow-up classification "absence of terrorism." This means that measures of undemocratic instability that increase the likelihood of terrorism define the scale. The lower the score, the more evidence there is of undemocratic instability.

The results of the regression reveal a positive and statistically significant relationship between political instability and government effectiveness. The interpretation is that, as one would expect, governments are more effective when threats of terrorism and undemocratic unrest are low. Because of these findings, it must be explained that when employing the scale, researchers should note that demonstrations, uprisings, and general revolt, which are the opposite of political stability by definition, here seem to either be excluded or their magnitude mitigated through the various weighing mechanisms the developers of the scale employ. Such an interpretation points to a substantial limitation for using this metric. In relation to a legacy of political activism, the literature points to the link between governance effectiveness and various forms of peaceful social unrest (Carty and Onyett, 2006; Edy, 2006; Giugni, 2004; Meyer, 2004). After all, the theories on economic sanctions examined in Chapter 1, posit that successful sanctions would lead to social unrest that would cause a change of government structure and or action.

In terms of the soft power technology metrics, the results indicate that increasing Internetsubscriptions contributed to improving government effectiveness. The interpretation is that improving access to venues that channel global ideas and information is a direct way of creating opportunities to pressure or incentivize local governments to improve their performance. The pressure or incentives can come from the electorate. Such an outcome can occur when people learn of international examples of alternatives to social policy issues they face at home. To that effect, the policy diffusion concept can be applicable not only in terms of governments learning from each other, but also ordinary people learning from the international citizenry. Because Internet connectivity is measured in terms of available access for average citizens, the interpretation of its impact is at that level of analysis. It suggests that as more people gained access to the Web in the MENA region, the stronger and more positive the policy changes of local governments became. This interpretation offers hope because much has been said about the disconnect between average Arab citizens and their government elites. As already noted, levels of repression have been reported in the region that posit a bleak democratic reality. The fact that there is a connection between access to new technology and improved governance may indicate a potential for future regime-changing, Web-based soft power initiatives.

Interestingly, the opposite relationship is observed with respect to cell phone subscriptions. As the number of new users increases, government effectiveness decreases slightly. This finding is counterintuitive and contrary to some previously examined arguments that social media, mainly accessed through cell phones, has been a key factor of mobilization during the Arab Spring, resulting in improvements to the local democratic process (Attia et al., 2011; Dunn, 2011; Khamis and Vaugh, 2011; Newsom and Lengel, 2012). It could be that adversaries of democracy are also increasingly using cellular technology. That interpretation is hard to link to an applicable example, as it is difficult to argue that citizens with strong motivation to undermine the performance of their governments are using their cell phones effectively to such an end. It is more feasible to link the result to business activity. The negative relationship can mean that in nations with relatively more "ineffective" governments, cell phone subscriptions grew more during the examined time frame. Through that prism, then an additional link can be made between poverty and technological proliferation, in terms of market development. The link lies in the argument that in the MENA nations, government ineffectiveness is correlated with poverty (Ali and Isse, 2005; Breisinger et al., 2012). Therefore, poverty is correlated with infrastructure underdevelopment. As discussed in Chapters 2, 3, and 4, poor nations lack in infrastructure, and as the examples from Myanmar and North Korea show, infrastructure development becomes a priority as trade and wealth increase. The literature on increased cell phone use in areas where traditional communication infrastructure, such as landline cable connectivity is lacking, shows that cell phones are an attractive and relatively inexpensive technological option because one cell tower is much cheaper to build than laying miles of cable (Agar, 2013; Aker and Mbiti, 2010). The results observed in table 5.1 could be a manifestation of such a dynamic, but prior lack of empirical evidence related to the strength of such a connection warrants further exploration.

Continuing with the interpretation of the results of the first regression, we see that foreign aid—one of the most often discussed direct soft power tools—does not significantly influence government effectiveness in the Middle East. Neither does the number of girls enrolled in school—a hypothesized outcome of soft power. The interpretation is that neither of those metrics reached critical mass to elicit institutional change in terms of government policies between 2004 and 2012.

Much has been written on the fairly low amounts of foreign aid, recipient nations actually get. Therefore, a possible proaid connection can be made from the results presented here. If the goal of foreign aid is to improve the governance institutions of recipient nations and if foreign aid by definition is a direct way to hand governments money under conditions—those conditions are soft power platforms—then either the money is not enough, or the conditions are not binding. Accountability of local governments has been discussed a lot, in how they use foreign aid. As previously noted, there is a link between foreign aid and corruption because of lack of accountability measures in the deployment of aid funds. The results of the regression in table 5.1, show that foreign aid did not have a beneficial effect on MENA governance, pointing to the need to evaluate quantity and application of aid disbursement in the region.

The results also indicate that the strongest predictor of government effectiveness in the region was foreign direct investment. The relationship is positive, which means that as FDI increased so did the government effectiveness score of the examined MENA countries.

When it comes to business opportunities, the strong relationship between FDI and government effectiveness offers support for the hypothesis that increasing the presence of foreign businesses in a nation leads to improvements of government performance. It is evidence that as a vehicle of soft power, FDI indeed causes governments in the Middle East to upgrade their services, possibly to create an improvement in terms of global standards and business effectiveness platforms. This link is important because augmenting foreign assets is connected to augmenting foreign-owned business operations. With foreign businesses come foreign products, foreign marketing, foreign managerial practices and behavior, as well as foreign compliance demands. This is the case because most FDI projects operate in coordination with multinational networks that are subject to international (or foreign) regulatory demands.

Such management applications of FDI assets are based on the proliferation of foreign information. The information can have ideological and political aspects. Ideologically, as other researchers have shown, the marketing and advertising of new products can alter local product consumption patterns, and such alterations can lead to changes in cultural habits. The literature on cultural imperialism notes how foreign advertising leads to change in behavior in developing nations (Kraidy, 2005; Petras, 1993; Tomlinson, 2001). This connection is generally portrayed with negative connotations, however, there is evidence that increasing the consumption of foreign products and being exposed to foreign advertising for the promotion of those products can lead to beneficial outcomes, particularly in such policy spheres as gender equality (Luke, 2001). For example, Jensen and Oster (2009) explain how watching American cable shows depicting the lives of women who enjoy higher degrees of economic and social emancipation led Indian women to change their own behavior and demand more equality and power from their husbands and male relatives. Also, Ibroscheva (2007) explains how the promotion of Western products in Eastern Europe after the end of Communist isolation has impacted the economic dynamics between men and women, where female consumerism is related to higher emancipation in order to emulate a more glamorous, but still, a more socially equitable Western lifestyle.

The political side of foreign information proliferation via increase in the investments of foreign firms lies in the connection to international production compliance standards. When projects are constructed with multilateral funding streams, such as World Bank loans, multilateral regulatory management practices must be followed. In that way, external operational management information can contribute to knowledge building in local management. As already noted, because those that comprise local business management are also the local political elite, then one can argue that a possible connection could exist between increasing business effectiveness and increasing government effectiveness. Still, much more research is needed to explore the magnitude of such a hypothetical link. Most prior studies have focused their attention on the connection between FDI and political stability.

A key argument in the literature on FDI location is that foreign investors prefer relatively more stable nations. In the case of the Middle East, this argument merits empirical testing because of the strategic importance of the region, and the presence of oil. These factors would suggest an incentive to manage the uncertainty of instability and continue to invest in the region despite instability, especially in light of current and future global energy needs. Such an incentive would have implications for sanction mitigation. The literature on economic sanctions explains that transaction costs of trade define sanction effectiveness with regard to finding alternative trading partners. The FDI literature concludes that political instability can be a prohibitive factor that deters foreign investment. Therefore, the expectation is that if FDI increases, then one would expect political stability to increase as well. However, the cases of Myanmar and North Korea showed that during the sanction years, while these countries were sponsoring and harboring terrorists, FDI increased. The interpretation is that today, MNCs may not be deterred by political instability as they had been in the past. In nations with strategic and precious natural resources, instability and terrorism may deter certain investors, but it may attract others.

Given the explored circularity in the relationships among FDI, government effectiveness, and political stability, an analysis of political stability as an outcome of FDI and soft power venue metrics is offered in table 5.2. Table 5.2 uses the score as a dependent variable. To control for reverse causality problems between political stability and government effectiveness in this case, the government effectiveness metric is lagged by one year.

The results show no statistical significance between any of the variables and political stability. This fact suggests that government effectiveness is not necessarily a predictor of political stability, in this case strongly defined by the absence of terrorism. Such a statement seems untrue in light of the link between the two represented in the general body of historical research. However, it could be a viable interpretation for the MENA nations. Based on noted recent terrorist activity in the region, it may be plausible that regardless of good local governance, terrorism can strike anywhere. It is an important issue to address in the context of the Middle East because it could offer insights as to whether terrorism activity increases in response to general Westernization of local governance. For example, there could be a link to the attack against Malala Yousafazi in 2012, or the abduction of the 300 schoolgirls in Nigeria by Boko Haram.

The fact that the soft power metrics do not impact political stability also suggests that if one defines political stability primarily through terrorism, then soft power policies can only go so far. The implication is that nations can become unstable and harbor terrorism regardless of the soft

Table 5.2 Fixed effects cross-sectional time series regression analysis, political stability[a]

Variables		Coefficient	Standard error	Significance
Internet subscribers (per 100)		−0.0000798	0.0039066	NS
Mobile subscribers (per 100)		0.0004995	0.0018609	NS
Government effectiveness$_{it-1}$		0.0641085	0.0775852	NS
FDI		1.01e−11	8.67e−12	NS
ODA & Foreign Aid		−5.04e−12	1.19e−12	NS
Female to male ratio secondary school enrollment		0.0037295	0.0054591	NS
Constant		−1.319343	0.137882	***
Prob. > F	< 0.0000			
R-squared	0.92			
Observations	179			

[a] Dependent variable: Political stability and absence of violence and terrorism—likelihood of government destabilization by violent means and or unconstitutional political participation and expression. Level of significance on a two-tailed test denoted by the following symbols: NS—not significant, ^p < 0.10, *p < 0.05, **p < 0.01, ***p < 0.001.
An explanation of the methodology behind building the score can be found at: http://info.worldbank.org/governance/wgi/index.aspx#doc.

power tactics of external and internal idea exchange. Such general statements may be overreaching based on the scale offered by the World Bank, mainly because it is unclear how the scale is constructed and how its components are weighted for magnitude of importance. The combination of the factors comprising the scores allows for significant discretion, both in terms of geographic data availability and the interpretation of qualitative data output by the World Bank researchers involved in the project. Further research could delve deeper into the scale components and examine robustness. It is important to keep applying the measures of both political stability, in all its definitions, and government effectiveness because they create outcomes. The goal of soft power diplomacy is to achieve tangible results. The challenge is quantifying the results with respect to specific policy outcomes. Therefore, literature from other disciplines that examine discipline-specific policy outcomes resulting from increased government effectiveness in developing nations can offer insights.

In the economic literature on industrial upgrading of developing countries, one of the most often studied outcomes is the ability of nations to attract FDI (Anguelov, 2014; Daud and Stein, 2007; Globerman and Shapiro, 2002, 2003; Wint and Williams, 2002). Based on that assumption, a test of both the government effectiveness and political stability measures as attractive factors for foreign investors is offered in table 5.3. Table 5.3 shows the results with FDI assets employed as the dependent variable.

The literature on FDI posits that an important attraction factor is gross national income per capita (GNI). Foreign investors favor nations with large and growing GNIs. For this reason, GNI is included in the regression in order to offer a more representative model. Although the goal here is to focus on soft power and governance, the wealth of the average citizen

Table 5.3 Cross-sectional time series regression analysis, FDI assets[a]

Variables		Coefficient	Standard error	Significance
Internet subscribers (per 100)$_{it-1}$		–3.71e+07	1.95e+07	*
Mobile subscribers (per 100)$_{it-1}$		–1.52e+07	8309629	^
Female to male ratio secondary school enrollment		–2779791	1.28e+07	NS
GNI $_{\text{per capita}}$		11627.95	17671.86	NS
Government effectiveness		1.56e+09	9.25e+08	^
Political stability		–1.06e+08	1.84e+08	NS
ODA & Foreign Aid		0.0905843	0.0733636	NS
Lagged dependent variable		0.9186849	0.1064782	***
Constant		2.70e+09	1.78e+09	^
Prob. > F	< 0.0000			
R-squared	0.81			
Observations	160			

[a] Dependent Variable: FDI—the overall balance of foreign assets to liabilities in a country measured in current US dollars. Level of significance on a two-tailed test denoted by the following symbols: NS—not significant, ^$p < 0.10$, *$p < 0.05$, **$p < 0.01$, ***$p < 0.001$.

cannot be ignored. As citizens earn more, they consume more and FDI responds to increasing local consumption demand.

Because of the addition of GNI to the model, a second Houseman test is performed. The results indicate that a fixed effects test is not necessary and therefore the method employed is a cross-sectional, panel-corrected time series regression analysis. Additionally, a time effect test is performed on this panel when employing FDI as the dependent variable as per Greene (2008) because of value similarity in FDI numbers from year to year. The results indicate indeed that a time effect is present, which is often the case with dollar amounts in investment and trade. Therefore, to correct for it, a lagged dependent variable is added.[37] Furthermore, because of possible endogeneity with respect to industrial sector, both Internet subscribers and mobile subscribers are lagged by one year.

It is noted that telecommunication technologies are often external to nations such as the MENA countries in the sample, and therefore FDI may be directed toward developing those sectors (Shirazi, 2008). The endogeneity may stem from the fact that a significant portion of foreign investment may be associated with each industry and therefore can cause Internet use and mobile subscriptions to change.

The results reveal an interesting outcome. An increase in both telecommunication variables causes yearly FDI to decline. This finding could signal market saturation typical with knowledge intensive economies that are not subject to diminishing returns. In such cases, notable increases in output, such as adding more cell and Internet users, do not require reciprocal linear investments. The curvilinear relationship denotes that minimal, and in many cases no, additional investment is needed to produce multiple product units. The implication is that in the MENA nations with fastest growing Internet and cell subscribers, the FDI associated with that growth decreases from year to year. A possible interpretation is that this fact indicates the high return on investment in the industries, also discussed by Shirazi (2008).

The results also reveal that government effectiveness was a positive predictor of increasing FDI, albeit the relationship is observed at the 0.10 level, while political stability does not seem to affect FDI in the region. Further research should focus on this very important finding as it suggests a possible relationship between FDI sources that do not value stability or increasing economic partnerships in unstable nations such as Iran and Syria with investors from Russia and China, as reported during the ArabS pring.[38]

Neither foreign aid nor female to male ratio in public education are shown to affect political stability. With respect to foreign aid, this finding again points to the ineffectual features of aid. Further research can examine if aid fails to improve political stability because of accountability factors, as some researchers suggest, or because of its limited amount, as the proponents of increasing aid argue.

With respect to the connection between reform of government policies in the Middle East toward the goal of improving human rights issues, as already discussed, much has been said about offering more opportunities for female education. Jeddah and Riyadh, in a story for the *Economist* magazine published on May 17, 2014 titled "Unshackling Themselves: Saudi Women are Gaining Ground, Slowly," explain that even with increasing government policies of women's political empowerment, public education is still "single-sexed," with the exception of one Saudi university. For those reasons Saudi women study abroad and many women-only universities are emerging in the Middle East. The will of women to gain access to education is evident, despite the difficulties. Women go to such lengths outside Saudi Arabia and in its women-only private education institutions that in 2014, the author argues, more women than men were in higher education. Keddie (2011) offers insight into the soft power nature of educating Muslim girls because the entire concept of female empowerment through education is still viewed as a "Western-informed viewpoint." For that reason, as is also noted by Riyadh in the *Economist* story, vocal local opposition exists against gender equality in education. But this issue is at the forefront of the cultural discussion with respect to improving government effectiveness in the region (Cooray and Potrafke, 2011; Gallant and Pounder, 2008; Hamdan, 2005; Keddie, 2011).

There is a general agreement that increasing the education of girls is, at its core, a successful outcome of soft power because the impetus for such a societal change, although embraced by Arab women, is external. It is Western values of gender equality and social opportunity that challenge local cultural legacies. For those reasons, a hypothesized successful outcome of soft power and government effectiveness would be an increase in the number of girls enrolled in schools. In the previously analyzed regressions, the metric is not a predictor of increases in government effectiveness scores, political stability scores, nor FDI amounts. As a dependent variable, it is also unaffected by the factors of the model, except for the one metric that the previous regressions found to be non-significant—foreign aid, as shownb yt able5 .4.

The results show a strong causal relationship between increasing foreign aid amounts and a rise in girls enrolled in public education in the MENA region. This fact denotes a direct link between foreign aid, as a tool of soft power, and an outcome of government effectiveness with respect to improving equitable public services. Because in the previously discussed regressions, foreign aid did not show a significant impact on increasing

Table 5.4 Cross-sectional time series regression analysis, female to male ratio, secondary school enrollment

Variables		Coefficient	Standard error	Significance
Internet subscribers (per 100)		−0.02	0.04	NS
Mobile subscribers (per 100)		0.00	0.01	NS
GNI $_{\text{per capita}}$		0.00	0.00	NS
Government effectiveness		−0.39	0.65	NS
Political stability		0.46	0.37	NS
FDI		−0.150e−11	3.00e−11	NS
ODA & Foreign Aid		2.38e−10	9.77e−11	**
Lagged dependent variable		0.92	0.02	***
Constant		7.36	2.12	***
Prob. > F	< 0.0000			
R-squared	0.96			
Observations	160			

Dependent Variable:Ratio of female to male secondary school enrollment—the percentage of girls to boys enrolled at secondary level in both public and private schools.[1] Level of significance on a two-tailed test denoted by the following symbols:
NS—not significant, ^p < 0.10, *p < 0.05, **p < 0.01, ***p < 0.001.

[1] h ttp://data.worldbank.org/indicator/se.enr.seco.fm.zs?display=default

government effectiveness directly, the implication is that in the MENA region aid is of a targeted nature. Government effectiveness has many outcomes. The results here indicate that foreign aid does not impact most of them, but is effective at improving gender equality in education. However, because of previously mentioned studies that find a connection between foreign aid and corruption, more research should be conducted empirically, and through applied case study examples. The focus should be on causal links to instances of policy change where foreign aid conditionality can be traced to its disbursement for education purposes. Still, the statistical significance of foreign aid, as a factor that increases the percent of girls enrolled in school, has implications for economic sanctions.

Foreign aid was the first soft power tool to be cut when sanctions against Myanmar were implemented. This is the reality in most cases of sanctions

(Brynen, 2000; Crawford, 1997; Kegley and Hook, 1991; Martens, 2008). Aid, particularly aid items classified as "non-humanitarian type aid," which would be all funds directed toward education exchange, diplomatic exchange, and community development programs, are the first to go. The aid that can be disbursed is for food and medicine, particularly in nations where famine or military unrest have resulted in direct life-threatening situations for local populations. Because of the overwhelming empirical evidence that aid may be unsuccessful in increasing overall government effectiveness or political stability, the findings here offer an insight into what particular outcomes of government effectiveness are closely contingent on aid. The central conclusion from the results in table 5.4 is that educational opportunities for marginalized segments of the population increase as a result of increasing foreign aid.

Education inequality and illiteracy are serious problems in the Middle East (Kuran, 2004; Moghadam, 2003; Omran and Roudi, 1993; Zaharna, 1995). It is heartening to know that they have improved in the MENA region since 2004, as a result of foreign aid. This conclusion is based on the fact that more girls are enrolling in schools and it has been among females that literacy rates have historically been lowest (Hammoud, 2006; Roudi-Fahimi and Moghadam, 2003). This positive outcome indicates that educating women is a central diplomatic issue. The importance of women's education is suggested by the interpretation of the results that significant portions of aid funds are directed toward female education programs. In addition, the previously noted reports of the power of women, as the new political voice of the Middle East during the Arab Spring, offer a further insight with implications for economic sanctions. Because foreign aid is a premium instrument in the sanction tool kit, its amount is likely to be decreased with ease and immediacy during discourses. Based on the findings here, it would follow that if aid is decreased, then empowerment of marginalized population segments will also decrease, which will diminish possibilities for developing viable local political oppositions. In that case, sanctions lowering nonessential and humanitarian aid can have unintended negative consequences for local democracy building. The development of a varied, inclusive, and educated local political opposition is a desired outcome of democracy building in nations with repressive political elites. The results here would suggest that soft power tools are much more viable mechanisms for building democratic platforms than economic sanctions.

Soft power is a complex concept with many definitions. Because it is a notion that is less than 30 years old, the literature is still developing. It has been measured in a variety of ways with mixed results. Therefore, it is a topic ripe for exploration. The results of the methodological query here show that a way forward is through a focus on vehicles, or channels, through which soft power messages travel. Nye (2010) advises a combined approach in the Middle East where hard power, that is, direct military action, against terrorists is tempered with soft power tactics. This prescription is important because terrorism does not exist in isolation. Rather, it depends on support from local peoples. It is through soft power that Western nations can minimize such support for extremist ideology via the spread of alternative ideals, and in that way, decrease the incentives for future insurgency.

The general conclusion of the query presented here is that information technology facilitates idea exchange. The results suggest that, in the Middle East, the expansion of telecommunication platforms, particularly Web and cellular technology, is a method through which such an idea exchange can lead to increased government effectiveness. Other analysts have discussed this fact, such as Sakr (2001), who examines how cable and satellite television penetration had political impacts in Arab countries. The contribution of this query is that it shows that the private investments in telecommunications of outside MNCs have strong soft power features. Therefore, money transferred via FDI is relevant when measuring soft power.

Further research should examine FDI assets and flows with particular focus on different sectors of foreign expansions. Understanding which sectors foreign firms favor can indicate product market gaps. By studying the product positioning tactics of foreign firms in addressing such gaps, diplomacy scholars can examine how the owners of the associated assets promote the merit of their products to local populations during their market development campaigns. These promotional tactics are image intensive and the image messages can be evaluated for soft power components. This is the case because today, the Internet, mobile phones, satellites, and cable communications platforms offer an emotional visual connection to media content (Kraidy, 2009; Mortensen, 2011; Pappé, 2014; Sakr, 2001). Therefore, modern soft power channels are stronger and more immediately absorbed than traditional print and radio media. Communications related to soft power are also more immediate. Such technological platforms increase the amount and scope of communication and, therefore, enable the spread of ideas necessary for soft power to be influential. In particular, as the results here indicate, FDI can transmit these ideas, most often through the advertising and promotion of foreign goods and services (Anguelov, 2014; Hayden, 2012; Jiang and Wei, 2012; Miller and Thorr, 2003).

Chapter 6

Sanctions or Soft Power: Implications for Competitiveness

This chapter links together the literatures on sanctions, soft power, international business, and foreign direct investment. FDI analysis of incentives is offered at the firm level, as vested in the production and operations management and international economics literatures, to explain how the growth of international business opportunities can diminish sanction impact. The mitigation is linked to lowering transaction and opportunity costs due to the augmenting scope of global market participation.

Firm Profitability in a Global Market

Although FDI is a direct outcome of economic sanctions, there is a surprising dearth of FDI analysis in the literature on economic sanctions. To that effect, the findings and examples in Chapter 5 detailing how FDI can be a vehicle for soft power dissemination are important. Insights for economic sanction effectiveness can come from understanding the incentives for investing internationally today.

Foreign investment is increasing in magnitude and changing in nature. According to United Nations Conference on Trade and Development's (UNCTAD) databank "Bilateral FDI Statistics," which offers FDI data for all countries since 1948, in the last two decades FDI's contributive portion to world economic growth has increased from 5 percent to over 30 percent. It has also diversified from mainly being linked to capital assets such as factories, buildings and land to financial instruments and general operational services ranging from research and development to logistics

(Damijan et al., 2003; Head and Reis, 2008). By definition the service component of FDI relies on information exchange, which is another reason why FDI is closely linked to soft power. At its core, soft power is the transmission of information. Therefore, the opportunities for soft power analysis via examining FDI in the services sector are significant.

Information exchange by itself is merely a component of FDI proliferation. FDI must lead to knowledge building for it to create significant soft power impacts that could offer alternative policies to the imposition of economic sanctions, or even, result in such levels of intergovernmental cooperation as to render sanctions obsolete. For this reason, the literature on knowledge sourcing through FDI offers important insights. It discusses how foreign investors amass knowledge for augmenting business profits. Increasing this knowledge base leads to improving operational efficiency, which in turn minimizes the transaction costs in trade partnerships. It is this process of knowledge building and knowledge transmission that occurs via the private investments of transnational firms as they expand globally.

At the firm level, an international knowledge base is both operational and ideological (Büthe and Milner, 2008). Both components are present because they depend on a critical level of reaching agreements for conducting business. Such a meeting of the minds, so to speak, denotes an ideological connection of mutual understanding with respect to how production processes are to be established and followed. Therefore, the various quantifiable forms of FDI can be used as proxies for channeling soft power by analyzing the legal establishment and execution of management practices. Through the process, diplomatic efforts can be improved. For example, the improvement can come from increasing incentives for firm-level information channeling with respect to training local workers and managers in ways congruent with international human rights norms. Because in sanctioned nations, firm management and political elites comprisethe same people, increasing the opportunities for business communication increases the opportunities for political communication.

As explained above, for FDI to grow, a critical level of mutually beneficial business agreement must be reached. When both investor and recipient of investment find benefits from the return on that investment, the incentives to increase the magnitude of the successful business relationship grow Therefore, even through discourse, if the local business entity is significantly dependent on foreign investment, the opportunities increase for the investor to demand compliance with their preferred platforms and standards. In other words, incentives exist where private firms can demand improvements in labor, environment or operational standard compliance from their local business partners. The incentives are created under the increased scrutiny placed on MNCs today by the large and constantly growing number of international nongovernmental organizations (INGOs). Evidence of such activity has been noted in the literature on corporate social responsibility (Aguilera et al., 2007; Campbell, 2007; Colas, 2013; Du, Bhattacharya, and Sen, 2010). The political connection is examined in the context of international civic activism. To understand the connection between global civic engagement and the powerful role international activism has on MNC profitability today, one needs to examine the difference between FDI today and in the past.

FDI's changing structure has been the focus in interdisciplinary work in studies on intrenational market development ranging from economics, sociology, and political science to business management. The core definition of international market development is in the explanation that FDI is changing in purpose. Its purpose today is to develop local markets, which is different from its historic legacy of being deployed for the exploitation of local natural resources without creating local commerce with respect to consumption.

From historically being employed for extraction of natural resources in well-separated industrial sectors, today most FDI is in multisector resource management (Blanton and Blanton, 2007; Helmsing, 2003; Huarng and Ribeiro-Soriano, 2014; Shafaeddin, 2005). This means that where in the past FDI firms engaged in one type of business activity in a recipient nation, today they perform multiple business activities in more than one industrial sector. An insight into how this proliferation process has increased comes from the analysis of MNC portfolio management with respect to FDI.

Today the main portion of FDI is in merger and acquisitions (M&As), rather than the past norm of financing the construction of new industrial facilities (Head and Reis, 2008). The M&A deals have increased in value and source, as developing nation MNCs join the world market and use FDI as a knowledge-sourcing tool (Di Minin, Zhang, and Gammeltoft, 2012; Song and Shin, 2008). They purchase firms in developed nations to gain access to markets and expertise. MNCs from developed and developing nations primarily use FDI today for that purpose—market access both in size and scope. The market scope component is referred to as diversification. MNCs are continuously diversifying their holdings (Schoar, 2002; Shapiro, 2008). This process is the definition of MNC portfolio management. The fact that increasing components of MNC portfolio management are in international assets has given impetus to the international portfolio management literature that is anchored in business and finance bodies of research. The transformation is important to put in context because it describes such business agglomeration activities as vertical integration. For MNCs vertical integration is the acquisition or development of the majority of production platforms in an industry. From extraction to manufacturing to sales, the ability to own all of the individual firms in the production link affects the incentives to invest in nations during sanctions. For example, as the cases of Myanmar and North Korea show, particularly with regard to rare earths and energy inputs, traditional FDI in commodity extraction is still an important part of international investment dynamics. But today, it is no longer done in isolation. Traditionally, extraction firms would be engaged in mining and refining ores, for example, but then they would sell the ores and metals to manufacturing firms for the follow-up processes in the production chain, typically outside of the nation in which extraction happens. However, today the MNCs engaged in extraction also own assets in the follow-up industries that use the extracted inputs. For example, Rio Tinto—one of the world's largest mining and extraction conglomerates, headquartered jointly in the United Kingdom and Australia—owns entire production platforms. The Rio Tinto Group either fully or partially owns subsidiaries in operations ranging from extraction of ores to their refinement to their use in the group's technology and innovation division. This, in essence, is the definition of MNC vertical integration.

In addition to vertical integration, today the asset management strategies of MNCs also include investing in multiple sectors and, if not directly producing, then acquiring financial assets in different sectors in multiple countries. An example of that dynamic with respect to soft power features of FDI is the portfolio of holdings of French telecommunications giant Vivendi. Vivendi owns movie and music production companies, software companies, newspapers, cable and television firms, ticket retailers, gaming console and online gaming platforms, as well as cell phone and mobile communication device firms. By definition, most of its product lines are channels of information exchange. Among Vivendi's holdings are American Universal Studios as well as American Bartlesmann Music Group, British cable television giant General Cable, Spanish software producer Anaya, Germany's subsidiary of VIVA television (which is wholly owned by Viacom, parent company of MTV, Comedy Central and Nickelodeon) and also Maroc Telecom—the only telecommunications firm in Morocco that handles all telephone and most media platforms. Morocco is part of the MENA nations examined in Chapter 5. The fact that its information technology sector is not only foreign owned, but by far the most diversified telecommunications MNC in the world, offers an example of how Western management of information can in itself be viewed as soft power. Understanding that Vivendi's interests would be to promote its product lines in its international markets would denote that cable programming in Morocco would include Spongebob Squarepants and the Daily Show. Moroccan movie theaters would show Universal Studio movies.

This strategy of product and market diversification allows MNCs to engage in international brand proliferation (Strebinger, 2014). The nature of international brand proliferation is to use FDI for developing local markets for the sale of their brands, which as already explained, is the new purpose of FDI in the modern global economy. With respect to historical use of FDI, this is a fairly modern business strategy. Its magnitude has grown as a result of the information technology revolution and the market liberalization policies that gained major impetus with the advent of the World Trade Organization in 1995. The creation of the WTO set forth an institutional platform for the internationalization of business, which directly changed the strategic possibilities FDI offered.

As already noted, FDI in the past had been primarily involved with resource-based industries such as mining, oil, agriculture, and general commodity trade. The investment focused, and often limited itself, to regions that possess natural resources, with extraction of these resources as a main goal (Blanton and Blanton, 2007; Sylwester, 2005). The sales took place in external markets that offered the highest profit margins. Sales in the countries of extraction did not primarily concern the firms investing overseas. Blanton and Blanton (2007) observe that the information systems' innovation that rapidly accelerated in the mid and late 1990s has led firms to change the purpose of their foreign investments, as explained earlier.

The change of purpose of FDI is contingent to the overall change of global economic activity (Gholami, Lee, and Heshmati, 2006). The same revolutionary changes that Blanton and Blanton (2007) discuss also led to the advent of the "new" economy. The new economy has been identified as the reality in which knowledge components employed in production increase significantly in relation to direct costs (Atkinson, 2004). Prior to the information technology revolution of the 1990s firms mostly relied on labor-intensive production in the value-added process. However, today knowledge-intensive components add a significant amount of product value and therefore are becoming increasingly important for firm profitability (Kelly, 1999). It is all based on higher rates of innovation and creative destruction. Creative destruction is the process of abandoning old production options for innovative ones that lead to efficiency improvements (Gordon, 2000). What is unique about modern day creative destruction is that it happens fast, (*i. e.),* in shorter than traditional time frames.

Creative destruction is dependent on information technology because the efficient transmission of information dictates the rates of information exchange (Atkinson, 2004). Those rates define the magnitude of creative destruction. The higher and more diverse the information exchange options become, the higher the rate of innovation and the higher the production value added options. This is the main reason why FDI has changed in both nature and scope. International investments in information exchange platforms are crucial in the modern economy (Gholami, Lee, and Heshmati, 2006). They are also the vehicles of soft power that influence the increase in global economic and political commonality. Even with the discourses examined in this book, it must be noted that international economic and political cooperation today is at an all time historical high (Kaul, Grunberg, and Stern, 1999; Keohane, 2005; Wight, 2014). It is all due to the increased options for communication. With respect to political information, a connection has been made between FDI and democratization through the deployment of information technology for the purpose of idea exchange (Addison and Heshmati, 2003).

Idea exchange dynamics at the government level is embodied in the notion of international policy diffusion (Simons and Elkins, 2004; Stone, 2001; Walter, 1999), that is, the process of governments learning from each other and locally applying policies observed outside their nations' realities. To that effect, we talk about global governance today and one global market—both are outcomes of the ability to transfer knowledge internationally at low direct and transaction costs. Low knowledge transfer cost is the core factor that has fueled the market change of global economic activity from the "old" to the "new" economy. Many argue that FDI fueled the global growth of the new economy (Addison and Heshmati, 2003; Cooke, 2001; Eichengreen, 2006).

The period prior to the change from the "old" to the "new" economy was when the bulk of economic sanction studies reported successful outcomes. The main reason being that during that period local market power in developing nations, in terms of purchasing magnitude, was insignificant in relation to the overall profits of MNCs. To put the difference in perspective, it must first be stated that firm profits are based on the successful final sale of finished products. In the old economy, MNCs relied on their developed nation markets for the majority of revenues because of the wealth and consumption habits of citizens in the developed world. Atkinson (2004) and Wolf (2004) explain that in the old economy, income levels in the developed world were the highest and discretionary spending brackets of consumers were the largest—when people earn a lot they can purchase a lot. In addition, as societies move up the industrialization ladder, their consumption bundles—as economists put it—increase. In other words, they not only can pay a lot for goods and services, but they also increase their consumption of the variety of goods and services. For these reasons, prior to the time of the new economy American and Western economic sanctions had purpose and impact. They controlled access to the markets with the highest purchasing power.

In the old economy, the single strongest market was the United States where hundreds of millions of customers consumed the largest and most diverse combination of goods and services in the world. Therefore, the volume of trade America offered had no parallel substitute. However, all of that changed when technological and political innovation led to the massive opportunities for developing new markets that drive the high economic growth rates of, what historically had been called, lesser developed countries (LDCs). Blanton and Blanton (2007) argue that FDI was and still is the core tool for the structural and institutional development of such new markets. It is the incentives of FDI's sources—the multinational corporations—that augment its importance. Those incentives shifted from reliance on mature markets for profit growth to strategic development of new consumption in developing markets. Therefore, the sectors of importance changed from primary commodities and products—such as raw agricultural exports, lumber, ores, coals, and metals to fast moving consumer goods (FMCGs) such as clothing, personal items, pharmaceuticals, electronics, information and telecommunication products, and financial services. The change of importance has to do with the internationalization of the manufacturing process. In the old economy, extraction was done in the developing world, as were (and still are) low-knowledge intensive manufacturing processes. High-knowledge intensive manufacturing remained concentrated in the developed world. However, in the new economy, with the aid of information technology, firms no longer have to rely on knowledge bases back in the developed world for the higher value-added manufacturing of finished goods. Information technology allows MNCs to disaggregate business processes and reduce the complexities associated with communication and coordination across organizational and geographic boundaries, as Contractor et al. (2010) explain. In this way, information technology assets became infrastructure assets. Today, they allow manufacturing functions to be developed closer to the extraction processes. The incentives are to concentrate more business activity closer to the site of extraction in order to minimize direct transportation costs, and also to benefit from the proximity to the end consumer. Such business activity consists of creating entire production networks, not just individual production links (Porter and Kramer, 2011). Therefore, today a global firm can develop production capabilities in diverse geographies and take advantage of cost saving opportunities in transportation and time management.

In the old economy, such approaches slowly developed over time and carried large risks for efficiency. But in the new economy, technology allows for the outsourcing process to include outsourcing knowledge instantaneously, which leads to the ability to outsource all components of production, not only those that are labor-intensive and based on low knowledge. Such an approach enables firms to reintegrate the outcomes of outsourced processes back into their internal operations. It provides a way to build competitive advantage at the firm level that can be measured by improvements in performance through, as Bardhan, Whitaker and Mithas (2006: 17) put it: "better codification and standardization of information exchange." Equally important, as already mentioned, is the fact that such an approach also allows for producing at local costs and therefore offering products at local prices. This is another important market development aspect that has changed the incentive to direct strategic investment from developed to emerging markets.

In the old economy when finishing production processes were in the relatively high-cost Western world, sales had to happen there as well. Reexportation back to the developed world would price products higher than local discretionary spending brackets for the majority of the population. Therefore, Western exports to LDCs were mostly in either commodities, such as food products or steel, or high-end industrial equipment such as machinery and airplanes, that could be purchased by governments and businesses, not average citizens. The FDI associated with such exports was also concentrated and limited in scope. For example, Panasonic could not sell many television sets in Zimbabwe, if it had to ship them from Japan and price them at world market levels. Its Zimbabwe investments could be in two production links: (1) low-end component assembly for export to final assembly in a more developed nation, or/and (2) setting up a retail operational structure in Zimbabwe through flagship stores or purchasing a retail outlet dedicated to the local sales of its finished electronics. In either or both instances of market presence, Panasonic could not sell many electronic products in Zimbabwe because few Zimbabweans (or other nationals who would make purchases while in the country) could afford to pay world market level prices. However, in the new economy, Panasonic can completely produce all components and their services in Zimbabwe. It can source all inputs locally or regionally and offer a television set priced according to local discretionary spending brackets. Local wages and local currency valuations set those brackets and, therefore, define local market purchasing power.

Discretionary spending brackets are growing in developing nations, but they are still much lower because wages are lower. Therefore, direct exports from high-wage nations would put the products at unattainable price points for average local consumers. Therefore, in order to penetrate developing markets in terms of introducing new products and growing the sales of those products, MNCs must produce locally. Evidence suggests that they do and this strategy is at the core of global firm profitability today (Adeyemi et al., 2014). To illustrate the magnitude of this global market power shift in relation to FDI, one can look at the types of modern aggregate FDI flows. The growth of FDI in service industries alone provides an important example.

Services encompass high-value added production link components such as finance, design, and customer service. They were traditionally undertaken in the developed world in the old economy, and are now increasingly channeled toward the developing world in the new economy (Dunning, 1998; Oehler-Şincai, 2011). For example, in 1990 FDI stock in services was $950 billion worldwide. By 2002, it had reached $4 trillion with FDI inflows into services accounting for two-third of all FDI inflows in 2001–2002 alone (Helpman, 2006). This metric is important because in relation to FDI stock—the overall balance of asset values—FDI inflows denote the annual increase of new investment at the country level. The averages suggest that at the onset of the 2000s, the annual growth of new FDI was four times as high as the value of FDI assets accumulated over time. When it comes to overall value estimates Choe (2003) posits that in the 1990s the dollar value of FDI inflows increased from $200 billion to $1.3 trillion. Choe (2003) further explains that during the same period the amounts of FDI inflows and outflows combined grew at least twice as fast as actual international trade amounts. The interpretation is that FDI stock—the value of investment after liabilities have cleared (such as debt and the general cost of acquisitions)—offers productivity options of a multiplier nature. Profits from FDI can quadruple, if judged by the numbers offered in Helpman (2006), through the spillover effects they generate for revenue streams in the multiple networks of modern MNCs. To put this growth in perspective of overall world economic activity in terms of value, it must be noted that in 1980 FDI stock represented 5 percent of world GDP (Lall and Rajneesh, 2004). By 2000, that percentage had almost tripled to 14 percent. By 2011, it had reached 30 percent as estimated by UNCTAD. These numbers indicate the importance of new internationalization. International trade was important in the past as well, but it only generated 5 percent of global wealth. Most wealth creation was internal, that is, within the defined boundaries of individual countries. Also, the developed world created most wealth, which is no longer the case today. Economists at Citigroup, as quoted by the *Economist* magazine, offer these important averages as examples of the change in wealth creation patterns from their historic legacy of being in developed nations toward developing nations. Between 1995 and 2007, 59 percent of global economic growth came form the developed world. Between 2010 and 2013, over 70 percent of global economic growth came from the developing world.[1] The article explains that because much of that growth happens within the borders of large developing nations, such as the BRICS (Brazil, Russia, India, China and South Africa) nations, it appears as though trade volumes have decreased and one could conclude that international trade is becoming less important. However, the real reason for the decrease in direct trade metrics—imports and exports—is that through FDI, firms develop local production systems in their entirety and as developing nations grow they face less need to import components. As the internal economies of developing countries diversify with respect to producing many goods and services, in large nations local sourcing options become available and substitute suppliers emerge to offer components that previously had to be imported. That reality makes it possible for a firm that sells products in Brazil, for example, to source all of the components for the final assembly of that product in Brazil and not import many, mainly technological components, as has been the case historically, from other nations. It is all possible because FDI from constantly increasing (in number and scope) sources are directed toward emerging markets and is deployed for the development of a diverse local industrial base. Since FDI is a component of international trade, the implication is that trade is becoming more important in the value creating process at the firm level, not less important if only judged by the direct balance of overall exports and imports.[2]

As already explained, not only have the FDI numbers grown, but also diversification across sectors has occurred. From investing in extracting raw materials, MNCs have shifted the focus of their FDI toward developing complete external networks with strategic backward linkages to local production entities and forward linkages with local retailers (Hayes et al., 2005; Weinstein, 2005). Those linkages with local retailers are growing in importance because of the focus on reaching new customers outside mature markets (Levy and Prakash, 2003).[3] Reaching those customers is contingent on successfully promoting the novelty of products and services to them. That promotion is the focus of the largest segment of business administration research—international marketing. By definition, and as explained by the literature on brand proliferation and even cultural imperialism, the marketing of foreign goods and services is soft power in application.

In an exhaustive volume on the modern dynamics of international marketing Terpstra, Foley, and Sarathy (2012) explain that it is all based on FDI. The assets of the firms promoting their products internationally are by definition FDI, because direct exports from home to host nations are the anomaly today (Cavusgil, Knight, and Riesenberger, 2012). As already noted, when MNCs promote products in new markets they look for local production platforms to either produce locally in entirety, or complete the final links in the production chain, in order to position the products close to the local consumer. In this way innovation can reach the customer fast, which helps minimize the transaction costs of promotion. Speed of reaching the customer allows producers to harness the power of excitement that innovation brings. In addition, this tactic minimizes not only direct costs such as transportation, but also indirect costs associated with prototyping and market testing. Innovation must be taste and preference specific, and therefore testing various options to study customer response is important in order to create the most satisfying, and therefore, the best positioned product (Beise, 2001). For that reason, the strategy for MNCs is to establish and grow favorable networks in component procurement (Porter and Kramer, 2011). Therefore, procuring locally is essential. MNCs must stay close to local cost structures in order to be able to offer local customers new products at competitive local prices. These are the strategies that have led to an international trade platform where direct exports from mature to emerging markets in finished products are the anomaly today.

The above examined dynamic of incentives in modern-day firm-level internationalization helps explain why the purpose of FDI in the new economy has changed. Among the many conclusions, with respect to diplomacy, a main point is that the information channels FDI offers are the foundations of its successful deployment. Then, it is counterintuitive that as a vehicle for soft power, FDI is less examined with respect to economic sanctions. When sanctions constrict FDI, they negatively impact the information transmitted through it. The reason for this oversight in making the connection could be that researchers and diplomats bear the legacy of ethnocentric guilt based on the historical findings of the pervasively negative impacts of Western FDI on the developing world. As a testament, Young (2001) raises the question, "what do researchers know about the global business environment" as the title of his work. He argues that surprisingly little has been said about the interconnected relationship between FDI and the governance structures of multilateral organizations such as the World Bank, the International Monetary Fund and activist nongovernmental organizations (NGOs). Those organizations are named because a lot of FDI penetration is championed via loans from the IMF and the World Bank in public-private partnerships (Hammami, Ruhashyankiko, and Yehoue, 2006; Hodge, Greve, and Boardman, 2010). When projects are executed with finances from such multilateral organizations, they deploy NGO networks in execution, monitoring, and local government mediation. Young (2001) also argues that the reason for focusing on that interplay is that informal governance influences formal governance. Therefore, guidelines promulgated through global governance structures and social activism are regarded with increased attention. This fact is also a result of the information technology revolution because advances in telecommunication technologies have allowed for higher degrees of monitoring. This growth of global social activism and the watchfulness placed on MNCs via cyber-civic engagement is a result of the much discussed historical legacy of the exploitative practices of Western MNCs. However, as global wealth balances shift, so do the investor characteristics.

As already discussed, the source of FDI historically had been in the developed world and most of its volume had been among the developed nations. Because of the dynamics in international production as examined above, starting in the mid 2000s FDI flows into developing countries have increased at the expense of developed countries. For example, at the end of 2008 FDI inflows into Africa had risen to a record value of $88 billion. FDI inflows into Asia had grown by 17 percent to a record $298 billion, FDI into Latin America and the Caribbean had grown by 13 percent to $144 billion, and FDI inflows to the former Eastern Bloc countries reached a record $114 billion. Meanwhile, FDI into the developed world decreased by more than 25 percent.[4] These averages are important because they reflect the economic crisis of that year. The rapid global diffusion of the crisis affected all financial markets. It constricted global capital liquidity by devaluing financial assets, lowering aggregate wealth, and impacting the ability of firms to invest (Tong and Wei, 2011). As expected, a drop in FDI inflows is observed by UNCTAD but only in the developed world. The strong growth of inward FDI into the developing world shows that global investors find value in allocating scarce financial resources there.

Also it must be noted that the investors are changing. Globalization has increased the wealth of the developing world and the wealth of its firms. The growing number of large MNCs from the developing world has been impressive. From 1996 to 2008, the number of developing country companies in the Fortune Global 500 increased 525 percent.[5] Such growth is the result of the explosion of international production networks and the increasing flows of FDI into the developing world.

The FDI going into the developing world from the developed had been studied with respect to mostly negative social outcomes associated with exploitation in the extraction process. When, as already noted, in the past FDI had been associated with the extraction of raw materials for export, the economic incentives of the investors were in cost-minimizing strategies for acquiring cheap inputs. As a result, since the 1970s two main theories developed to explain the negative impact of developed nations' investments in the developing world—World-System Theory and Dependency Theory. Both are based on the assumption that FDI comes from the West and is deployed to exploit the East and South. That assumption may have very well been the reality in the old economy. But today increasing amounts of FDI come from the East. A major and growing portion of that investment is directed toward the West as a competitive tool that MNCs from the developing world employ to acquire new technologies and gain access to new markets (Anguelov, 2014; Barnard, 2008; Dunning, Van Hoesel, and Narula, 1996; Gammeltoft, 2008; Klein and Wöcke, 2007). These findings, and the general platform of international business operations explained here, indicate that things have changed. Therefore, theoretical platforms must account for those changes. It would be far too optimistic to dismiss both theories and declare the end of exploitation. But, it must be understood how their assumptions hold today and if they are valid. Even though there is evidence that contradicts the main premise of both theories, it does not mean that in all cases developed nations' control over developing markets is diminished.

World-System Theory states that there is a global capitalist system that allows Western (core) nations to exploit developing and less-developed (semi-periphery and periphery) nations by bringing them closer in or further out from the global economic core (London and Smith, 1988). Dependency Theory states that dependence on foreign capital by underdeveloped nations causes decreased economic productivity and negative conditions in general (Kardulias, 1999; Robertson, 1992). In both theoretical frameworks, FDI is portrayed as a tool for foreign capital dependence in a negative light. The concept denotes a gradual increase of domination and control of developing nations by their developed partners achieved through the proliferation of FDI (Kellner, 2002; Kentor, 2001; Kentor and Boswell, 2003; Rudra, 2002; Wimberley an Bello, 1992).

There are two measures of dependence: investment dependence—the penetration of a country by foreign capital—and debt dependence—the dependence of a government on foreign credit. Both are contingent on MNC activities because, as already explained, most direct economic penetration is accomplished through the private investments of MNCs. Multilateral organizations can aid in providing financial incentives for economic penetration, but ultimately it is MNCs that acquire the property rights associated with new industrialization. Acquiring those property rights has been equated by both theories to economic imperialism. For example, Kentor (2001) finds foreign capital dependence to have a negative effect on domestic problems in developing nations by promoting income inequality, accelerating population growth, and slowing economic growth. A significant body of socioeconomic research by Kentor and the above cited scholars reflects the old economy incentive structures of trade. The pervasively negative aspects of globalization embodied by the investments of MNCs are observed because of the extraction-based nature of trade. It is also worth noting that the literature comes from the field of sociology with little regard to other fields that study international trade such as operations management.

The fields of productions and operations management and international marketing bring insights into current changes of incentive structures in international business. Those are the changes that give MNCs impetus to engage in a lower degree of exploitation and put more effort into improving institutional cultures in developing nations. The incentives are due to two main factors—one is purely economic and based on the transaction costs of increasing marginal sales. In terms of sales growth, transaction costs are the costs of introducing new products in markets (also referred to as product development), advertising, promotion, and customer and public relations services. In developed countries those costs are high because many brands compete in an overcrowded market place for limited market share. The owners of those brands look at emerging markets for future increases in sales volume in two important aspects that were discussed previously: direct export sales, which is the traditional approach of exporting, and more importantly, local manufacturing for sales in local markets (Aizenman, 2006). To offer an example of how important the local manufacturing for local sales component is, Drezner (2006) estimates that of all the production done in China by foreign companies, over 80 percent of the products are sold in China and not exported for sale outside the country. This shift in market concentration not only toward China, but toward the majority of emerging markets, did not occur with significant force until the mid-2000s (Zakaria, 2011). The change is the core factor behind the new incentives of MNCs to engage in behavior that increases the welfare of the populations of developing nations. This increase in welfare is likely to be spent on new products and services offered by MNCs, because as already noted, increased product and market diversification allow the MNCs to offer a growing variety of goods and services.

The second main factor contributing to the observed general improvement of social behavior in MNC platforms is contingent on soft power. It comes in two facets—the soft power of monitoring from formal and informal governance structures and the soft power MNCs themselves wield through information dissemination in teaching and learning (Campbell, 2006; Cheng, Ngok, and Huang, 2012; Lensink and Morrissey, 2006, Levy, 2008, Vogel, 2008). Much has been said about the increased power of international nonprofit organizations (INGOs) and social activists in raising awareness of social justice issues of exploitation by MNCs in the developing world (Ayoub, 1998; Momin, Ahmed, and Parker, 2013; Monshipouri, Welch, and Kennedy, 2003; Santoro, 2003). A whole discipline has developed around the monitoring of human rights abuses due to business practices. This very fact has changed the power dynamic and

MNCs tread with caution, aware that in the information technology age, bad publicity can cause significant damage in customer relations (Ali, 2013; Lompo and Trani, 2014; Vogel, 2008).

With respect to MNCs as sources of soft power that can lead to improvements in social conditions via teaching and learning, an explanation lies in the definition of FDI linkage and training channels. FDI channels are classified in terms of competition, innovation, and human development (Seck, 2012; Winkler, 2013). With respect to human development, the linkage channel provides a venue for technology transfer. Foreign firms transfer new technology to domestic firms through transactions with these firms (Ernst and Kim, 2002; Martin and Salomon, 2003; Smeets, 2008; Wang, 2009). Then the training channel provides a venue for knowledge transfer because the introduction of new technologies by foreign firms encourages "an upgrading of human capital" (Lensink and Morrissey, 2006: 479). This knowledge transfer is not only technological, but also political. As already noted, FDI by MNCs is increasingly monitored for global civic society (Barrientos and Smith, 2007; Levy, 2008). The higher scrutiny provides incentives for foreign firms that engage in new production to follow international standards in operations management (Campbell, 2006; Vogel, 2008). In the process, they can positively impact local social justice. Research again has focused on examples from China (Bergsten et al., 2007; Cheng, Ngok, and Huang, 2012; Subramanian, 2011). Examples from China are important with respect to human condition improvements because of the negative legacy of human rights set by the Chinese government. It is well documented and discussed that the Chinese government represses its people in order to prevent dissent. Therefore, it can be concluded that there would be few internal incentives to improve human rights policies in China. But external factors can create such incentives. Bergsten et al. (2007) show how increased presence of foreign firms, investment, and managers in China has impacted Chinese companies with respect to increasing competition for local labor. The competition has led to monetary gains for employees and also to the Central Communist Party taking a firm stand in policies that improve the working conditions and pension plans for Chinese workers.

Another positive example of this process is the noted interest in mutually beneficial labor relations. Even while some criticize certain aspects of globalization, economists and sociologists have observed a current and steady rise in wages in developing nations as a result of trade liberalization and MNC market penetration (Henry, 2007; Henry and Sasson, 2008; Irwin, 2009; Krugman, 2008; Stulz, 2005; Subramanian, 2011). There is a well accepted connection by scholars between general economic growth and rising wages that is attributed to multiple factors.

Today among those factors is a general economic interest by multinational employers in labor issues in emerging markets. What in the past was referred to solely as "labor" is now viewed as "a consumer" (Basile et al., 2008; Grossman et al., 2006; Navaretti et al., 2007). Today MNCs have vested interests in the purchasing power of their workers in the countries they penetrate, because they look for opportunities to sell to those workers. Firms are now less concerned with keeping wages low in host nations to maintain low production costs, as they have been and as is the convenient argument for the critics of free-trade. In the modern interconnected global marketplace, MNCs have an interest in increasing wages because the wage increase is likely to be spent on the products and services that the MNC is selling.

Unfair Competitive Advantage and Its Implications for Political Resilience under Economic Sanctions

For global firms, market presence is no longer a choice but a necessity. Therefore, any sanctions that prohibit firms from optimally choosing their locations negatively impact firm competitiveness not only in a specifically sanctioned nation, but overall. When in the past firms could strategically choose markets based on institutional stability, today the interconnectedness of business activity makes location options less important than strategic necessities. In the developing world unattractive markets have become attractive because trade liberalization has changed the structure of market participation. The general growth of economic activity that has resulted from the proliferation of globalization has caused an increase in the number of market participants. Townsend, Yeniyurt, and Talay (2009) explain that all markets—developed and developing—once had a well-defined set of competitors. Today, both in terms of firms and countries, the set of competitors has expanded and become harder to define, because of the international fragmentation in production. The higher the fragmentation, the more links in the production chain, the more market participants there are, and the less clear it becomes which links bear the critical value-adding features that lead to firm profitability. Another cause for the increase in the number of international market participants is the growth of global brand proliferation and diversification. Brand proliferation refers to the internationalization of firm assets and sales. Brand diversification refers to the variety of products and services modern day transnational firms provide.

For these reasons, the profit growth of MNCs today is simultaneously tied to geographic and product diversification.

Product diversification offers opportunities for achieving economies of scale and scope (Chang and Wang, 2007). Economies of scale are savings in production costs per unit that firms gain when they grow in size. Going global allows modern firms to increase their size drastically. Therefore, with the growth of international operations comes savings on production costs per unit because many more units are sold than in one national market. It is important to remember though, that because of the above-discussed fragmentation of the production function, such growth is contingent on partnerships. As firms increase the number of countries in which they operate, they increase the number of business intermediaries that help them establish operations and or connect to local consumers. In this way, as a firm grows outward with respect to its national economy, the number of participants in the firm's market operations also grows. In the process, per unit costs of manufacturing additional products decrease because fixed costs—those of buildings, machinery, and rents become average costs when firms do not have to construct new factories, for example when they grow, but can outcontract the increased production to intermediaries.

Economies of scope are similar in the fact that they are achieved on an average cost per unit bases, but in this case that cost is spread out across multiple products. The savings are achieved in two ways. One is by the reliance on a common indivisible asset, such as a specific technological know-how. The other is in lowering transaction costs of promotion in reaching new customers. In other words, when MNCs make many products and bundle them in product packages, for example, they promote multiple product lines with the aid of common advertising platforms. For example, Apple Inc. offers many products. They all have a similar brand design. Apple uses the same marketing experts and designers to create the promotion tools for all its products from laptops to cell phones to iTunes and Apple TV services. Economies of scope are achieved because the costs of producing the main campaigns and their design are spread out across many products. As the number of products promoted grows, more people can be reached per unit of money spent. This would imply that there is no need to hire additional designers to keep creating new logos for the new products. Those products all bear the same packaging and image, and therefore, Apple Inc. achieves wage savings per unit with respect to advertising and promotion. For these reasons, the general economic theory of international trade states that the unique benefits of increasing trade are the achieving of economies of scale and scope (Ethier, 1982). This is the main reason why in the new economy firms have incentives to set up international operations.

As mentioned above, when they diversify in location, MNCs have the opportunity to identify gaps in newly penetrated markets. In developing nations that are climbing the industrialization ladder, the possibility to fill such gaps offers an additional diversification incentive—product diversification. As emerging market populations increase their wealth, they increase their consumption needs in scale and scope. To cater to these needs, diversified in terms of product breadth, MNCs can easily introduce new products for the local population, products that have been previously developed in mature markets. This is the definition of market development. This is different from product development, which was discussed earlier with respect to customer proximity in prototyping during the innovation process in order to minimize transaction costs. The difference is that market development refers to the sale of products already developed in other markets and introduced in a new market. They are not invented in the new market, which is the process of product development. Specific features of these products can be tailored to local taste and preferences, but the main product attributes do not need to be reinvented. Therefore, in order to be best poised to fill gaps in developing nation markets, MNCs increase diversification of holdings and product lines. Many product lines allow firms to introduce products already tested for success in other nations, while improving their features, based on the knowledge of all the international markets where the products have been sold as well as local market-specific knowledge.

Product diversification increases MNC value because it offers options for multiproduct, multimarket expansion, which is essential for the profit growth of MNCs today (Schoar, 2002). As a result, MNC investment has morphed from foreign direct investment into foreign portfolio investment (FPI) (Blanton and Blanton, 2007; Lensink and Morrissey, 2006). The management of FPI is a continuous process of acquisition and divestment, expansion and contraction, and overall restructuring of operations through reallocating assets in different countries by leveraging competitive capabilities, as Oliveira, Roth and Ponte (2003) put it. In this process, location-specific knowledge spillovers occur because of the many trade partnerships that are developed. In both forward supply chain operations—from manufacturing to retail—and backward supply chain operations—from sourcing of manufactured parts and components to the mining and extraction of oars, metals, and energy for their production—MNCs share best practices managerial input with their partner firms (Rozenweig, Roth, and Dean Jr., 2003). Because in many cases partner firms are themselves entities from MNC conglomerate groups that provide inputs based on their own international firm-specific platforms, international information spillovers occur. They are regional in nature because of proximity needs. It is the combination of these reasons that creates a spillover effect with respect to economic sanctions.

The reason for the spillovers lies in the fact that economic sanctions impact the major trading partner nations of both the sender and receiver country. At the firm level economic sanctions may disproportionately affect the firms of the sender nation because of the nature of regional production fragmentation noted in MNC operations management. The sender nation's firms may incur higher loss of value in their entire regional operations because restriction of production activity in one country can result in restriction of contingent business operations in neighboring countries. The reasons for this disproportional loss of value are related to agglomeration economies.

Regional economies define modern international production because of the proliferation of agglomeration economies globally. By definition, agglomeration economies are region specific. They are marked by benefits to be gained by proximity to certain markets, inputs, and knowledge. Because of the international fragmentation of production, which as already explained is the location of specific production processes for the final assembly of one product in different countries, industrial agglomeration has become very important. It is based on specialization (Peri, 2002). Certain nations and, by association, their regional trading networks become leading specialists in specific industrial activity. To this effect, industrial agglomeration refers to the creation and proliferation of global industrial clusters (Lazzeretti, Sedita, and Caloffi, 2014; Markusen, 1996).

Alfred Marshall first identified cases of industrial agglomeration, or clusters, in 1890 and described their spillover effects in knowledge that are created when firms benefit from the production and innovation activities of neighboring firms in the same and related industries (Marshall, 1890). Because of the specific spatial costs of that time period, Marshall's clusters were within nations. Today they are among nations. Cluster activity has been much studied in international production contexts because in the knowledge economy, informational spillovers can give clustered firms a better production function than that of isolated producers (Krugman, 1991). However, as already noted and discussed at length in Weinstein (2005), at large, there is no such thing as isolated producers anymore. All components of production depend on international production networks that are situated within clusters. It is because of the agglomeration effect of these factors that economies of scale and scope are created (Lazzeretti, Sedita, and Caloffi, 2014). Economies of scope are achieved in clusters because firms reduce their average cost in making multiple products in a concentrated geographic area.

In summary, in the new global market, economies of scale and scope are the goal of MNC business strategies. They are achieved in two main ways—by diversification in products and markets, and by being strategic in cluster location. Being part of old and new clusters has become so important as to merit its own policy description—spatial management (Dunning, 1998, 2009; Porter, 2011).

The benefits of proximity contribute to two main reasons for the emergence and growth of clusters globally. First, the concentration of firms in a specific region offers a pooled labor market with industry-specific skills, ensuring both a lower probability of unemployment and a lower probability of labor shortages. Second, localized industries can support the production of nontradable specialized inputs (Martin and Sunley, 2003). Such inputs can be in human capital, when a region such as Silicon Valley has many entrepreneurial information technology professionals. Nontradable specialized inputs can also come in the form of specific infrastructure, such as large military industrial complexes around which firms want to locate, or large ports where processing and logistic cervices create their own operational knowledge incubators.

It is these factors that shape the ability to produce multiple goods efficiently in concentrated locales that has magnified the level of diversification of firms. Because of this diversification, location becomes even more important for MNCs as emerging markets take the lead in overall corporate profits. Being close to those markets in all aspects of operations provide essential benefits that range from knowledge spillovers in innovation to knowledge sharing in best practices with suppliers and intermediaries, to have a better understanding of customer needs and to be able to respond fast to changes in those needs, and to taking advantage of lower production and transportation costs. An essential thing to remember is the fact that the quest to attain those benefits happens in a context of increasing competition. As emerging markets grow, so do their firms. In a world with rapidly growing market players, the magnitude of competition increases for all those players. Because of this reality, economic sanctions can end up providing competitive advantages to the firms of those nations that do not comply with them.

The proliferation of multinational corporate business interconnectedness, combined with the market opportunities in the developing world, sheds light on the ability of sanctioned nations to frustrate American and Western efforts. In all cases examined previously, sanctioned nations find effective alternative options for trade. Today they do so speedily and efficiently, as the data in Chapters 2, 3, and 4 from Myanmar and North Korea indicate and the examples of Russia and Iran offered in Chapter 1 show. A reason for this agility lies in the fact that it is local political elites in the sanctioned nations that comprise the local business establishment. Its members may be bad politicians according to Western definitions of good governance, but that does not mean they are bad business people in terms of international trade. For example, the magnitude of growth in each industrial sector in Myanmar examined in Chapter 3 indicates that there was significant learning associated with trade during the sanction years. The implication is that non-American trading partners contributed to substantial industrial upgrading with respect to building operational knowledge capacity in Myanmar. This fact is related to the nature of knowledge spillovers in regional contexts. It indicates that firm management—be it private or government controlled—learns from the managers of other firms. To that effect, Luo (2005) describes the incentives for MNCs to share operational knowledge with their trading partners. The incentives are significant and go beyond subsidiary to ancillary partner networks. As Luo (2005) puts it, there is more of a coopetition process than a competition process in international market development. Coopetition occurs when in one aspect firms compete with each other, but then they provide cooperative advice, technology, and investment to common ancillary networks. This effect is particularly strong in developing nations where multiple firms rely on one common transportation firm, for example. In that context, all businesses that use the services of that transportation firm end up sharing input in their supply chain management strategies. The common provider of transportation services becomes a communication hub where the information is shared. It is shared because knowledge flows both from the top down and bottom up in management. Keeping these facts in mind can help understand why political dictatorships become so good at evading sanctions. The longer they stay in power, the longer they stay in business. While controlling all business operations in the absence of market competitors, they learn the best ways to increase their business profitability through international information exchange. When their business profitability grows, so does the political resilience of the government because the economic benefits can be used to increase political rents. As authoritarian regimes become richer, the economic and political rents they can extract, protect, and bestow on their supporters increase. For these reasons we see the resilience to international diplomatic pressures in Myanmar, China, North Korea, Egypt, Iran, Cuba, and Russia.

The constriction of information also fuels resilience. As discussed in Chapter 5, FDI is a vehicle for information transmission and knowledge. When Western firms are told to scale down or seize further investment in sanctioned nations, external information flow becomes unidirectional with respect to ideology. Local political information becomes dominated by one-sided information sources—those who support the local regime.

Therefore, alternative information dissemination is negatively impacted. In other words, when Western nations impose sanctions, they limit the amount of information that can be used to build local political coalitions that would support the ideals congruent with those of the sender nations.

For these reasons, the political resilience of rogue and repressive regimes must be examined in terms of the economic incentives to remain repressive. Their resilience is based on the fact that the local politicians are also the local businessmen. Through the growth of international production networks, their business opportunities augment and the rents associated with that growth also increase. As business opportunities grow in the absence of competition, so does the amount of rent extraction and protection. Rent protecting leads to strengthening economic and political leadership, because the wealth is used for creating further rents by providing economic benefits to the regime supporters. This reliance on economic rents delivers strong political rents and lowers opportunities for the development of viable political oppositions because it has a path-dependent component. As we see in the case of Myanmar, path dependence keeps the economic and political life of the country unchanged after the end of sanctions.

In summary, as long as sanctioned governments are not significantly isolated from the global market, sanctions can disproportionately harm the sender nation. This harm can result in two main outcomes. One is through the direct loss of market share for the sender nation's MNCs that can have regional and global profitability sides. This is a serious competitive advantage problem because MNC production and management platforms in any country rely on the business partnerships of the country in question and its major trade links in regional supply chains. The sender nation MNC affiliates in neighboring countries can be dependent on economic activity in the sanctioned nation, and when that activity is contracted, so is the activity of their affiliates in the region. Therefore, they can become more competitively vulnerable. The result can be a decrease in the overall earnings of the sender nation MNCs.

The other way that sanctions can harm the sender nation is by lowering its credibility on the international political arena if the effect of the sanctions is not evident. The lower the credibility, the lower the support for the social or humanitarian cause that the sanctions aim to alleviate. The result is a loss of moral ground. When the sender nation is questioned, so are its legitimacy, diplomacy and policy positions.

Chapter 7

Engage or Not? Conclusions and Policy Implications

This chapter puts the combined findings on sanction limitations in the context of transaction cost assumptions of firm-level asset internationalization. The link is exemplified through the agenda setting dynamic of the November 2014 APEC summit during which policy formation on issues affecting the future of Myanmar's democracy and Russo-American relations points to the futility of sanctions. An insight comes from the soft power analysis of information exchange. As sanctions lower the number and scope of international sources of information that challenge local political elites, they provide an information exchange rent platform that repressive regimes can use to augment their domestic and international diplomatic power.

Sanctions and Market Power

The contribution of this book is that it examines how the imposition of sanctions can creates market rents for competing multinational corporations (MNCs). MNCs from the sender nation are at a disadvantage because when told to scale down operations in target nations, MNCs from nonparticipating nations can gain competitive market positions. The example of Myanmar indicates that an eagerness exists to engage in such "market grabbing" because it lowers local market competition within the nation as well as regionally. Lower local market competition has nonlocal spillover effects on firm profitability because in a global market-place, overall firm profitability is contingent on the degree of internationalization. Absence and/or late arrival in one market can have nonlinear negative spillover effects on overall firm growth (Agrawal et al., 2014; Parola, Satta, and Persico, 2013). This is the case because, as explained in Chapter 6, the fragmentation of what economists call the "international production function" necessitates the building of multiple linkages that are geographic in scope (Mahutga, 2012; Suder et al., 2014). Those linkages involve not only the sender and receiver nation MNCs, but also their regional partners. Firms that build those linkages first can control entire supply chains and co-opt backward and forward related businesses in resisting late market arrivals.

For those reasons, as Verčič (2008) notes, hard power methods of physical coercion, such as economic sanctions, become more expensive in terms of direct dollar amounts, loss of lives, and loss of political clout. Therefore, soft power may become an increasingly attractive way to ameliorate international relations. This is a possibility today because of the dramatic growth in cross-border interactions among state and nonstate actors. To that effect, Smith and Wiest (2005: 290) call to scholars of transnational relations to expand the traditional "state-bounded notions of civil society to account for a transnational public sphere." This transnational public sphere has many facets. It has been studied for a while and it has been defined by its public nature. The term offered to describe transnational activism is "global civil society" (Wapner, 1996). Based on Wapner's description of the new global public sphere, Smith (2002) provides the following definition of global civil society:

> It is that dimension of transnational collective life in which citizens organize themselves—outside their identity with a particular state or their role as a producer or consumer—to advance shared agendas and coordinate political activities throughout the world (Smith, 2002: 204).

As with most definitions, there is a broad scope for interpretation. With respect to economic sanctions, it could be deduced that "advancing a shared agenda" can be executed with coordinated hard power. However, the examples of ineffective sanction policies overwhelmingly show that it is the coordination of sanction consistency among sender nation governments that is problematic. This is the case because incentives for firm profitability can outweigh international political commitment. This fact changes the traditional view of international civic activism as a public good. It is much more dependent on private profits, or as is increasingly the case with the global growth of centrally planned economies in emerging markets, a combination of public and private profits. Understanding the options to increase profits in a global context for private and public firms, as well as the relationship between such growth in wealth and political action, is imperative in understanding the limitations of hard power diplomacy.

Additionally, shifting market power balances toward the East have augmented the economic and, therefore, diplomatic clout of emerging market giants such as the BRICS nations. For example, starting in 2007 China has contributed more to global growth than the United States (Zakaria, 2011). Zakaria argues that doing business with China today is no longer a choice but a necessity, discussing shifting geopolitical structures and changing diplomatic power balance. In support of such arguments, Enright (2009) offers an empirical example in analyzing location decisions of 352 MNCs in 2005. Every single firm in the study sample had presence in China. Of the Western firms surveyed, 84 percent sold their products in China and 54 percent had production facilities there. Because of such facts, analysts have identified China as the driver of the overall growth in the developing world both economically and geopolitically (Bremmer, 2010; Chin and Thakur, 2010; Felipe et al., 2013; Kaplan, 2011 Perkins, 2012; Rodrik, 2014; Wong and Zhou, 2014; Zakaria, 2011).

The starting point of this leadership can be identified with China's admission into the World Trade Organisation (WTO) in December, 2001. This move changed the world dynamic and balance of trade because it altered investment incentives. The largest country in the world became fully integrated into the legal global commercial system, agreeing to obey the rules of international trade adjudication. There is much debate today on how well China obeys WTO directives. Whether and how well China is complying with WTO rules is an ubiquitous topic of daily discussion, but the fact remains that even with charges of noncompliance, structural changes within China had a spillover effect on incentives for FDI locations for several reasons.

The most important reason is to reach 1.3 billion new customers with growing purchasing power who are eager to improve their standard of living by consuming products and services they had never enjoyed before (Zakaria, 2011). Second, in addition to benefiting from the already vast and continuously growing opportunities of China's market, MNCs investing in China improve their market access to Asia and other regions where establishing their presence may be challenging, particularly for Western firms (Midler, 2009). Third, the growth in China serves as a catalyst to the increasing importance of lower developed nations in international trade and relations, as China strategically pursues improving its own trade ties with those countries (Kaplan, 2011). For example, in 2009 when most nations were scaling back on investment as a result of the financial crisis, China was aggressively increasing its investments in Africa. At the Forum on China-Africa Cooperation on November 20, 2009, the Chinese prime minister, Wen Jiabao, announced that China would double the amount of low-interest loans to African nations to $10 billion in the following three years, increase the number of scholarships, and reduce tariffs on products from the poorest nations.[1] China's expansion in Africa has received much attention and has been tied to economic incentives (Alden, Large, and De Oliveira, 2008; Carbone, 2011; Large, 2008; Tan-Mullins, Mohan, and Power, 2010). Its political implications have also been analyzed in the context of democracy. It has been noted that China extends a diplomatic hand to undemocratic African governments and endorses command-style economic and political systems (Kolstad and Wiig, 2011; Wasserman, 2013; West, 2014).

China's geopolitical power has added an urgency component to investment incentives that impact transaction costs of sanction evasion.[2] Transaction costs in this context mean the economic and noneconomic efforts of doing business with alternative nations rather than the sender nations. In the past, the general economic inequality of the world made it difficult if not impossible to find such alternative nations that could offer sanctioned countries viable trading options. But today, as the wealth of developing nations increases, transaction costs of sanction evasion become lower. China, Russia, India, Indonesia, Saudi Arabia, and others look to expand their international influence through forging economic and diplomatic partnerships that are no longer dependent on the West. The wealth in such nations, and the high rates of marginal growth of that wealth, not only lowers the transaction costs of sanction mitigation in targeted countries, but also impacts the transaction costs of overall international business. The change has to do with risk and willingness of firms to bear higher risks of internationalization, when expanding investments in nations with underdeveloped institutional environments. In the past investors from the developed world could wait strategically to penetrate an emerging market based on such transaction costs of investing that include transparency and accountability in financial contracting, the ability to acquire property rights, the ability to appropriate profits, and a general ease of doing business, but today the explosive growth in competition for local market share in developing regions makes it necessary to build market presence there fast, even at high transaction costs of legal uncertainty.

Economic sanction analysts must understand such dynamics because today market power is global. Home markets are becoming secondary to foreign markets because internationalization has exponentially increased the size of the whole concept of a firm's market. With respect to size, national markets, even those of large countries, remain decidedly small in relation to the global market. In addition, because the economic growth rate of emerging markets is higher than mature markets (Kaplan, 2011), the marginal sale volumes in developing world markets are stronger for most products in relation to marginal sales volumes in developed world markets (Dunning, 2013; Melitz and Trefler, 2012; Taylor and Thrift, 2012). Furthermore, based on market equalization assumption arguments, future growth rate potential in emerging markets is higher. The assumptions of liberalizing markets state that under factor or price equalization efficiency, as barriers to market participation decrease and markets expand, they expand in scope, where increased competition leads to the equalization of market activity in terms of rates (Balassa, 2012; Jovanovic, 2014). This means that consumption functions, subject to budget constraints, equalize.

In unevenly balanced markets, individual consumption functions move toward convergence. That means that as poorer nations climb the industrialization ladder, their consumers—those with lower consumption functions—gradually increase their consumption rates to match up with the average consumption rate of the overall global market population. The opposite does not occur. The higher consuming segments of the market population, (*i. e.),* developed nation consumers, do not lower their rates of consumption toward downward equalization because of the nonsatiation assumption of utility theory (Debreu, 1987). The nonsatiation assumption is behind the core definition of consumer theory. It describes the fact that customers would choose to increase their consumption bundles in both size and scope toward maximization under their individual budget constraints. This means that all world consumers, both in the developed and developing world, are predisposed to marginal increases in their consumption patterns. The rate of those increases is different because, given the fact that all consumers will choose to consume more, those with faster growing discretionary incomes will be able to enjoy higher rates of marginal consumption. In other words, people in the developing world will be able to increase the amount of purchases they make more than their developed world counterparts.

Because, as noted, the above discussed dynamic is subject to budget constraints, the assumption only holds true when significant economic growth is observed. That growth must impact wealth creation in the general population with respect to increasing its purchasing power. Today, volumes of literature point to just such an outcome in the developing world. Therefore, in the current uneven, but rapidly changing, structure of global market consumption patterns, consumers with low consumption functions will keep on gradually augmenting them until they equalize with consumers with large consumption functions (Adams, 2013). In applied terms, Dresner (2009) explains the process by offering examples of comparative consumption. According his estimates, in the 1990s the average person in North America consumed more than 20 times the amount of goods and services than the average person in China and India, and as much as 70 times more than the average person in Bangladesh. Those metrics are given in the context of sustainability, warning that as equalization of consumption increases, its ecological impacts could be very significant. However, in general context those numbers, as well as other research on rapid market and economic growth in the developing world with respect to consumption rates (Adams, 2013; Hassett, 2012; Kaplan, 2011; Weinstein, 2005; Wolf, 2004), suggest that future global growth rates there will be higher.

Evidence toward this case is already present. The world's largest by value company, American Apple Inc. reports total sales of $158 billion in 2013 on its website. Bloomberg.com estimates close to $50 billion to be profitable revenue. Almost $30 billion of that revenue came from its developing world markets with the highest growth rates observed in China, Russia, and Brazil according to Techcrunch.com. In China, iPhone sales alone grew 67 percent between 2012 and 2013, according to Bloomberg.com.[3] By the end of the third fiscal quarter of 2014, total sales were recorded at $165.2 billion, with only $26 billion in domestic sales, leaving 84 percent of total sales to international markets. Once again the strongest growth rate was in China where all sales, including retail, app downloads, and other services increased by 26 percent. Apple itself reports that 20 percent of its total sales in 2014 are from China alone.[4] If 84 percent of its total sales are international, that means 16 percent are domestic, and at 20 percent sales in China alone, China becomes more important to Apple's overall global profitability than its home nation market—the United States.

Such averages are approximations because, as the *New York Times* explains, the company reports operational expenses as deductions from total sales in a way that the lowest overall profit is noted for the sake of saving on tax burdens.[5] According to those *New York Times* estimates, in 2012 Apple officially reported $34 billion in profit for fiscal 2011 for purposes of itemizing corporate tax deductions. But the profits from overseas affiliates that are not eligible for domestic tax credit are not repatriated and, therefore, do not have to be reported. The implication is that Apple makes a lot more profit in emerging market nations than it reports even to its shareholders back home. Therefore, those profits add to the high marginal growth rates of the company's overall earning. This fact adds to understanding the importance of international market sales, particularly emerging market sales, when compared to the volumes of domestic sales of MNCs from the developed world. When the strategic markets of importance are in nations such as China and Russia, then the priorities in firm strategic planning become directed to those markets. At the firm level, strategic growth investments are placed on segments where the marginal growth rates are highest. For those reasons, not only is presence in China important, but for businesses continuously improving strategic operational expansions there, it becomes essential because of future growth possibilities.

Market Power and Global Diplomatic Clout

As the main black knight nation that counteracts American economic and diplomatic hegemony, China's role in economic sanction discourses must be understood, because for rogue nations it provides not only an alternative trading partner to the United States, but also a willing diplomatic partner. But it should be known that China does not operate in isolation when it comes to international alliance building. Ding (2008) explains how China uses soft power effectively to foster a diplomatic and economic leadership position in the general developing world. In particular, researchers have noted that China has been aggressively building its network of international support among nations with historic anti-Western legacies (Alden and Alves, 2008; Armijo, 2007; Ding, 2008; Menon, 1997; Roy, 1996; Walt, 2009; Zhimin, 2005). Among the most examined of those forging alliances is the relationship between China and Russia. In light of the recent crises in Crimea, Chinese support for Russia, both diplomatically and economically, has offered a strong example of the ideological disconnect between Western diplomacy values and their applicability in the modern global political sphere.

With Russia defying sanction pressures, China offered a strategic hand and issued a signal to other nations of the need to support Russia through increasing economic partnerships. A 2014 editorial published at the onset of sanction deployment in 2014 by the first 24-hour Russian English language international network RT (formerly Russia Today)—Russia's response to the Voice Of America on the web—clearly explains the economic alternatives for Russia that the other BRIC nations offer.[6] Understood as a source of pro-Russian propaganda, it is important to offer this example of the official Russian government's point of view to understand the salience and the promotion of its position internationally. As the title suggests, and the article explains with undeniable data points, Russia's economic interests prioritize developing relations with the economies of China, Brazil, India, South Africa, and their respective cohorts of economic and political allies. The article's stance was validated when Russia and China signed the largest bilateral natural gas agreement in recent history, which offers Russia not only an alternative market to Western Europe for its main export, but a more favorable alternative market.[7] The deal was signed during the

November 2014, Asia Pacific Economic Cooperation (APEC) CEO summit in Beijing, China, after Western sanctions and threats against Russia had been in place since March, 2014. The fact that the deal was signed at the APEC summit is important because US president Barack Obama attended the summit to forge better cooperation in light of the difficulties with Russian resistance.

Hoping to lobby for support from Russia's partners, which includes putting more economic pressures on Russia by China, prior to the trip the US administration stressed the importance of a united international stance against territorial aggression, as exemplified by the developments in Crimea. However, as the noted gas deal indicates, achieving international unity on putting economic stress on Russia did not seem to be a popular notion. The breakdown of the summit agenda shows that impressive economic cooperation initiatives involving Russia were established.[8] Among them is a deal between Iran and Russia's state-owned nuclear energy company, Rosatom, to build up to eight new nuclear reactors in Iran.

A main accomplishment for American foreign policy at the summit was the signing of a climate bill between the United States and China that sets goals for reducing carbon emissions.[9] The success of the agreement took the majority of discussion of the summit outcomes. It is a significant international development toward reaching global policies for climate change mitigation. However, with respect to economic sanction diplomacy, the signing of the bill has another interpretation. It shows the power of China to even out the playing field of setting international agendas for such summits around issues that range in importance. The fact that the deal took central stage in the news spotlight after the summit merits note because before the summit it was not mentioned as part of the summit agenda.

The agenda for the US president to achieve at the forum focused on a few main points that all centered around Asian politics with respect to China's role in those political dynamics: (1) pressuring Russia on Ukraine; (2) the meeting with Myanmar president Sein to address stalled democratic reforms in Myanmar and then meeting with famous opposition leader Aung San Suu Kyi to indicate support for her future run for president; (3) facilitating dialogue for easing the territorial disputes in the South China Sea—mostly between China and US ally the Philippines; (4) further economic integration of ASEAN to morph into a common market similar to the European Union post–2015; (5) the president's tone to indicate the US administration's policy toward reaching a general rebalance and commitment to improving US relations with the region; and (6) a reaction or even note from the American president on the Hong Kong protests.[10] No analysts included a climate bill as a part of the summit agenda.

As the summit progressed and came to an end, and President Obama made speeches, attended meetings, and continued on his post-summit visits to the G20 meeting in Australia and then the ASEAN summit in Myanmar, the above-mentioned six points were not even parts of any of the post-summit analysis. The climate bill took the news spotlight. The Myanmar visit did not offer much clarification with respect to well-defined policy change in the nation. The official conclusion is that the United States continues to "urge" the Myanmar government to follow through with democratic reforms.

For those reasons one can conclude that what in effect happened at the summit was a showmanship of agenda setting. Pre-summit, the American diplomatic goals were to be focused on Russia, Myanmar, South China Sea dispute resolution, and a direction toward aiding the Hong Kong protesters to achieve democratic policy changes from the Beijing government. In addition to the coverage of the summit goals by the media, the agenda is implied by the schedule of events posted by the White House.[11] Post-summit, the result was a different outcome altogether—a climate bill. It appears as though the climate bill was a symbolic carrot thrown at America to appease it for not being able to exercise its influence toward achieving its summit agenda.

In the aftermath of the summit, achieving progress on the pre-summit goals of the American agenda from President Obama's trip looks discouraging. Russia increases its military presence in Crimea and around the Ukrainian border; more demonstrators were arrested in Hong Kong on November 26, 2014;[12] and in Myanmar Aung San Suu Kyi will not be able to run for president in the 2015 elections. Even after urges from the US president and offers of economic incentives made during the trip to elicit political change, the regime is not allowing Suu Kyi's main ethnic Muslim supporters to be granted citizenship. With significant portions of those ethnic potential voters excluded from the voting process and forced into refugee status, Suu Kyi cannot hope for a viable chance to run for the presidency.[13]

Why Are We still Confused

Despite all of these facts, and in light of the examples illustrated by the case studies of this book, China's economic and political power is still largely discounted by extant economic sanction analysis. There are a few reasons for this oversight. One is that its economic might is questioned with respect to sustainability (Roy, 1996; Shane and Gale, 2004; Wen and

Chen, 2008; Yang, 2006). The Chinese planned model defies Western economic efficiency theories. Therefore, the legacy of analysis of national industrial upgrading policies would suggest that its growth rate will diminish and be replaced by inflation problems, decreasing market competition, and lower innovative and resilience capabilities. It is all based on the Western laissez-faire economic assumptions that government intervention in market activity leads to inefficiencies over time. However, China's growth rates are not significantly decreasing. The economy seems to be managed fairly well by the central government. It withstood the economic crisis of 2008–2009 and as it stands today, contributes more to the growth of international trade, based on its export volumes, than any other nation, including the United States (Bergsten, Hufbauer, and Miner, 2014; Gao, Whalley, and Ren, 2014). Analysts are waiting for signs of significant economic malaise, and only time will tell if such an outcome will occur, as Western economic theory predicts. China's average GDP growth rate since 2001 has been between 8 percent and 10 percent, dropping down to about 7 percent during the worst of the "great recession." In comparison, since 2001 Western nations annual GDP growth rates range from negative to, in the most optimistic cases, upward of 5 percent.[14]

As China's economy grows, so does its diplomatic power because its role in international trade becomes central. It is important to remember this dynamic because its command structures make it easy for the Chinese government to retaliate against the local business interests of foreign firms on its soil. In an eventual case of discourse, the governments of centrally controlled economies can execute policies with immediacy that can hurt the business interests of foreign MNCs. Those policies can be at the macro- and microlevel, effecting all aspects of business from finance to cost management to legal issues of taxation and compliance. Therefore, general diplomacy today is defined by policy formation that protects business interests first. Political discourse is put on a back burner if favorable local market positions are at stake.

Another reason why China and the growing importance of other black knight nations is downplayed by academics is the nature of economic sanction research analysis. It largely excludes operational management works that study the economic incentives of private global firms with respect to how those incentives are growing toward business strategies in the developing world. The exclusion of that literature leads to not accounting for, or largely discounting, the importance of market development. As explained in Chapter 6, the soft power tools of product promotion spearhead market development. The importance of this platform needs to be accounted for in sanction analysis studies. Therefore, the fairly recent findings of the international brand proliferation literature on global product positioning should not be excluded from the analysis of sanction effectiveness, which seems to be the case currently, based on the volumes of interdisciplinary research examined during the writing of this book. Chapter 6 examines that body of work and relates its conclusions on market development incentives to the lowering transaction costs of sanction mitigation.

Sanction analysis has its historic bases in political science foundations, and it has seldom examined international economic and production incentive literatures and the changes in it due to globalization assumptions. By definition economic sanctions depend on economics, therefore understanding the economic activities that result from their impact is imperative. To that effect, an important distinction in economic research must be noted. Economic outcomes of international trade, such as growth or decline of GDP, exports, imports, or FDI are most directly analyzed by macroeconomics. However, economic incentives are more directly examined by welfare economics. Therefore, both literatures should be consulted in depth when analyzing incentive changes with strategic implications because economic sanctions cause strategic behavior. Firms and governments impacted by sanctions plan out a mitigation strategy of future action. Therefore, the incentives of such strategies need to be the focus of sanction research, not only the direct outcomes of sanction imposition.

It is also imperative that sanctions are studied in context. Most of the sanction literature is based on old data. Analysts fall prey to continuing the empirical tradition of analyzing metrics that are not congruent with current economic and global power balance realities because of the methodological demands of academic model building. Models need to be large and offer many data points. For that reason mainly, most published longitudinal economic sanction studies start with the most recent data and count backward. The further back the count goes, the larger and therefore, in statistical demands, the better the dataset. If one chooses to define goodness of model fit, so to speak, in that statistical context, then one can conclude that the results of such large, backward-reaching datasets would have the strongest validity. The interpretations of their results would be applied toward policy recommendations. The problem is that they would be applicable to a time period when the United States and its Western allies had no equal power match in the world. Therefore, the influence of those Western nations in international sanction dynamics would be of stronger magnitude than it is today. Hence, interpreting factors that contribute to sanction success would be defined by the strength of persuasive power of the sender nation, which in the overwhelming cases of sanctions has been the United States. If interpretations from past realities are applied in the current context, then they would assume a level of American persuasive power that is possibly much higher than it actually is. For example, one of the most widely used datasets of sanctions is the Threat and Imposition of Economic Sanctions (TIES) database put forth by the University of North Carolina, Chapel Hill—a leading institution in the international relations field of political science. The problem is that the last year with data is 2005. In a 2013 publication, expert sanction political scientists with one of the TIES database creators as the lead author—Navin Bapat—suggest in the title of their paper "Determinants of Sanctions Effectiveness: Sensitivity Analysis Using New Data," that it is sufficient to consider data "new" when they end in 2005 (Bapat et al., 2013. The question is, should one look at effectiveness of sanctions over time and construct longitudinal models that meet statistical requirements, in terms of number of observations, if past time frames are unrepresentative of current realities. In other words, if researchers continue to use old data, such as the TIES database, they would have to only include four years that can reflect even a semblance to the economic and diplomatic power that China has today.

It is well accepted by general international trade and relations scholars that China stepped into its new global role post-admission to the World Trade Organization in 2001 (Kurlantzick, 2002; Lieberthal and Lieberthal, 2003; Kong, 2010; Zeng, 2013). Its significant economic growth was not noted until around 2004, when its GDP annual growth rate first surpassed 10 percent. With respect to sanction effectiveness in the context of black knights, as illustrated by the findings in this book, studying time frames prior to 2004 would be akin to analyzing the historic performance of a sports team in order to predict future performance, when that team's most valuable player was a newborn. An example is the case analysis of Myanmar examined in Chapters 2 and 3 of this book. As shown in these chapters, Myanmar's massive economic growth escalated in 2004, as the most restrictive round of sanctions came into effect. The main contributor to that growth was China—both directly and indirectly—through its impact on augmenting regional economic demand. The example offered in Chapter 4 that North Korea's economic growth in the past five years has been significant and much higher than that in previous time periods, as well as driven by its partnerships with Chinese business and political entities, also indicate a role of China's economic position that is uniquely modern.

The current size of the Chinese economy and its wealth define demand levels of Chinese business partners. Those demand levels are high, and therefore offer high trade volume options. High volumes mean a lot of business, and therefore, trade with China today generates the significant profitability as noted in Chapters 2, 3, and 4. In addition, as the case of Myanmar shows, Chinese regional partners add more volume to trade options because they are also growing economically at significant rates. This was not the case a mere ten years ago.

Another oversight noted while examining the volumes of literature on sanctions is that the body of political science literature stays vested in itself. Even works that discuss the black knight phenomenon, at large, do not examine other bodies of literature that study international business. The earlier example of the work by Bapat et al. (2013) only includes three articles from economics journals in its list of references, mainly cited because of methodological references on regression analysis and not for their general findings on the economic outcomes of sanction implementation. The rest of the cited works are important political science publications, many also cited in this book, but in those publications there is also a general lack of discussion on current international trade dynamics.

Sanctions are an interdisciplinary phenomenon. Their effectiveness is subject to a vast number of mitigating factors. A main part of those factors is contingent on the ability of sanctioned nations to evade negative outcomes of hard power diplomacy by finding alternative trade partners to sender nations. Therefore, international production and asset management research should be thoroughly consulted in understanding the modern assumptions of international firm-level profitability. For these reasons, the interdisciplinary case study approach employed in this book proves fruitful in analyzing incentive dynamics in the cases of Myanmar and North Korea. A case-based analysis approach allows for examining how individual nations mitigate sanction impact through understanding the economic interests of their ruling elites.

Studying ruling elites' abilities to augment wealth provides insights into commonalities of coping with sanctions. The evidence overwhelmingly points to the common thread of China. For this reason future sanction analysis, particularly that focused on the impact of United States-led initiatives, should study China's incentives for response. These incentives should be viewed in the context of theirability today to offer an economic alternative to trade with the United States that is viable, and, maybe even, more attractive.

Market Power, Soft Power, and the Power of Image—Interconnectivity, Visibility, and Immediacy

In addition to direct economic benefits, the evidence presented in this book suggests that China, Russia, and their allies use sanctions as an opportunity to show the growing importance of their international diplomatic power. Put in the context of the APEC 2014 agenda analysis, their diplomatic power seems to be of such magnitude today, as to dictate the agenda setting in modern global international relations.

For these reasons, the recommendation is to engage rogue regimes. Western punishment today leads to little, if any, repercussion. If Eastern rivals use Western political action, including sanctions, as an opportunity to justify their own importance, Western isolationism can result in a *de facto* support for local repressive regimes. This can be the case, as the soft power analysis offered in this book suggests, because sanctions limit the channels through which alternative political information flows. When that information flow is lowered, local political opposition movements are affected. It becomes harder for them to communicate with the general public and with supporters outside of their borders. To that effect, the ability to reach critical mass support for the development of viable local political oppositions can be decreased. When alternatives to the local elite political organizations do not gain critical mass—in terms of size and the ability to contribute to local policy formation processes—policy change becomes harder. The examples in this book of Myanmar's stalled democratic reforms post-sanctions explain how that dynamic can endure. Bret Stephens, Pulitzer Prize–winning columnist for the *Wall Street Journal*, critical of the Obama administration's foreign policy legacy, argues that the stalled reforms in Burma (he does not address Myanmar by the name the military dictatorship has given the nation, presumably as a gesture for not recognizing its legitimacy) show how lifting sanctions only enables dictators. Stephens used the example as a caution of possible negative democratic impacts in Cuba as the United States pursues normalization of relations.[15] The missing component in such a line of argument is the regimes' use of sanctions for their own enrichment. Chapters 2 and 3 track how profitable sanctions became for the Myanmar government and therefore, little incentives exist currently for that government to change any of its policies. Its wealth continues to grow and arguably would have continued to grow regardless of the ease of sanctions. What the Obama administration had to decide was whether to join in the Myanmar market growth or continue to allow non-American business interests to keep fueling the regime's wealth. In light of the fact that ASEAN is set to move toward a common market, having sanctions in place against a member state that can be a crucial strategic entity in the near future is not wise. However, as Stephens points out, there is also no need for the general appeasement of the US government toward the regime. America must remain honest in its stance against the lack of democracy in Myanmar. It must find ways to continue to highlight the fact that today in Myanmar the old regime remains in power and continues its repressive legacies. The lifting of sanctions offers nations and their firms a choice—do business with despots, or choose not to. As the literature examined here on brand proliferation shows, such a choice may not be a viable option in the strong competition for market share of the rapidly growing Southeast Asian economy. However, there are costs associated with choosing to do business with repressive governments. Those costs impact national- and firm-level credibility with respect to perception and judgment of values. The issue is that media and technology today have provided an opportunity for oversight of both government and private commercial actions that is unprecedented.

The research on soft power in Chapters 5 and 6 indicates that the proliferation of civic activism has transcended borders and drives global passions toward augmenting levels of engagement from nonstate actors. Social activism is aided by information technology in offering an immediate venue for input from the general public that increases its ability to apply political pressure for an official policy response from governments. It happens in an environment of visibility where soft power information exchange channels grow and diversify. This growth and diversification allows for the inclusion of large numbers of types of social activists and their collective impact can raise visibility on a wide range of issues, as it can change the platforms in international political dynamics with respect to agenda setting. Today, the global political agenda can be set outside of the sphere of government action when private entities engage in behavior that has political features. An example is the recent controversy with Sony Picture's film *The Interview*. The film plot on assassinating North Korean leader Kim Jong-un unsurprisingly offended the regime to reaction, which allegedly was a cyber attack on Sony Films perpetrated by the North Korean government.[16] The outcomes are: (1) an official position and a much-discussed speech by US president Barack Obama on Sony's decision to cancel the release of the film, (2) North Korea's refusal to participate in UN talks, and (3) heated debates on freedom of expression, cyber terrorism, and the connection of the Japanese nationality of Sony the corporation to the Japanese political legacy in the Korean Peninsula.[17] The serious nature of the incident is creating a precedent in which the American government's response was needed with respect to protecting the commercial interests of a private Japanese firm. The confusion stems from the perception of the whole incident. It was not seen by the political and lay community as a mockery of a Japanese private firm or of North Korea. It was seen as an American wielding of soft power because its manifestation is a Hollywood film.

As already discussed in Chapter 5, American popular culture is seen as the greatest incarnation of American soft power. The North Korean incident is an example of how strong and immediate a response to an exercise of this type of soft power can be in relation to past instances of intergovernmental and intercultural censorship issues. It also points to the high standard of scrutiny America faces. In comparison, when in 1989 British citizen Salman Rushdie published *The Satanic Verses*—a satirical book of fiction, Ayatollah Khomeini, then the Shah of Iran, called for the assassination of Rushdie because the author offered a critical view of the prophets Abraham and Muhammad, which in the interpretation of the satire, the Shah saw as blasphemous. Then, the British government placed Rushdie under armed protection, and the world rallied around the author in solidarity for the defense of free speech, freedom of artistic expression, and support for the values of secular democracy.[18] Bald (2006) includes the incident in a volume that examines literary censorship in the Islamic world. Amid all the discussion then, it is hard to recall or find evidence of stopping the distribution of the book. Today, the immediate reaction to the *Interview's* controversy was to not release the film. The reaction is so strong because the point of the film can be seen and felt immediately. Unlike a book that must be read and analyzed for its main message, the promotional trailers for a Hollywood film offer the film's point in mere seconds. When in 1989 Iran's reaction to a book was a threat against an individual, today a serious cyber attack against a multinational entertainment giant serves as a chilling signal of the possibilities for retaliation of displeased national leaders.

The literatures on soft power and information technology's impact on international civic society stress that the ability to transmit information fast, through a variety of ways, and in multidirectional formats, has increased interconnectivity of individuals, governments, and businesses. It has increased transparency because many organizations have vested monetary and nonmonetary interests in monitoring the actions of governments and corporations. As diplomatic options, such as the imposition or removal of sanctions, are considered today, policy makers must remain aware that they operate in an environment of immediate reaction. The global citizenry judges government actions in an instant. Activists not only in countries impacted by sanctions, but anywhere in the world analyze the reasons for governments to engage in hard power actions. Such actions create lasting future outcomes. These outcomes influence the formation of public opinion in future generations because those generations shape their views based on personal experiences. As a reminder of how strong this dynamic is, Chapter 5's literature on America's diplomatic legacy in the Middle East offers the summation that post 9/11, the hard power US tactics in the region have contributed to a negative outlook toward America in the Arab World. America is judged by the actions of its government. More than few of the studies describe America's behavior as hypocritical. In light of such a legacy, and in the context of the strong impact soft power,

American policy makers must remember that they are judged to a standard of leadership that is both economic and cultural. As the strongest wielder of soft power in the world, America is looked at with both admiration and disdain. For supporters of both positions soft power can offer ammunition. Therefore, as the 2014 controversy in releasing the CIA records of the alleged torture of prisoners in the War on Terror shows, American foreign policy must stay aligned with American ideals. When evidence of divergence emerges, American legitimacy can be significantly damaged. The torture report revelations serve as an additional example of American hypocrisy. On one hand, as Chapters 2, 3, and 4 indicate, America is a vocal critic of the torture of prisoners in nations such as Myanmar and North Korea. When evidence emerges that it engages in the same actions it criticizes and uses as evidence for the imposition of sanctions, American critics are given evidence of what has been described as the arrogance of American exceptionalism (Bacevich, 2008).

Perhaps because of such policy inconsistencies, stability and democracy building in the Middle East is a pervasive problem. It is disheartening to read, as shown in Chapter 5, as well as witness in the media every day, that given both the soft and hard power efforts the United States has exerted in the Middle East since 2001, its image has suffered. Possibly because of this negative legacy, today we see the birth of ISIS. Its members have grown under the impact of the War on Terror, as well as the impacts of the soft power tools employed in the region designed to ameliorate the negative attitudes toward American and Western societies. The fact that extremist groups such as ISIS in Iran and Syria, the Muslim Brotherhood in Egypt, and the Ennhada party in Tunisia all developed and grew alongside Hezbollah, Al-Qaeda, the Taliban, and Hamas, and all rally around the American policies in the Arab World post 9/11, shows how much stronger the negative legacy of hard power policies is in relation to soft power's ability to offer an amending impact. This is the case because hard power tactics disproportionately impact the poorest segments of the population while soft power tactics are most fruitful when fully deployed through sophisticated modern telecommunication platforms. The problem is that in a world of economic inequality, soft power reaches the fairly wealthy citizens—those that can afford the technology and are drawn to the cultural allure of foreign glamor, while hard power exacerbates the destitute living condition of the poorest, the angriest, and the most desperate citizens. As their conditions deteriorate, these citizens face incentives for engaging in extremism and offering support to their local governments as a way of looking to improve their hopeless economic situations.

Notes

1 Economic Sanctions: An Overview

1. For a thorough discussion of transaction costs in governance see: Douglass Cecil North, *Transaction Costs, Institutions, and Economic Performance* (San Francisco, CA: ICS Press, 1992).
2. See: Jeffrey J. Schott, June 3, 1998, "US Economic Sanctions: Good Intentions, Bad Execution," Statement before the Committee on International Relations, United States House of Representatives, Washington D.C, retrieved from http://www.iie.com/publications/papers/paper.cfm?ResearchID=314
3. See: "Obama Should End the Embargo on Cuba," *The New York Times Sunday Review*, October 11, 2014.
4. See: Alan Yuhas, "Obama and Castro Hail Historic Breakthrough For US-Cuba Relations—As it Happened," *The Guardian*, December 17, 2014.
5. See: Venessa Mock and Laurence Norman, "Ukraine, Russia Reach Deal on Natural Gas Dispute," *The Wall Street Journal*, October 30, 2014.
6. As quoted by BBC on July 30, 2014, story available at http://www.bbc.com /news/world-europe-28551391.
7. For a thorough discussion see: William Taylor, Steven Pifer, and John E. Herbst, "Don't Forget Crimea," *The New York Times*, June 8, 2014.
8. See: David M. Herszenhorn, "Fears Rise As Russian Military Units Pour into Ukraine," *The New York Times*, November 13, 2014.
9. See: Stephen Beard, "Europe Faces Produce Glut After Russian Ban," Marketplace.org, August 12, 2014.
10. For a list of the sanctions see the European Union's website: europa.eu /ne wsroom/highlights/special-coverage/eu_sanctions/index_en.htm.
11. See: Fareed Zakaria, "The EU is The World's Greatest No Show," *The Washington Post*, July 24, 2014.
12. Available at: http://www.opec.org/opec_web/static_files_project/media /downloads/publications/momrjuly2014.pdf
13. Data come from the United States Energy Information Administration, eia. gov.
14. See: Anthony DiPaola and Golnar Motevalli, "Iran's Oil Revenue Falls 30% Because of Global Price Decline," Bloomberg.com, October 30, 2014.

15. China still enjoys the same benefits today, after the official end of sanctions in Myanmar in 2010.
16. As reported by Julian Borger, "Burma Suspected of Forming Nuclear Link with North Korea," *The Guardian*, July 21, 2009.
17. See: John Sifton, "Dispatches: A Scathing Verdict on Burma's Stalled Reform," October 17, 2014. The Human Rights Watch online, available at: https://www.hrw.org/news/2014/10/17/dispatches-scathing-verdict-burma-s-stalled-reforms.
18. For a thorough discussion see: Glenys Baroness Kinnock, "ASEAN Stands up to Myanmar?" *The Diplomat Online*, May 18, 2011.
19. For a thorough discussion see: "Politics In Myanmar: Not So Fast—Aung San Suu Kyi's Road to the Presidency Grows Longer and More Winding," *The Economist Magazine*,F ebruary8 ,2 014.

2 Myanmar—20 Years of Sanctions and Their Lasting Effect

1. For a chronology of the political changes in Myanmar see: Jayshree Bajoria,, "Understanding Myanmar," June 21, 2013, US Council On Foreign Relations, available at: http://www.cfr.org/human-rights/understanding-myanmar/p14385.
2. For a discussion on the legacy of rice production—the most significant export crop—see: Sergiy Zorya, June 11, 2014, "A Bigger and Better Harvest: Myanmar's Rice Export Opportunities," theworldbank.org, available at: http://blogs.worldbank.org/eastasiapacific/bigger-and-better-harvest-myanmar-s-rice-export-opportunities.
3. BBC News, August 11, 2009, "Burma Court Finds Suu Kyi Guilty," available at:h ttp://news.bbc.co.uk/2/hi/asia-pacific/8194596.stm.
4. BBC News, November 13, 2010, "Burma Releases Pro-Democracy Leader Aung San Suu Kyi," available at: http://www.bbc.co.uk/news/world-asia-pacific-11749661.
5. US Department Of State, April 17, 2006, "Conditions in Burma and US Policy toward Burma For The Period September 28, 2005–March 27, 2006." availablea t:h ttp://merln.ndu.edu/archivepdf/eap/state/66449.pdf.
6. For a thorough discussion on the issues see: Human Rights Watch, August 29, 2004. "Statement to the EU Development Committee," available at: http://www.hrw.org/en/news/2004/08/29/statement-eu-development-committee.
7. According to the Assistance Association of Political Prisoners. For the story and more go to:
8. Human Rights Watch, October 31, 2007. "Sold to Be Soldiers: The Recruitment and Use of Child Soldiers in Burma," available at: http://www.hrw.org/en/reports/2007/10/31/sold-be-soldiers.
9. Paul Roberts, November 24, 1997, "A Growing Menace to Free Trade: US Sanctions." *Businessweek*,3 554,2 8.

10. By definition only the Myanmar government would be able to purchase US militarye quipment.
11. OER GDP represents the market value of all final goods and services produced within the nation in a given year that are traded internationally. Values obtainedf rom:h ttp://unctadstat.unctad.org.
12. Forr awd ataa ndr eportsg ot o:e library-data.imf.org.
13. Tibshiriani proves that point with step-wise regression. Therefore, his findings are linked to Aiken and West (1991) who argue the same point to be applicable for all types of multiple regressions.

3 Myanmar's Sanction Legacy: The Results of Nonengagement

1. Membership estimates and definitions of USDA's nature come from: BBC News, July 15, 2010, "Burma Junta Support Group USDA Disbands," availablea t:h ttp://www.bbc.co.uk/news/world-asia-pacific-10651760.
2. Central Intelligence Agency, 2010, Country Profiles, Burma, *CIA World Factbook,* available at: https://www.cia.gov/library/publications/the-world-factbook/geos/th.html.
3. Available at: http://www.treasury.gov/resource-center/sanctions/documents/13448.pdf.
4. See: L. K. Jha, July 30, 2008, "Bush Signs Burma Jade Act, Adds to Sanctions List," *The Irrawaddy*, available at: http://www.irrawaddy.org/article.php?art_id=13628.
5. See: L. K. Jha, "Bush Signs Burma Jade Act, Adds to Sanctions List."
6. http://unstats.un.org/unsd/iiss/international-standard-industrial-classification-of-all-economic-activities-isic.ashx.
7. https://unstats.un.org/unsd/snaama/introduction.asp.
8. See: Gripas, Uri, May 14, 2014, "Obama Extends Some Sanctions against Myanmar Despite Reforms," Reuters, available at: http://www.reuters.com/article/2014/05/15/us-myanmar-usa-obama-idusbrea4e0w820140515.
9. See: "Reality Check: Optimism about Business Prospects on the Final Frontier May Be Overblown," *The Economist*, January 4, 2014, available at: http://www.economist.com/news/asia/21592658-optimism-about-business-prospects-final-frontier-may-be-overblown-reality-check.
10. See: "Trade on the Rise along Myanmar's Busy Borders," *The Bangkok Post*, May 19, 2014, available at: http://www.bangkokpost.com/business/news/410573/trade-on-the-rise-along-myanmar-busy-borders.
11. Article available at: http://www.usatoday.com/story/money/business/2014/06/07/gap-to-be-1st-us-retailer-to-enter-myanmar-market/10161841/.
12. For a discussion see: "Politics in Myanmar: Not So Fast," *The Economist*, February 8, 2014 available at: http://www.economist.com/news/asia/21595920-aung-san-suu-kyis-road-presidency-grows-longer-and-more-winding-not-so-fast.

13. Report can be found at: http://www.treasury.gov/resource-center/faqs/sanctions/pages/ques_index.aspx.
14. Jeffrey. J Schott, June 3, 1998, "US Economic Sanctions: Good Intentions, Bad Execution." Statement before the Committee on International Relations, United States House of Representatives, Washington DC Retrieved from http://www.iie.com/publications/papers/paper.cfm?ResearchID=314.

4 Absorb and Control: How North Korea Responds to Economic Sanctions

1. Also see the Reuters, report from May 26 2014, "China Agrees North Korea's Nuclear Activities a Serious Threat, Says South," available at: http://uk.reuters.com/article/2014/05/26/uk-northkorea-nuclear-idukkbn0e61lj20140526.
2. See Mitchell Learner, 2008, "Making Sense of the 'Hermit Kingdom: North Korea in the Nuclear Age," Origins 2 (3), available at: http://origins.osu.edu/print/826.
3. For a discussion on the US government's assessment of the threat see: Thom Shanker, David Sanger, and Eric Schmitt, "Pentagon Finds Nuclear Strides by North Korea," *The New York Times*, April 11, 2013, available at: http://www.nytimes.com/2013/04/12/world/asia/north-korea-may-have-nuclear-missile-capability-us-agency-says.html.
4. Also see: Andrei Lankov, "The North Korean Economy: Between Myth And Reality," Eastasiaform.org, Februrary 8, 2011, available at: http://www.eastasiaforum.org/2011/02/08/the-north-korean-economy-between-myths-and-facts/.
5. Report available at: http://www.hrw.org/world-report/2013/country-chapters/north-korea.
6. For more on the famine see: Barbara Crossette, "Korean Famine Toll: More Than 2 Million," *The New York Times*, August 20, 1999, available at: http://www.nytimes.com/1999/08/20/world/korean-famine-toll-more-than-2-million.html.
7. For a related discussion, also see: UNICEF, *State Of The World's Children* (London: Oxford University Press, 1996).
8. The report can be accessed at: http://oai.dtic.mil/oai/oai?verb=getrecord&metadataprefix=html&identifier=ada485982.
9. Read Resolution 1540 at: http://www.un.org/en/ga/search/view_doc.asp?symbol=S/RES/1540%20(2004).
10. Read selected documents pursuant Resolution 1718 at: http://www.un.org/sc/committees/1718/selc_docs.shtml.
11. Read Resolution 1874 at: http://www.un.org/news/press/docs/2009/sc9679.doc.htm.
12. See Aiden Foster-Carter, "South Korea Has Lost The North to China," *The Financial Times*, February 20, 2014.

13. See industry classifications under "Economy" in The CIA World FactBook, Country Profiles—Korea, North, available at: https://www.cia.gov/library/publications/the-world-factbook/geos/kn.html.
14. Data collected from The United Nations' National Accounts Database availablea t:h ttp://unstats.un.org/unsd/snaama/dnllist.asp.
15. For additional estimates of particular current sector growth, see the work of Frank Ruediger, professor of East Asian economy and society at the University of Vienna, head of the Department of East Asian studies, and an adjunct professor at Korea University and the University of North Korean studies. Availablea t:h ttp://38north.org/2012/07/rfrank071612/.
16. Data collected from the CIA World FactBook country profiles database available at: https://www.cia.gov/library/publications/the-world-factbook/geos/kn.html.
17. The phenomenon is explained in depth by: David Albright and Paul Brannan, "Taking Stock: North Korea's Uranium Enrichment Program," The Institute For Science And International Security, October 8, 2010, available at: http://isis-online.org/uploads/isis-reports/documents/isis_dprk_uep.pdf.
18. As reported by Foster-Carter, "South Korea Has Lost the North to China."
19. See: Charlie Zhu, "China Moves Ahead with North Korea Trade Zone Despite Nuclear Test," Reuters, February 28, 2013, available at: http://www.reuters.com/article/2013/03/01/us-china-northkorea-trade-idusbre92005i20130301.
20. See discussion under "Economy," available at: https://www.cia.gov/library/publications/the-world-factbook/geos/kn.html.
21. See: Dexter Roberts, "North Korea, New Land Of Opportunity?" *Businessweek*, January 19, 2012, available at: http://www.businessweek.com/magazine/north-korea-new-land-of-opportunity-01192012.html.
22. For a discussion the Trans-Siberian initiatives both in rail and natural gas transportation, see Joseph O'Reilly, "Russia Rushed to Develop Trans-Siberian Rail Line," Global Logistics, April 2013, available at: http://www.inboundlogistics.com/cms/article/global-logistics-april-2013/.
23. See: Frik Els, "Largest Known Rare Earth Deposit Discovered in North Korea," Mining.com, December 5, 2013, available at: http://www.mining.com/largest-known-rare-earth-deposit-discovered-in-north-korea-86139/.
24. See: Zachary Keck, "North Korea May Have Two-Thirds of the World's Rare Earths," *The Diplomat Magazine*, Janurary 22, 2014, available at: http://thediplomat.com/2014/01/north-korea-may-have-two-thirds-of-worlds-rare-earths/.
25. See: Tae-Jun Kang, "North Korea Resumes Rare Earth Exports to China." *The Diplomat Magazine*, July 30, 2014, available at: http://thediplomat.com/2014/07/north-korea-resumes-rare-earth-exports-to-china/.

5 Alternatives to Sanctions

1. Availablea t:h ttp://www.state.gov/documents/organization/207305.pdf.
2. An example from BBC is available at: http://www.bbc.com/news/world-asia-pacific-11388628.

3. Available at: http://www.businessinsider.com/the-dictators-wives-club-2014-1?op=1.
4. Much less reaching a critical level of mind and value change for the majority of a population.
5. Availablea t:h ttp://www.worldvaluessurvey.org/wvs.jsp.
6. Zakaria was Samuel Huntington's PhD student at Harvard University.
7. Fareed Zakaria, "The Politics of Rage: Why Do They Hate Us?" Newsweek.com, October 14, 2001, available at: http://www.newsweek.com/politics-rage-why-do-they-hate-us-154345.
8. Fareed Zakaria, "Why Do They Still Hate Us, 13 Years Later," *The Washington Post*, September 4, 2014.
9. Murtaza Hussain, "Sanctioning Society: From Iraq to Iran," *Al-Jazerra America* 3, October 3, 2012, available at: http://www.aljazeera.com/indepth/opinion/2012/10/201210373854792889.html&gt.
10. Glenn Greenwald, "Iran Sanctions Now Causing Food Insecurity, Mass Suffering," *The Guardian*, October 7, 2012.
11. Pew Research Global Attitudes Project, "Global Public Opinion in The Bush Years (2001–2008)," December 18, 2008, available at: http://www.pewglobal.org/2008/12/18/global-public-opinion-in-the-bush-years-2001-2008/.
12. The poll and interpretation of the results can be accessed at: http://static.squarespace.com/static/52750dd3e4b08c252c723404/t/538deedde4b008372f20a182/1401810653450/five%20years%20after%20the%20cairo%20speech%206_2.pdf.
13. Websitei sm epi.state.gov.
14. Forc ontenta ndp rogrammingg ot o:w ww.radiosawa.com.
15. For a thorough discussion of the initiative and its impact see: Sheldom Rapton, "Shared Values Revisited," Center For Media And Democracy's prwatch.org/, October 17, 2007, available: http://www.prwatch.org/node/6465.
16. See:h ttp://www.zogbyanalytics.com/about-us.
17. The report is available at: http://www.arabvoices.net/docs/2004_impressions_of_america_poll.pdf.
18. For analysis of the findings and a copy of the full report go to: http://www.pewglobal.org/2009/07/23/lessons-from-the-2009-global-attitudes-survey-transcript/.
19. Given that Pakistan is notoriously disapproving of the United States, even amongy outh.
20. It is worth specifying that the popularity of American business is noted both in approval of US science and technology, as well as its popular culture.
21. Report can be found at: http://www.pewglobal.org/files/2012/06/pew-global-attitudes-u.s.-image-report-final-june-13-20123.pdf.
22. Report can be found at: http://eca.state.gov/files/bureau/youth-exchange-and-study-yes-full-report-aug-2009.pdf.
23. For a complete description of the methodology go to: http://info.worldbank.org/governance/wgi/index.aspx#doc-sources.

24. The series can be accessed at: http://www.instituteforgovernment.org.uk/publications?field_publication_authors_nid=1204&sort_by=field_publication_date_value&sort_order=desc.
25. Namely Busse and Hefeker's (2007) model has similarities to the one offered here but examines 1990 to 1999—years prior to the turbulence of current Middle Eastern dynamics.
26. Definition available at: http://info.worldbank.org/governance/wgi/index.aspx#faq.
27. Definition available at: http://info.worldbank.org/governance/wgi/index.aspx#faq.
28. http://data.worldbank.org/indicator/bx.klt.dinv.wd.gd.zs.
29. http://data.worldbank.org/indicator/ny.gnp.pcap.cd?display=default.
30. http://data.worldbank.org/indicator/dt.oda.alld.cd.
31. http://data.worldbank.org/indicator/ne.imp.gnfs.zs.
32. http://data.worldbank.org/indicator/it.net.user.p2?display=default.
33. http://data.worldbank.org/indicator/it.cel.sets.p2?display=default.
34. For a recent recount on the issue see Jeddah andRiyadh, "Women In Saudi Arabia Unshackling Themselves: Saudi Women are Gaining Grown, Slowly," *The Economist*, May 17, 2014.
35. http://data.worldbank.org/indicator/se.enr.seco.fm.zs?display=default.
36. other sources include unesco, unicef, and investment map. data available at: http://mecometer.com/compare/armenia+west-bank-and-gaza/internet-users/. http://www.pdwb.de/archiv/weltbank/gnipc06.pdf. http://www.tradingeconomics.com/djibouti/gni-per-capita-atlas-method-us-dollar-wb-data.html. http://www.pdwb.de/archiv/weltbank/gnipc10.pdf. http://www.unicef.org/infobycountry/iran_statistics.html. http://www.unicef.org/infobycountry/kuwait_statistics.html. http://www.unicef.org/infobycountry/oman_statistics.html. http://www.unicef.org/infobycountry/syria_statistics.html. http://www.pipa.gov.ps/economic_indicators.asp. http://www.indexmundi.com/facts/syrian-arab-republic/foreign-direct-investment. http://www.investmentmap.org/prioritysector.aspx. http://stats.uis.unesco.org/unesco/tableviewer/tableview.aspx?reportid=3983&if_language=eng. http://stats.uis.unesco.org/unesco/tableviewer/tableview.aspx. http://www.nationsencyclopedia.com/worldstats/edu-gender-parity-index-education3.html. http://www.unicef.org/infobycountry/bahrain_statistics.html.
37. Controlling for time effect is done by adding a lagged dependent variable to the model as per King (1986) and Greene (2008), Chapter 9.
38. For a thorough discussion the Russo-Arab relationships during the Arab Spring see Mark Katz, "Russia and the Arab Spring," Washington, DC: The Middle East Institute, 2012, available at: http://www.mei.edu/content/russia-and-arab-spring. For a synopsis of the history and economic interests of China in the Middle East see Jonathan Pollack, "Unease From Afar," Washington, DC: Brookings Institute, 2011, available at: http://www.brookings.edu/research/articles/2011/11/18-arab-awakening-china-pollack.

6 Sanctions or Soft Power: Implications for Competitiveness

1. See: *The Economist* magazine December, 14, 2014. "A Troubling Trajectory: Fears Are Growing That Trade's Share of The World's GDP Has Peaked. But That is Far from Certain."
2. For more on the blurring distinctions between exports, imports, and foreign and domestic assets see Anguelov (2014), Chapters 1 and 2.
3. Mature markets are a definition of developed world markets.
4. Data compiled from the United Nations Conference on Trade and Development. (2010). World Investment Report series, 2005–2009. Available atu nctad.org.
5. See: US Council On Competitiveness "Compete 2.0" Report Series, available at: compete.org.

7 Engage or Not? Conclusions and Policy Implications

1. See: Sharon Lafraniere, "China Helps The Powerful in Namibia," *The New York Times*, November 20, 2009.
2. For transaction cost discussion see Coase (1988) and Williamson (1981, 1998, 2005).
3. See: http://www.bloomberg.com/news/2013-01-24/apple-china-revenue-jumps-67-as-sales-outlets-double.html.
4. As reported by Jared Newman, "Why Apple Is Winning in China," macworld.com, May 1, 2014, available at: http://www.macworld.com/article/2150281/why-apple-is-winning-in-china.html.
5. See: Charles Duhigg and David Kocieniewski, "How Apple Sidesteps Billions in Texas," *The New York Times*, April 28, 2012.
6. See: Irina Sukhoparova, "Sanction Effect: Russia to Change Its Economic Partners… For The Better." rt.com, March 21, 2014.
7. See: Mike Bird, "Putin's Revenge: China and Russia Try to End The Dominance of The Dollar," Businessinsider.com, November 10, 2014.
8. See: David Francis and Sabine Musca, "FP's Situation Report: China and The United States Make Climate, Military Deals; Iran and Russia Make a Nuclear Deal; Iran Has a Role in the Fight against the Islamic State; Kurds Make Gains in Kobani; and Much More," foreignpolicy.com, November 12, 2014.
9. See: Matt Hoye, "White House and China Set Historic Green House Emissions Levels," cnn.com, November 12, 2014.
10. See: Mary Bruce, "Five Things to Watch For during President Obama's Asia Trip," ABCnews.com, November 10, 2014.Also See: Carol E. Lee and Jeremy Page, "Obama Seeks Common Ground with China at APEC," *The Wall Street Journal*, November 10, 2014.

11. See: Tanya Somanader, "The Road Ahead: President Obama Travels to The Asia Pacific," Whitehouse.gov, November 7, 2014.
12. See: Andrew Stevens and Tim Hume, "Hong Kong Student Leader Joshua Wong Arrested in Mong Kok Clearance," cnn.com, November 26, 2014.
13. See: Bruce Einhorn, "Obama Visits Myanmar: A Success Story That has Soured," BloombergBusiness.com, November 13, 2014.
14. Averagesb asedo nd ataf romT radingEconomics.com.
15. Stephens discussed the example during CNN's Global Public Square, which aired on December 21, 2014, For more also see: Bret. Stephens, "What Obama Knows," *The Wall Street Journal*, September 22, 2014.
16. For a discussion on the unraveling of the events and an explanation of the political response for different governments see: Peter Walker, "North Korea Threaten US, Claiming White House was Involved in Film Plot," *The Guardian*, December 22, 2014.
17. For a discussion see: Devlin Barrett and Danny Yadron, "North Korean Role in Sony Hack Presents Quandary for US: Issue Elevated from Question of Corporate Security to National Security," *The Wall Street Journal*, December 17,2 014.
18. For more see the chronology in "Looking Back at Salman Rushdie's *The Satanic Verses*: Writers, Broadcasters, Friends and Publishing Insiders Recall What It was Like to Be Caught up in The Most Controversial Story in Recent Literary History, The Satanic Verses and the Ensuing Fatwa against Its Author, As Salman Rushdie Prepares to Bring out His Eagerly Awaited Memoir," *The Guardian*, September 14, 2012, available at: http://www.theguardian.com /books/2012/sep/14/looking-at-salman-rushdies-satanic-verses.

References

Abdelfattah, Yasmine M., Aamer S. Abu-Qarn, J. Paul Dunne, and Shadwa Zaher. (2014). "The Demand for Military Spending in Egypt." *Defence and Peace Economics* 25, (3): 231–245.

Abdon, Arnelyn, Jesus Felipe, Utsav Kumar, and Norio Usui. (2013). "Why Has China Succeeded? and Why it Will Continue to Do So." *Cambridge Journal of Economics* 37, (4): 791–818.

Acemoglu, Daron, Simon Johnson, James A. Robinson, and Pierre Yared. (2005). "From Education to Democracy?" *American Economic Review* 95, (2): 44–49.

Adams, Gerard F. (2013). *Globalization; Today and Tomorrow.* London: Routledge.

Adamopoulos, Antonios, Melina Dritsaki, and Chaido Dritsaki. (2004). "A Causal Relationship between Trade, Foreign Direct Investment and Economic Growth for Greece." *American Journal of Applied Sciences* 1, (3): 230–235.

Addison, Tony, and Almas Heshmati. (2003). "The New Global Determinants of FDI Flows to Developing Countries: The Importance of ICT and Democratization." Discussion Paper No. 2003/45, Helsinki: World Institute for Development Economics.

Adeyemi, Oluseyi, Harry Boer, Dmitrij Slepniov, Brian Vejrum Wæhrens, and Xiaobo Wu. (2014). "Exploring the Changing Roles of Western Subsidiaries in China: Balancing Global Priorities with Local Demands." In *International Operations Networks,* Johansen, John, Sami Farooq, and Cheng Yang (eds), 67–80. London: Springer.

Agar, Jon. (2013). *Constant Touch: A Global History of the Mobile Phone.* London: Icon Books.

Agrawal, Ajay, Iain Cockburn, Alberto Galasso, and Alexander Oettl. (2014). "Why are Some Regions More Innovative Than Others? The Role of Small Firms in The Presence of Large Labs." *Journal of Urban Economics* 81, (May): 149–165.

Aguilera, Ruth V., Jyoti Ganapathi, Deborah E. Rupp, and Cynthia A. Williams.. (2007). "Putting the S Back in Corporate Social Responsibility: A Multilevel Theory of Social Change in Organizations." *Academy Of Management Review* 32, (3): 836–863.

Ahmed, Shamima. (2011). "The Impact of NGOs on International Organizations: Complexities and Considerations." *Brooklyn Journal of International Law* 36: 817–1183.

Ahmed, Abdullahi D., Enjiang Cheng, and George Messinis. (2011). "The Role of Exports, FDI and Imports in Development: Evidence From Sub-Saharan African Countries." *Applied Economics* 43, (26): 3719–3731.

Aiken, Leona S., and Stephen G. West. (1991). *Multiple Regression: Testing and Interpreting Interactions.* Newcastle, UK: Sage.

Aizenman, Joshua. (2006). "International Reserves Management and the Current Account." *Working Paper No.12734.* National Bureau of Economic Research. Washington, DC.

Alden, Chris, and Cristina Alves. (2008). "History & Identity in The Construction of China's Africa Policy." *Review of African Political Economy* 35, (115): 43–58.

Ali, Abbas J. (2013). "Global Economic Challenges: The Pressing and Visible Issues." *Competitiveness Review* 23, (3): 192–198.

Ali, Abdiweli M., and Hodan S. Isse. (2005). "An Empirical Analysis of the effect Effect of Aid on Growth." *International Advances in Economic Research* 11, (1): 1–11.

Allen, Susan H. (2008). "Political Institutions and Constrained Response to Economic Sanctions." *Foreign Policy Analysis* 4, (3): 255–274.

Al-Roubaie, Amer, and Wajeeh Elali. (1995). "The Financial Implications of Economic Sanctions against Iraq." *Arab Studies Quarterly* 17, (3): 53–69.

Aiken, Leona S., and Stephen G. West. (1991). *Multiple Regression: Testing and Interpreting Interactions.* Newcastle, UK: Sage.

Aker, Jenny, and Isaac Mbiti. (2010). "Mobile Phones and Economic Development in Africa." *Center for Global Development Working Paper,*2 11.

Alden, Chris, Daniel Large, and Ricardo Soares De Oliveira. (2008). *China Returns to Africa: A Rising Power and A Continent Embrace.* New York: Columbia University Press.

Alamgir, Jalal. (2008). "Myanmar's Foreign Trade and Its Political Consequences." *Asian Survey* 48, (6): 977–996.

Alesina, Alberto and David Dollar. (2000). "Who Gives Foreign Aid to Whom and Why?" *Journal of Economic Growth* 5, (1): 33–63.

Ali, Hamid E. (2012). "Military Expenditures and Inequality in the Middle East and North Africa: A Panel Analysis." *Defence and Peace Economics* 23, (6): 575–589.

Al-Riffai, Perrihan, Clemens Breisinger, Olivier Ecker, and Bingxin Yu. (2012). *Beyond The Arab Awakening: Policies and Investments for Poverty Reduction and Food Security.* Washington, DC: International Food Policy Research Institute.

Anguelov, Nikolay. (2014). *Policy and Political Theory in Trade Practice: Multinational Corporations and Global Governments.* New York: Palgrave Macmillan.

Armijo, Leslie Elliott. (2007). "The BRICS Countries (Brazil, Russia, India, and China) as Analytical Category: Mirage Or Insight?" *Asian Perspective* 31, (4): 7–42.

Aron, Leon. (2013, Spring). "The Political Economy of Russian Oil and Gas." Washington, DC: American Enterprise Institute.

Askari, Hossein, John Forrer, Tarek Hachem, and Jiawen Yang. (2005). "Measuring Vulnerability to US Foreign Economic Sanctions." *Business Economics* 40, (2): 41–55.

Åslund, Anders. (1994). "Lessons of The First Four Years of Systemic Change in Eastern Europe." *Journal of Comparative Economics* 19, (1): 22–38.

Aslund, Anders. (2002). *Building Capitalism: The Transformation of the Former Soviet Bloc*. Cambridge: Cambridge University Press.

Assaad, Ragui, and Farzaneh Roudi-Fahimi. (2007). *Youth in The Middle East and North Africa: Demographic Opportunity Or Challenge?* Washington, DC: Population Reference Bureau.

Asteriou, Dimitrios. (2009). "Foreign Aid and Economic Growth: New Evidence from a Panel Data Approach to Five South Asian Countries." *Journal of Policy Modeling* 31, (1): 155–161.

Atkinson, Robert D. (2004). *The Past and Future of America's Economy: Long Waves of Innovation That Power Cycles of Growth*. Cheltenham, UK: Edward Elgar Publishing.

Atkinson, Carol. (2010). "Does Soft Power Matter? A Comparative Analysis of Student Exchange Programs 1980–2006." *Foreign Policy Analysis* 6, (1): 1–22.

Attia, Ashraf M., Nergis Aziz, Barry Friedman, and Mahdy F. Elhusseiny. (2011). "Commentary: The Impact of Social Networking Tools on Political Change in Egypt's '"Revolution 2.0'" *Electronic Commerce Research and Applications* 10, (4): 369–374.

Ayoub, Lena. (1998). "Nike Just Does It – And Why the United States Shouldn't: The United States' International Obligation to Hold MNCs Accountable for Their Labor Rights Violations Abroad." *DePaul Business Law Journal* 11: 395–426.

Bacevich, Andrew J. (2008). *The Limits of Power: The End of American Exceptionalism*. New York: Palgrave Macmillan.

Baharum, Adam, and M. Ataharul Islam. (2010). "The Analysis of Transitions in Economic Performance Using Covariate Dependent Statistical Model." *Journal of Developing Areas* 43, (2): 289–298.

Balassa, Bela. (2012). *The Theory of Economic Integration (Routledge Revivals)*. London: Routledge.

Bald, Margaret. (2006). *Literature Suppressed on Religious Grounds*. New York: Infobase Publishing.

Baltagi, Badi H. (2008). "Forecasting with Panel Data." *Journal of Forecasting* 27, (2): 153–173.

Baltagi, Badi H., Peter Egger, and Michael Pfaffermayr. (2008). "Estimating Regional Trade Agreement Effects on FDI in an Interdependent World." *Journal of Econometrics* 145, (1): 194–208.

Bapat, Navin A., Tobias Heinrich, Yoshiharu Kobayashi, and T. Clifton Morgan. (2013). "Determinants of Sanctions Effectiveness: Sensitivity Analysis Using New Data." *International Interactions* 39, (1): 79–98.

Bardhan, Indranil, Sunil Mithas, and Jonathan Whitaker. (2006). "Information Technology, Production Process Outsourcing, and Manufacturing Plant Performance." *Journal of Management Information Systems* 23, (2): 13–40.

Bardhan, Pranab. (2002). "Decentralization of Governance and Development." *Journal of Economic Perspectives* 16, (4): 185–205.

Barnard, Helena. (2008). "Capability Development and the Geographic Destination of Outbound FDI by Developing Country Firms." *International Journal of Technology and Globalisation* 4, (1): 39–55.

Barrientos, Stephanie, and Sally Smith. (2007). "Do Workers Benefit from Ethical Trade? Assessing Codes of Labour Practice in Global Production Systems." *Third World Quarterly* 28, (4): 713–729.

Basile, Roberto, Davide Castellani and Antonello Zanfei. (2008). "Location Choices of Multinational Firms in Europe: The Role of EU Cohesion Policy." *Journal of International Economics* 74, (2): 328–340

Beise, Marian. (ed.). (2001). Lead Markets: Country Specific Success Factors of the Global Diffusion of Innovations; with 8 Tables. *ZEW Economic Studies* Vol. 14, Manheim: Springer.

Bergsten, Fred, Bates Gill, Nicholas Lardy and Derek Mitchell. (2007). *China: The Balance Sheet. What the World Knows about the Emerging Superpower.* New York: Public Affairs Press.

Bergsten, C. Fred, Gary Clyde Hufbauer, and Sean Miner. (2014). *Bridging The Pacific: Toward Free Trade and Investment between China and the United States.* Washington, DC: Peterson Institute for International Economics.

Bhattacharya, C. B., Shuili Du, and Sankar Sen. (2010). "Maximizing Business Returns to Corporate Social Responsibility (CSR): The Role of CSR Communication." *International Journal of Management Reviews* 12, (1): 8–19.

Bjørnskov, Christian. (2010). "Do Elites Benefit from Democracy and Foreign Aid in Developing Countries?" *Journal of Development Economics* 92, (2): 115–124.

Blanton, Shannon L., and Blanton, Robert G. (2007). "What Attracts Foreign Investors? An Examination of Human Rights and Foreign Direct Investment." *Journal Of Politics* 69, (1): 143–155.

Boardman, Anthony E., Carsten Greve, and Graeme A. Hodge (eds). (2010). *International Handbook on Public-Private Partnership.* Cheltenham, UK: Edward Elgar Publishing.

Bougheas, Spiros, Panicos O. Demetriades, and Edgar LW Morgenroth. (1999). "Infrastructure, Transport Costs and Trade." *Journal Of International Economics* 47, (1): 169–189.

Boswell, Terry and Jeffrey Kentor. (2003). "Foreign Capital Dependence and Development: A New Direction." *American Sociological Review* 68, (2): 301–113.

Bratton, Michael. (1989). "The Politics of Government-NGO Relations in Africa." *World Development* 17, (4): 569–587.

Bremmer, Ian. (2010). "The End of the Free Market: Who Wins the War between States and Corporations?" *European View* 9, (2): 249–252.

Breslin, Julia and Sanja Kelly. (eds). (2010). *Women's Rights in the Middle East and North Africa: Progress amid Resistance.* Lanham, MD: Rowman and Littlefield Publishers.

Briere, Col Andre, and William Wunderle. (2007). "Uncertain Future: A Strategic Review of the Middle East and Implications for the United States." *Comparative Strategy* 26, (3): 205–214.

Brown, Graham K., Arnim Langer, and Frances Stewart. (2008). *A Typology of Post-Conflict Environments: An Overview Centre for Research on Inequality, Human Security and Ethnicity*. Oxford, UK: University of Oxford Press.
Brynen, Rex. (2000). *A Very Political Economy: Peacebuilding and Foreign Aid in The West Bank and Gaza*. Washington, DC: US Institute of Peace Press.
Bu, Liping. (2003). *Making the World Like Us: Education, Cultural Expansion, and the American Century*. Westport, CT: Praeger Publishers.
Butt, Muhammad Sabihuddin, Muhammad Shahbaz, and Muhammad Shahbaz Shabbir. (2013). "Does Military Spending Explode External Debt in Pakistan?." *Defence and Peace Economics* 24, (2): 1–24.
Buckley, Peter J., and Pervez N. Ghauri. (2004). "Globalization, Economic Geography and the Strategy of Multinational Enterprise." *Journal of International Business Studies* 35, (2): 81–98.
Busse, Matthias, and Carsten Hefeker. (2007). "Political Risk, Institutions and Foreign Direct Investment." *European Journal of Political Economy* 23, (2): 397–415.
Büthe, Tim, and Helen V. Milner. (2008). "The Politics of Foreign Direct Investment into Developing Countries: Increasing FDI through International Trade Agreements?" *American Journal Of Political Science* 52, (4): 741–762.
Byman, Daniel, and Jennifer Lind. (2010). "Pyongyang's Survival Strategy: Tools of Authoritarian Control in North Korea." *International Security* 35, (1): 44–74.
Campante, Filipe R., and Davin Chor. (2012). "Why was The Arab World Poised for Revolution? Schooling, Economic Opportunities, and the Arab Spring." *The Journal of Economic Perspectives* 26, (2): 167–187.
Campbell, John L. (2007). "Why Would Corporations Behave in Socially Responsible Ways? An Institutional Theory of Corporate Social Responsibility." *Academy Of Management Review* 32, (3): 946–967.
Campbell, Tom. (2006). "A Human Rights Approach to Developing Voluntary Codes of Conduct For Multinational Corporations." *Business Ethics Quarterly*: 255–269.
Charap, Samuel. (2014). "The Ukraine Impasse." *Survival* 56 (5): 225–232.
Carbone, Maurizio. (2011). "The European Union and China's Rise in Africa: Competing Visions, External Coherence and Trilateral Cooperation." *Journal of Contemporary African Studies* 29, (2): 203–221.
Carter, Barry E. (1987). "International Economic Sanctions: Improving the Haphazard US Legal Regime." *California Law Review* 75, (4): 1162–1278.
Carty, Victoria, and Jake Onyett. (2006). "Protest, Cyberactivism and New Social Movements: The Reemergence of the Peace Movement Post 9/11." *Social Movement Studies* 5, (3): 229–249.
Cavusgil, S. Tamer, Gary Knight, and John R. Riesenberger. (2012). *International Business*. Upper Saddle River, NJ: Pearson Education Publishing.
Cha, Victor D., and David C. Kang. (2013). *Nuclear North Korea: A Debate on Engagement Strategies*. New York: Columbia University Press.
Chan, Kitty K., and Edward R. Gemayel. (2004). "Risk Instability and the Pattern of Foreign Direct Investment in the Middle East and North Africa Region."

International Monetary Fund Working Paper 04/139, available at http://papers.ssrn.com/sol3/papers.cfm?abstract_id=878964.
Chan, Steve. (2009). "Strategic Anticipation and Adjustment: Ex Ante and Ex Post Information in Explaining Sanctions Outcomes." *International Political Science Review* 30, (3): 319–338.
Chang, Shao-Chi, and Chi-Feng Wang. (2007). "The Effect of Product Diversification Strategies on The Rélationship between International Diversification and Firm Performance." *Journal of World Business* 42, (1): 61–79.
Chazan, Naomi. (1992). "Africa's Democratic Challenge." *World Policy Journal* 9, (2): 279–307.
Chenery, Hollis B., and Alan M. Strout. (1966). "Foreign Assistance and Economic Development." *American Economic Review* 56, (4): 679–733.
Cheng, Joseph Yu-shek, Yan Huang, and King-lun Ngok. (2012)."Multinational Corporations, Global Civil Society and Chinese Labour: Workers' Solidarity in China in the Era of Globalization." *Economic and Industrial Democracy* 33, (3): 379–401.
Chen, Jining and Zongguo Wen. (2008). "A Cost-Benefit Analysis for the Economic Growth in China." *Ecological Economics* 65, (2): 356–366.
Chesters, Graeme. (2004). "Global Complexity and Global Civil Society." *Voluntas: International Journal of Voluntary and Nonprofit Organizations* 15, (4): 323–342.
Chin, Gregory, and Ramesh Thakur. (2010). "Will China Change the Rules of Global Order?" *The Washington Quarterly* 33, (4): 119–138.
Cho, Ilsoo David, and Meredith Jung-En Woo. (2007). "North Korea in 2006: The Year of Living Dangerously." *Asian Survey* 47, (1): 68–73.
Choe, Jong Il. (2003). "Do Foreign Direct Investment and Gross Domestic Investment Promote Economic Growth?" *Review Of Development Economics* 7, (1): 44–57.
Choi, Seung-Whan, and Shali Luo. (2013). "Economic Sanctions, Poverty, and International Terrorism: an Empirical Analysis." *International Interactions* 39, (2): 217–245.
Chow, Peter C. Y. (1987). "Causality between Export Growth and Industrial Development: Empirical Evidence from the NICs." *Journal of Development Economics* 26, (1): 55–63.
Chowdhury, Abdur, and George Mavrotas. (2006). "FDI and Growth: What Causes What?" *World Economy* 29, (1): 9–19.
Coase, Ronald Harry. (1988). *The Firm, the Market, and the Law.* Chicago: University of Chicago Press.
Colas, Alejandro. (2013). *International Civil Society: Social Movements in World Politics*. Hoboken, NJ: John Wiley & Sons.
Contractor, Farok J., Vikas Kumar, Sumit K. Kundu, and Torben Pedersen. (2010). "Reconceptualizing the Firm in a World of Outsourcing and Offshoring: The Organizational and Geographical Relocation of High-Value Company Functions." *Journal of Management Studies* 47, (8): 1417–1433.

Cooke, Philip. (2001). "Regional Innovation Systems, Clusters, and the Knowledge Economy." *Industrial and Corporate Change* 10, (4): 945–974.

Cooray, Arusha, and Niklas Potrafke. (2011) "Gender Inequality in Education: Political Institutions or Culture and Religion?" *European Journal of Political Economy* 27, (2): 268–280.

Craig, Timothy C., and Richard King. (2002). *Global Goes Local: Popular Culture in Asia*. Vancouver: University of British Columbia Press.

Crawford, Gordon. (1997). "Foreign Aid and Political Conditionality: Issues of Effectiveness and Consistency." *Democratization* 4, (3): 69–108.

Croco, Sarah E., and Tze Kwang Teo. (2005). "Assessing the Dyadic Approach to Interstate Conflict Processes: Aka "Dangerous" Dyad-Years." *Conflict Management and Peace Science* 22, (1): 5–18.

Crothers, Lane. (2012). *Globalization and American Popular Culture*. Lanham, MD: Rowman and Littlefield Publishers.

Cumings, Bruce. (2013). *North Korea: Another Country*. New York: The New Press.

Caloffi, Annalisa, Luciana Lazzeretti, and Silvia Rita Sedita. (2014). "Founders and Disseminators of Cluster Research." *Economic Geography* 14, (1): 21–43.

Carriere, Michael, and Daniel Morrow. (1999). "The Economic Impacts of the 1998 Sanctions on India and Pakistan." *The Nonproliferation Review* 6, (4) 1–16.

Chang, Semmon andSuk Hi Kim. (2007). *Economic Sanctions against a Nuclear North Korea: An Analysis of United States and United Nations Actions since 1950*. Jefferson, NC: McFarland.

Damijan, Jože P., Mark Knell, Boris Majcen, and Matija Rojec. (2003). "The Role of FDI, R&D Accumulation and Trade in Transferring Technology to Transition Countries: Evidence from Firm Panel Data for Eight Transition Countries." *Economic Systems* 27, (2): 189–204.

Dashti-Gibson, Jaleh, Patricia Davis, and Benjamin Radcliff. (1997). "On The Determinants of the Success of Economic Sanctions: An Empirical Analysis." *American Journal of Political Science* 41, (2): 608–618.

Daude, Christian, and Ernesto Stein. (2007). "The Quality of Institutions and Foreign Direct Investment." *Economics & Politics* 19, (3): 317–344.

Davison, Roderic H. (1960). "Where Is the Middle East?" *Foreign Affairs* 38, (4): 665–675

De Boef, Suzanna, and Luke Keele. (2008). "Taking Time Seriously." *American Journal of Political Science* 52, (1): 184–200.

Dean Jr., James W., Eve D. Rosenzweig, and Aleda V. Roth. (2003). "The Influence of an Integration Strategy on Competitive Capabilities and Business Performance: An Exploratory Study of Consumer Products Manufacturers." *Journal of Operations Management* 21, (4): 437–456.

Debreu, Gerard. (1987). *Theory of Value: An Axiomatic Analysis of Economic Equilibrium No. 17*. Connecticut: Yale University Press.

de Bruijn, Frank. (2005). "The Current Status of Fuel Cell Technology for Mobile and Stationary Applications." *Green Chemistry* 7, (3): 132–150.

de Jonge Oudraat, Chantal. (2010). *"Making Economic Sanctions Work."* (2010). New York: Taylor and Francis.

Derksen, S. and H. J. Keselman. (1992). Backward, Forward and Stepwise Automated Subset Selection Algorithms: Frequency of Obtaining Authentic and Noise Variables. *British Journal of Mathematical and Statistical Psychology* 45, (2): 265–282.

Diamond, Larry Jay. (2002). "Thinking about Hybrid Regimes." *Journal of Democracy* 13, (2): 21–35.

Dingli, Shen. (2008). "Can Sanctions Stop Proliferation?" *Washington Quarterly* 31, (3): 89–100.

Ding, Sheng. (2008). "To Build a "Harmonious World:" China's Soft Power Wielding in the Global South." *Journal of Chinese Political Science* 13, (2): 193–213.

Di Minin, Alberto, Peter Gammeltoft, and Jieyin Zhang. (2012). "Chinese Foreign Direct Investment in R&D in Europe: A New Model of R&D Internationalization?" *European Management Journal* 30, (3): 189–203.

Dobbin, Frank, Geoffrey Garrett, and Beth Simmons. (2007). "The Global Diffusion of Public Policies: Social Construction, Coercion, Competition, or Learning?" *Annual Review of Sociology* 33: 449–472.

Doxey, Margaret. (1971). *Economic Sanctions and International Enforcement.* Oxford: Oxford University Press.

Dresner, Simon. (2009). *The Principles of Sustainability.* London: Earthscan

Drezner, Daniel W. (1999). *The Sanctions Paradox: Economic Statecraft and International Relations.* Cambridge, UK: Cambridge University Press.

Drezner, Daniel. (2006). *US Trade Strategy. Free Versus Fair.* New York: The Brookings Institution Press.

Drury, A. Cooper. (1998). "Revisiting Economic Sanctions Reconsidered." *Journal of Peace Research* 35, (4): 497–509.

Drury, A. Cooper. (2001). "Sanctions as Coercive Diploimacy: The US President's Decision to Initiate Economic Sanctions." *Political Research Quarterly* 54, (3): 485–508.

Drury, A. Cooper, and Dursun Peksen. (2009). "Economic Sanctions and Political Repression: Assessing The Impact of Coercive Diplomacy on Political Freedoms." *Human Rights Review* 10, (3): 393–411.

Dryzek, John S. (2012). "Global Civil Society: The Progress of Post-Westphalian Politics." *Annual Review of Political Science* 15: 101–119.

Dunn, Alexandra. (2011). "Unplugging a Nation: State Media Strategy during Egypt's January 25 Uprising." *Fletcher Forum of World Affairs* 35, (2): 15–24.

Dunning, John H. (1998). "Location and the Multinational Enterprise: A Neglected Factor?" *Journal of International Business Studies* 29, (1): 45–86.

———. (2009). "Location and The Multinational Enterprise: John Dunning's Thoughts on Receiving the Journal of International Business Studies 2008 Decade Award." *Journal of International Business Studies* 40, (1): 20–34.

Dunning, John H. (2013) *International Production and the Multinational Enterprise* Abingdon, UK: Routledge.

Dunning, John H., Roger Van Hoesel, and Rajneesh Narula. (1996). "Explaining The 'New' Wave of outward FDI from Developing Countries: The Case of Taiwan and Korea." *Research Memoranda* 9: 1–25.

Early, Bryan R. (2011). "Unmasking The Black Knights: Sanctions Busters and Their Effects on The Success of Economic Sanctions." *Foreign Policy Analysis* 7, (4): 381–402.

Early, Bryan R. (2009). "Sleeping with Your Friends' Enemies: An Explanation of Sanctions—Busting Trade." *International Studies Quarterly* 53, (1): 49–71.

Ernst, Dieter, and Linsu Kim. (2002). "Global Production Networks, Knowledge Diffusion, and Local Capability Formation." *Research Policy* 31, (8): 1417–1429.

Edy, Jill. (2006). *Troubled Pasts: News and The Collective Memory of Social Unrest.* Philadelphia, PA: Temple University Press.

Edwards, Michael, and John Gaventa, (eds). (2014). *Global Citizen Action.* London: Routledge.

Egreteau, Renaud. (2008). "India's Ambition in Burma: More Frustration than Success." *Asian Survey* 48, (6): 936–957.

Eichengreen, Barry. (2006). "Global Imbalances: The New Economy, the Dark Matter, the Savvy Investor, and the Standard Analysis." *Journal of Policy Modeling* 28, (6): 645–652.

El-Nawawy, Mohammed. (2006). "US Public Diplomacy in the Arab World: The News Credibility of Radio Sawa and Television Alhurra in Five Countries." *Global Media and Communication* 2, (2): 183–203.

Elliott, Kimberly Ann, Gary Clyde Hufbauer, Barbara Oegg, and Jeffrey J. Schott. (2007). *Economic Sanctions Reconsidered.* Washington, DC: Peterson Institute for International Economics.

Elliott, Kimberly Ann, Gary Clyde Hufbauer, Barbara Oegg, and Jeffrey J. Schott. (2009). *Economic Sanctions Reconsidered* 3 ed. Washington, DC: Peterson Institute for International Economics.

Elliott, Kimberly Ann, Gary Clyde Hufbauer, and Jeffrey J. Schott. (1990). *Economic Sanctions Reconsidered: History and Current Policy.* Washington, DC: Institute for International Economics.

Enright, Michael J. (2009). "The Location of Activities of Manufacturing Multinationals in the Asia-Pacific." *Journal of International Business Studies* 40, (5): 818–839.

Esposito, John L. (2002). *Unholy War: Terror in the Name of Islam.* Oxford: Oxford University Press.

Ethier, Wilfred J. (1982). "National and International Returns to Scale in the Modern Theory of International Trade." *The American Economic Review* 72, (3): 389–405.

Ewing-Chow, Michael. (2006). "First Do No Harm: Myanmar Trade Sanctions and Human Rights." *Northwestern University Journal of International Human Rights* 5, (2): 153–180.

Fan, Ying. (2008). "Soft Power: Power of Attraction or Confusion?" *Place Branding and Public Diplomacy 4,* (2): 147–158.

Fawn, Rick (ed.). (2003). *Realignments in Russian Foreign Policy.* London: Frank Cass Publishers.

Fisher, William F. (1997). "Doing Good? The Politics and Antipolitics of NGO Practices." *Annual Review of Anthropology* 26: 439–464.

Fosu, Augustin K. (1996). "The Impact of External Debt on Economic Growth in Sub-Saharan Africa." *Journal of Economic Development* 21, (1): 93–118.

Foley, James, Ravi Sarathy, and Vern Terpstra. (2012). *International Marketing.* Naperville, IL: Naper Press, 2012.

Frank, Ruediger. (2005). "Economic Reforms in North Korea (1998–2004): Systemic Restrictions, Quantitative Analysis, Ideological Background." *Journal of the Asia Pacific Economy* 10, (3): 278–311.

Fischer, Stanley, Gordon Hughes, Jeffrey Sachs, and Wing Thye Woo. (1994). "Structural Factors in the Economic Reforms of China, Eastern Europe, and the Former Soviet Union." *Economic Policy* 9, (18): 102–145.

Frey, Bruno S., and Friedrich Schneider. (1985). "Economic and Political Determinants of Foreign Direct Investment." *World Development* 13, (2): 161–175.

Fullerton, Jami A., and Alice Kendrick. (2006). *Advertising's War on Terrorism: The Story of the US State Department's Shared Values Initiative.* Spokane, WA: Marquette Books.

Fujita, Kōichi, Fumiharu Mieno, and Ikuko Okamoto. (2009). *Myanmar After 1988: Market Economy versus State Control.* Singapore: National University of Singapore Press.

Furia, Peter and Russell E. Lucas. (2006). "Determinants of Arab Public Opinion on Foreign Relations." *International Studies Quarterly* 50, (3): 585–605.

Gale, Fred, and Mathew D. Shane. (2004). "China: A Study of Dynamic Growth." *Outlook Report # WRS0408.* US Department of Agriculture. Washington, DC.

Gallant, Monica, and James S. Pounder. (2008). "The Employment of Female Nationals in the United Arab Emirates (UAE): An Analysis of Opportunities and Barriers." *Education, Business And Society: Contemporary Middle Eastern Issues* 1, (1): 26–33.

Galtung, Johan. (1967). "On the Effects of International Economic Sanctions: with Examples from The Case of Rhodesia." *World Politics* 19, (3): 378–416.

Gammeltoft, Peter. (2008). "Emerging Multinationals: outward FDI from The BRICS Countries." *International Journal of Technology and Globalisation* 4, (1): 5–22.

Ganesan, Narayanan. (1999). *Bilateral Tensions in Post-Cold War ASEAN.* Singapore: Institute of Southeast Asian Studies.

Ganesan, Narayanan. (2001). "Thailand's Relations with Malaysia and Myanmar in Post-Cold War Southeast Asia." *Japanese Journal of Political Science* 2, (1): 127–146.

Gao, Yue, Yonglei Ren, and John Whalley. (2014). "Decomposing China's Export Growth into Extensive Margin, Export Quality and Quantity Effects." *China Economic Review* 29, (June): 19–26.

Gause III, F. Gregory. (2011). "Why Middle East Studies Missed the Arab Spring: The Myth of Authoritarian Stability." *Foreign Affairs* 90, (4): 81–90.

Gebert, Konstanty. (2013) "Shooting in the Dark? EU Sanctions Policies." Policy Brief # ECFR71, Brussels: European Council on Foreign Relations.

Geiger, Linwood T. (1990). "Debt and Economic Development in Latin America." *Journal of Developing Areas* 24, (2): 181–194.

Genser, Jared M., and Robert L. Hose. (2007). "Are EU Trade Sanctions on Burma Compatible with WTO Law." *Michigan Journal of International Law* 29: 165–196.

Gentilini, Ugo, and Andy Sumner. (2012). "What Do National Poverty Lines Tell Us about Global Poverty?" *IDS Working Papers*, #392: 1–48.

Gholami, Roghieh, Almas Heshmati, and Sang-Yong Tom Lee. (2006). "The Causal Relationship between Information and Communication Technology and Foreign Direct Investment." *The World Economy* 29, (1): 43–62.

Gibbons, Elizabeth D. (1999). *Sanctions in Haiti: Human Rights and Democracy Under Assault.* Westport, CT: Praeger.

Globerman, Steven, and Daniel Shapiro. (2002). "Global Foreign Direct Investment Flows: The Role of Governance Infrastructure." *World Development.* 30, (11): 1899–1919.

Globerman, Steven, and Daniel Shapiro. (2003). "Governance Infrastructure and US Foreign Direct Investment." *Journal of International Business Studies* 34, (1): 19–39.

Greene, William H. (2008). *Econometric Analysis* 6th ed., Upper Saddle River, NJ: Pearson/Prentice Hall

Grossman, Gene, Elhanan Helpman and Adam Szeidl. (2006). "Optimal Integration Strategies for the Multinational Firm." *Journal of International Economics* 70, (1): 216–238.

Golan, Guy J., and Sung-Un Yang. (2013). "Diplomat in Chief? Assessing the Influence of Presidential Evaluations on Public Diplomacy Outcomes among Foreign Publics." *American Behavioral Scientist* 57, (9): 1277–1292.

Goodwin, Jeff, and Theda Skocpol. (1989). "Explaining Revolutions in the Contemporary Third World." *Politics and Society* 17, (4): 489–509.

Goodwin, Jeff. (2011). "Why We Were Surprised (Again) by the Arab Spring." *Swiss Political Science Review* 17, (4): 452–456.

Goldsmith, Benjamin E., and Yusaku Horiuchi. (2012). "In Search of Soft Power: Does Foreign Public Opinion Matter for US Foreign Policy?" *World Politics* 64, (3): 555–585.

Gordon, Robert J. (2000). Does The" New Economy" Measure up to the Great Inventions of the Past? *Discussion Paper No. W7833.* National Bureau Of Economic Research, Washington, DC.

Greene, William H. (2008). *Econometric Analysis* 6th ed., Upper Saddle River, NJ: Pearson/Prentice Hall.

Giugni, Marco, (ed.). (2004). *Social Protest and Policy Change: Ecology, Antinuclear, and Peace Movements in Comparative Perspective.* Lanham, MD: Rowman and Littlefield.

Giurcanu, Magda, andBryon Moraski. (2013). “European Reactions to the 2008 Georgian-Russian War: Assessing the Impact of Gas Dependence.” *Studies in Comparative International Development* 48, (4): 432–456.

Gvosdev, Nikolas and Ray Takeyh. (2002). “Do Terrorist Networks Need a Home?” *Washington Quarterly* 25, (3): 97–108.

Haacke, Jürgen. (2006). *Myanmar's Foreign Policy: Domestic Influences and International Implications.* New York: Routledge.

Haaland, Jan, Giorgio Navaretti, and Anthony Venables. (2007). *Multinational Corporations and Global Production Networks: The Implications for Trade Policy.* London: European Commission Directorate General for Trade, Center for Economic Policy Research.

Haggard, Stephan and Marcus Noland. (2007). *Famine in North Korea: Markets, Aid, and Reform.* New York : Columbia University Press.

Haggard, Stephan, and Marcus Noland. (2012). “Networks, Trust, and Trade: The Microeconomics of China-North Korea Integration.” *East-West Center Working Paper Series, Working paper # 12–8.* Honolulu, Hawaii.

Hajzler, Christopher. (2014). “Resource-based FDI and Expropriation in Developing Economies.” *Journal of International Economics* 92, (1): 124–146.

Hamdan, Amani. (2005). “Women and Education in Saudi Arabia: Challenges and Achievements.” *International Education Journal* 6, (1): 42–64.

Hammami, Mona, Jean-Francois Ruhashyankiko, and Etienne B. Yehoue. (2006). “Determinants Of Public-Private Partnerships in Infrastructure.” *Working Paper # 06/99.* International Monetary Fund. Washington, DC.

Hammoud, Hassan R. (2006). “Illiteracy in the Arab World.” *Adult Education and Development* 66: 83–101.

Harris, James C. (2012). “Daw Aung San Suu Kyi: Freedom to Lead.” *Archives of General Psychiatry* 69, (7): 657–659.

Hart, Robert A. (2000). “Democracy and the Successful Use of Economic Sanctions.” *Political Research Quarterly* 53, (2) 267–284.

Hassett, Kevin. (ed.). (2012). *Rethining Competitiveness.* Lanham, MD: Rowman and Littlefield.

Hayden, Craig. (2012). *The Rhetoric of Soft Power: Public Diplomacy in Global Contexts.* Lanham, MD: Lexington Books.

Hayes, Robert, Gary Pisano, David Upton and Steven Whe,elwright. (2005). *Operations, Strategy, and Technology: Pursuing the Competitive Edge.* Malden, MA: John Wiley and Sons, Inc.

Head, Keith, and John Ries. (2008). “FDI as an Outcome of the Market for Corporate Control: Theory and Evidence.” *Journal of International Economics* 74, (1): 2–20.

Helmsing, A. H. J. (Bert). (2003). “Local Economic Development: New Generations of Actors, Policies and Instruments For Africa.” *Public Administration and Development* 23, (1): 67–76.

Helpman, Elhanan. (2006). “Trade, FDI, and the Organization of Firms.” *Journal of Economic Literature* 44, (3): 589–630.

Henriksen, Thomas H. (2001). “The Rise and Decline of Rogue States.” *Journal of International Affairs* 54, (2): 349–371.

Hill, M. Anne and Elizabeth M. King. (eds). (1997). *Women's Education in Developing Countries: Barriers, Benefits, and Policies*. World Bank Publications.

Henry, Peter Blair. 2007. "Capital Account Liberalization: Theory, Evidence, and Speculation." *Journal of Economic Literature* 45, (4): 887–935.

Henry, Peter Blair, and Diego Sasson. (2008). "Capital Account Liberalization, Real Wages, and Productivity." *Working Paper No.13880*. National Bureau of Economic Research. Washington, DC.

Hilson, Gavin. (2014). "'Constructing'Ethical Mineral Supply Chains in Sub-Saharan Africa: The Case of Malawian Fair Trade Rubies." *Development and Change* 45, (1): 53–78.

Holliday, Ian. (2011). *Burma Redux: Global Justice and the Quest for Political Reform in Myanmar*. New York: Columbia University Press.

Hook, Steven W., andCharles W. Kegley Jr. (1991). "US Foreign Aid and UN Voting: Did Reagan's Linkage Strategy Buy Deference or Defiance?" *International Studies Quarterly* 35, (3): 295–312.

Hovi, Jon, Robert Huseby, and Detlef F. Sprinz. (2005). When Do (Imposed) Economic Sanctions Work?" *World Politics* 57, (4): 479–499.

Huarng, Kun-Huang, and Domingo Enrique Ribeiro-Soriano. (2014). "Developmental Management: Theories, Methods, and Applications in Entrepreneurship, Innovation, and Sensemaking." *Journal of Business Research* 67, (5): 657–662.

Hubert, Franz, and Svetlana Ikonnikova. (2011). "Investment Options and Bargaining Power: The Eurasian Supply Chain for Natural Gas." *The Journal of Industrial Economics* 59, (1): 85–116.

Hufbauer, Gary Clyde, and Barbara Oegg. (2003). "Economic Sanctions: Public Goals And Private Consumption." *Chicago Journal of International Law* 4, (2): 305–328.

Hufbauer, Gary Clyde and Barbara Oegg. (2000). "Targeted Sanctions: A Policy Alternative." *Law and Policy in International Business* 32, (1): 11–20.

Hughes, Christopher W. (2013). *Japan's Economic Power and Security: Japan and North Korea*. London: Routledge.

Huntington, Samuel P. (1993). "The Clash of Civilizations?" *Foreign Affairs* 72, (3): 22–49.

Husted, Bryan. W., and Instituto Tecnologico y de Estudios. (1999). "Wealth, Culture, and Corruption." *Journal of International Business Studies* 30, (2): 339–359.

Ibroscheva, Elza. (2007). "Caught between East and West? Portrayals of Gender in Bulgarian Television Advertisements." *Sex Roles* 57, (5–6): 409–418.

Inomata, Satoshi, Peter W. Liesch, Irina Mihailova, Bo Meng, and Gabriele Suder. (2014). "The Evolving Geography of Production Hubs and Regional Value Chains across East Asia: Trade in Value-Added." *Journal of World Business*. Available at: doi:10.1016/j.jmb.2014.05.003.

Irwin, Douglas A. (2009). *Free Trade under Fire*. Princeton, NJ: Princeton University Press.

Jeffries, Ian. (2012). *North Korea, 2009–2012: A Guide to Economic and Political Developments*. London: Routledge.

Jensen, Robert, and Emily Oster. (2009). "The Power of TV: Cable Television and Women's Status in India." *The Quarterly Journal of Economics* 124, (3): 1057–1094.

Jewitt, Sarah. (1995). "Europe's Others'? Forestry Policy and Practices in Colonial and Postcolonial India." *Environment and Planning* D, (13): 67–67.

Jiang, Jing, and Ran Wei. (2012). "Influences of Culture and Market Convergence on the International Advertising Strategies of Multinational Corporations in North America, Europe and Asia." *International Marketing Review* 29, (6): 597–622.

Jin, Jang C. (2003). "Openness and Growth in North Korea: Evidence from Time-Series Data." *Review of International Economics* 11, (1): 18–27.

Jovanovic, Miroslav. (2014). *International Economic Integration: Limits and Prospects*. London: Routledge.

Jreisat, Jamil. E. (2006). "The Arab World Reform or Stalemate." *Journal of Asian and African Studies* 41, (5–6): 411–437.

Jung, Woo S., and Peyton J. Marshall. (1985). "Exports, Growth and Causality in Developing Countries." *Journal of Development Economics* 18, (1): 1–12.

Kaempfer, William H., and Anton D. Lowenberg. (1988). "The Theory of International Economic Sanctions: A Public Choice Approach." *American Economic Review* 78, (4): 786–793.

Kaempfer, William H., Anton D. Lowenberg, and William Mertens. (2004). "International Economic Sanctions against a Dictator." *Economics & Politics* 16, (1): 29–51.

Kaempfer, William H. and Stephen V. Marks. (1993). "The Expected Effects of Trade Liberalisation: Evidence from US Congressional Action on Fast—Track Authority." *The World Economy* 16, (6): 725–740.

Kalyoncu, Huseyin and Ilhan Ozturk. (2007). "Foreign Direct Investment and Growth: An Empirical Investigation Based on Cross-Country Comparison." *Economia Internazionale* 60, (1): 75–82.

Kamalipour, Yahya R., and Nancy Snow, (eds). (2004). *War, Media, and Propaganda: A Global Perspective*. Lanham, MD: Rowman and Littlefield.

Kamat, Sangeeta. (2003). "NGOs and the New Democracy." *Harvard International Review* 25, (1): 65–69.

Kanbur, Ravi, and Xiaobo Zhang. (2005). "Fifty Years of Regional Inequality in China: A Journey through Central Planning, Reform, and Openness." *Review of Development Economics* 9, (1): 87–106.

Kang, In-Bong, and Kenneth Greene. (1999). "A Political Economic Analysis of Congressional Voting Patterns on NAFTA." *Public Choice* 98, (3–4): 385–397.

Kaplan, Robert D. (2011). *Monsoon: The Indian Ocean and the Future of American Power*. New York: Random House.

Kardulias, Nick (ed.) et al. (1999). *World-Systems Theory in Practice: Leadership, Production, and Exchange*. Lanham, MD: Rowman and Littlefield Publishers.

Kaufmann, D., A. Kraay, A., and P. Zoido-Lobatón. (1999). "Aggregating Governance Indicators Vol. 2195." *World Bank Publications*.

Kaul, Inge, Isabelle Grunberg, and Marc Stern. (1999). *Global Public Goods: International Cooperation in the 21st Century*. Oxford: Oxford University Press.

Keddie, Amanda. (2011). "Framing Discourses of Possibility and Constraint in the Empowerment of Muslim Girls: Issues of Religion, Race, Ethnicity and Culture." *Race Ethnicity and Education* 14, (2): 175–190.

Kennedy, Evan T., Mahmood Monshipouri, andClaude Emerson Welch. (2003). "Multinational Corporations and The Ethics of Global Responsibility: Problems and possibilities." *Human Rights Quarterly* 25, (4): 965–989.

Kim, Jeong-Nam, and Seong-Hun Yun. (2008). "Soft Power: From Ethnic Attraction to National Attraction in Sociological Globalism." *International Journal of Intercultural Relations* 32, (6): 565–577.

Kellner, Douglas. (2002). "Theorizing Globalization." *Sociological Theory* 20, (3): 285–305.

Kelly, Kevin. (1999). *New Rules for the New Economy*. London: Penguin.

Keohane, Robert O. (2005). *After Hegemony: Cooperation and Discord in the World Political Economy*. Princeton, NJ: Princeton University Press.

Kentor, Jeffrey. (2001). "The Long Term Effects of Globalization on Income Inequality, Population Growth, and Economic Development." *Social Problems* 48, (4): 435–455.

Khamis, Sahar, and Katherine Vaughn. (2011). "Cyberactivism in The Egyptian Revolution: How Civic Engagement and Citizen Journalism Tilted the Balance." *Arab Media and Society* 13, (3): 1–37.

Khine, Thandar. (2008). "Foreign Direct Investment Relations between Myanmar and ASEAN." *Discussion Paper #149*. Institute of Developing Economies Discussion Paper, Japan. Available at: http://www.ide.go.jp/English/Publish/Download/Dp/149.html.

Kimura, Mitsuhiko. (1999). "From Fascism to Communism: Continuity and Development of Collectivist Economic Policy in North Korea." *Economic History Review* 52, (1): 69–86.

King, Gary. (1986)."How Not to Lie with Statistics: Avoiding Common Mistakes in Quantitative Political Science." *American Journal of Political Science* 30, (3): 666–687.

Kirshner, Orin. (2005). "Triumph of Globalism: American Trade Politics." *Political Science Quarterly* 120, (3): 479–503.

Klein, Saul, and Albert Wöcke. (2007). "Emerging Global Contenders: The South African Experience." *Journal of International Management* 13, (3): 319–337.

Knack, Stephen. (2004). "Does Foreign Aid Promote Democracy?" *International Studies Quarterly* 48, (1): 251–266.

Kolstad, Ivar, and Arne Wiig. (2011). "Better the Devil You Know? Chinese Foreign Direct Investment in Africa." *Journal Of African Business* 12, (1): 31–50.

Kong, Qingjiang. (2010). "Trade Disputes between China and the EU: Are They Manageable?" *Global Trade and Customs Journal* 5, (2): 47–55.

Kozhanov, Nikolay A. (2011). "US Economic Sanctions against Iran: Undermined by External Factors." *Middle East Policy* 18, (3): 144–160.

Kraidy, Marwan. (2005). *Hybridity, othe Cultural Logic of Globalization.* Philadelphia, PA: Temple University Press.

Kraidy, Marwan M. (2009). *Reality Television and Arab Politics: Contention in Public Life.* Cambridge: Cambridge University Press.

Kramer, Mark R., and Michael E. Porter. (2011). "Creating Shared Value." *Harvard Business Review* 89, (1/2): 62–77.

Krugman, Paul R. (1991). *Geography and Trade.* Cambridge, MA: MIT Press.

Krugman, Paul R. (2008). "Trade and Wages, Reconsidered." *Brookings Papers on Economic Activity* 1: 103–154.

Kudo, Toshihiro. (2006). "Myanmar's Economic Relations with China: Can China Support the Myanmar Economy?" *Discussion Paper # 66.* Institute of Developing Economies, Japan. Available at: http://www.ide.go.jp/English/Publish/Download/Dp/066.html.

Kuran, Timur. (2004). "Why the Middle East Is Economically Underdeveloped: Historical Mechanisms of Institutional Stagnation." *Journal of Economic Perspectives* 18, (3): 71–90.

Kurlantzick, Joshua. (2002). "China: Economic Power, Political Enigma." *Washington Quarterly* 25, (3): 59–67.

Lall, Sanjaya, and Rajneesh Narula. (2004). "Foreign Direct Investment and its Role in Economic Development: Do We Need a New Agenda?." *The European Journal of Development Research* 16, (3): 447–464.

Lam, Peng Er. (2007). "Japan's Quest For "Soft Power:" Attraction and Limitation." *East Asia* 24, (4): 349–363.

Lankov, Andrei. (2008). "Staying Alive: Why North Korea Will Not Change." *Foreign Affairs* 87, (2): 9–16.

Large, Daniel. (2008). "Beyond "Dragon in The Bush": The Study of China–Africa Relations." *African Affairs* 107, (426): 45–61.

Lee, Chung Min. (2007). "Nuclear Sisyphus: The Myth of Denuclearising North Korea." *Australian Journal of International Affairs* 61, (1): 15–22.

Lee, Soo-Young, and Andrew B. Whitford. (2009). "Government Effectiveness in Comparative Perspective." *Journal of Comparative Policy Analysis* 11, (2): 249–281.

Lee, Sook Jong and Jan Melissen. (eds). (2011). *Public Diplomacy and Soft Power in East Asia.* New York: Palgrave Macmillan.

Lee, Seung-Ook and Seung-Hyun Yoon. (2013). "From Old Comrades to New Partnerships: Dynamic Development of Economic Relations between China and North Korea." *The Geographical Journal* 179, (1): 19–31.

Lieberthal, Kenneth, and Geoffrey Lieberthal. (2003). "The Great Transition." *Harvard Business Review* 81, (10): 70–81.

Lektzian, David, and Mark Souva. (2007). "An Institutional Theory of Sanctions Onset and Success." *Journal of Conflict Resolution* 51, (6): 848–871.

Lensink, Robert, and Oliver Morrissey. (2006). "Foreign Direct Investment: Flows, Volatility, and the Impact on Growth." *Review of International Economics* 14, (3): 478–493.

LeoGrande, William M. (1996). "Making the Economy Scream: Sanctions against Sandinista Nicaragua." *Third World Quarterly* 17, (2): 329–348.

Leogrande, William M., and Julie M. Thomas. (2002). "Cuba's Quest for Economic Independence." *Journal of Latin American Studies* 34, (2): 325–363.
Levy, David L. (2008). "Political Contestation in Global Production Networks." *Academy of Management Review* 33, (4): 943–963.
Levy, David L., and Aseem Prakash. (2003). "Bargains Old and New: Multinational Corporations in Global Governance." *Business And Politics* 5, (2): 131–150.
Lengel, Lara, and Victoria A. Newsom. (2012). "Arab Women, Social Media, and the Arab Spring: Applying the Framework of Digital Reflexivity to Analyze Gender and Online Activism." *Journal of International Women's Studies* 13, (5): 30–45.
Lewis, Bernard. (1990). "The Roots of Muslim Rage." *The Atlantic Monthly* 266, (3): 47–60.
Little, Douglas. (2008). *American Orientalism: The United States and the Middle East since 1945*. Chapel Hill, NC: UNC Press.
Loeffler, Rachel L. (2009). "Bank Shots." *Foreign Affairs* 88, (2): 101–110.
Lompo, Kevin, and Jean-Francois Trani. (2013). "Does Corporate Social Responsibility Contribute to Human Development in Developing Countries? Evidence from Nigeria." *Journal of Human Development and Capabilities* 14, (2): 241–265.
London, Bruce and David A. Smith. (1988). "Urban Bias, Dependence, and Economic Stagnation in Non-Core Nations." *American Sociological Review* 53, (3): 454–463.
Luke, Carmen. (2001). *Globalization and Women in Academia: North/West-South/East*. London: Routledge.
Luqmani, Mushtaq, Zahir A. Quraeshi, and Ugur Yavas. (2013). "Towards a Framework for Applying US Economic Sanctions." *World Review of Entrepreneurship, Management and Sustainable Development* 9, (1): 114–130.
Luo, Yadong. (2005). "Toward Coopetition within a Multinational Enterprise: A Perspective from Foreign Subsidiaries." *Journal of World Business* 40, (1): 71–90.
Luo, Yadong, and Rosalie L. Tung. (2007). "International Expansion of Emerging Market Enterprises: A Springboard Perspective." *Journal of International Business Studies* 38: 481–498.
Mahutga, Matthew C. (2012). "When Do Value Chains Go Global? A Theory of the Spatialization of Global Value Chains." *Global Networks* 12, (1): 1–21.
Manby, Bronwen. (1992). "South Africa: The Impact of Sanctions." *Journal of International Affairs* 46, (1): 193–217.
Manyin, Mark E., and Mary Beth Nikitin. (2008). "US Assistance to North Korea." *Congressional Research Service Report*, Library of Congress. Washington, DC.
Manyin, Mark. E. (2012). *The Kaesong North-South Korean Industrial Complex*. Darby, PA: Diane Publishing.
Manyin, Mark E., and Dick K. Nanto. (2011). "China–North Korea Relations." *North Korean Review* 7, (2): 94–101.
Marinov, Nikolay. (2005). "Do Economic Sanctions Destabilize Country Leaders?" *American Journal of Political Science* 49, (3): 564–576.

Marks, Stephen P. (1999). "Economic Sanctions as Human Rights Violations: Reconciling Political and Public Health Imperatives." *American Journal of Public Health* 89, (10): 1509–1513.

Markusen, Ann. (1996). "Sticky Places in Slippery Space: A Typology of Industrial Districts." *Economic Geography* 72, (3): 293–313.

Marshall, Alfred. (1890). *Principles of Economics*. New York: Palgrave Classics.

Martens, Bertin. (2008). *The Institutional Economics of Foreign Aid*. Cambridge: Cambridge University Press, 2008.

Martin, Ron, and Peter Sunley. (2003). "Deconstructing Clusters: Chaotic Concept or Policy Panacea?" *Journal of Economic Geography* 3, (1): 5–35.

Martin, Xavier, and Robert Salomon. (2003). "Knowledge Transfer Capacity and its Implications for The Theory of The Multinational Corporation." *Journal of International Business Studies* 34, (4): 356–373.

Massari, Stefania, and Marcello Ruberti. (2013). "Rare Earth Elements as Critical Raw Materials: Focus on International Markets and Future Strategies." *Resources Policy* 38, (1): 36–43.

Matheny, Kenneth J. (2009). "Trends in the Aggregate Labor Force." *Federal Reserve Bank of St. Louis Review* 91, (4): 297–310.

Mattern, Janice Bially. (2005). "Why Soft Power isn't So Soft: Representational Force and the Sociolinguistic Construction of Attraction in World Politics." *Millennium Journal of International Studies* 33, (3): 583–612.

Maung, Mya. (1970). "The Burmese Way to Socialism beyond the Welfare State." *Asian Survey* 10, (6): 533–551.

Mazarr, Michael J. (1995). *North Korea and the Bomb: A Case Study in Nonproliferation*. New York: St. Martin's Press.

McAlister, Melani. (2005). *Epic Encounters: Culture, Media, and US Interests in the Middle East since 1945*. Berkeley: University of California Press.

McCarthy, Stephen. (2000). "Ten Years of Chaos in Burma: Foreign Investment and Economic Liberalization under the SLORC-SPDC, 1988 to 1998." *Pacific Affairs* 73, (2): 233–262.

McKay, John. (2005). "How Significant and Effective are North Korea's "Market Reforms"?" *Global Economic Review* 34, (1): 83–97.

McLean, Elena V., and Taehee Whang. (2010). "Friends or Foes? Major Trading Partners and The Success of Economic Sanctions." *International Studies Quarterly* 54, (2): 427–447.

Melissen, Jan. (2005). "Wielding Soft Power: The New Public Diplomacy." *Clingendael Diplomacy Paper* No. 2, Netherlands Institute of International Relations, The Hague.

Melitz, Marc J., and Daniel Trefler. (2012). "Gains from Trade When Firms Matter." *The Journal of Economic Perspectives* 26, (2): 91–118.

Menon, Rajan. (1997). "The Strategic Convergence between Russia and China." *Survival* 39, (2): 101–125.

Meyer, David S. (2004). "Protest and Political Opportunities." *Annual Review of Sociology* (30): 125–145.

Michaels, Jon D. (2012). "Private Military Firms, the American Precedent, and the Arab Spring." *Stanford Journal of International Law* 48, (2): 277–288.

Mickelson, Sig. (1983). *America's Other Voice: The Story of Radio Free Europe and Radio Liberty*. New York: Praeger.
Midler, Paul. (2009). *Poorly Made in China*. Hoboken, NJ: John Wiley and Sons.
Miljkovic, Dragan. (2002). "Economic Sanctions as the Prepositional Satisfiability Problem." *Policy Sciences* 35, (1): 1–15.
Miller, Brena and James D. Thorr. (2003). *Developing Nations*. Farmington Hills, MI: Greenhaven Press.
Miyagawa, Makio. (1992). *Do Economic Sanctions Work?* New York: St. Martin's Press.
Moghadam, Valentine M. (2003). *Modernizing Women: Gender and Social Change in the Middle East*. Boulder, CO: Lynne Rienner Publishers.
Momin, Mahmood Ahmed, and Lee D. Parker. (2013). "Motivations for Corporate Social Responsibility Reporting by MNC Subsidiaries in an Emerging Country: The Case of Bangladesh." *The British Accounting Review* 45, (3): 215–228.
Morgan, T. Clifton, and Valerie L. Schwebach. (1997). "Fools Suffer Gladly: The Use of Economic Sanctions in International Crises." *International Studies Quarterly* 41, (1) 27–50.
Mortensen, Mette. (2011). "When Citizen Photojournalism Sets the News Agenda: Neda Agha Soltan as A Web 2.0 Icon of Post-Election Unrest in Iran." *Global Media And Communication* 7, (1): 4–16.
Moghadam, Valentine M., and Farzaneh Roudi-Fahim. (2003). *Empowering Women, Developing Society: Female Education in The Middle East and North Africa*. Washington, DC: Population Reference Bureau.
Niemann, Ulrich. (2005). "Sunshine in the Darkness? Where Will North Korea's Economic Reforms Lead?" *Asia Europe Journal* 3, (3): 309–312.
Niksch, Larry A., and Martin A. Weiss. (2009). *"Burma: Economic Sanctions."* Washington, DC: Congressional Research Service Report, Library of Congress.
Nincic, Miroslav, and Bruce Russett. (1979). "The Effect of Similarity and Interest on Attitudes toward Foreign Countries." *Public Opinion Quarterly* 43, (1): 68–78.
Nisbet, Erik C., Matthew C. Nisbet, Dietram A. Scheufele, and James E. Shanahan. (2004). "Public Diplomacy, Television News, and Muslim Opinion." *The Harvard International Journal of Press and Politics* 9, (2): 11–37.
Noland, Marcus. (2009). "The (Non-) Impact of UN Sanctions on North Korea." *Asia Policy* 7, (1): 61–88.
Noland, Marcus. (2004). *Korea after Kim Jong-Il*. Washington, DC: Institute for International Economics.
Nooruddin, Irfan. (2002). "Modeling Selection Bias in Studies of Sanctions Efficacy." *International Interactions* 28, (1): 59–75.
Norris, Pippa and Ronald Inglehart. (2002). "Islamic Culture and Democracy: Testing the "clash of Civilizations" Thesis." *Comparative Sociology* 1, (3): 235–263.
Nossal, Kim Richard. (1989). "International Sanctions as International Punishment." *International Organization* 43, (2): 301–322.

Nye, Joseph. (2002). "Hard and Soft Power in a Global Information Age." In Mark Leonard (ed.). *Reordering the World.* London: Foreign Policy Centre (FPC).
Nye, Joseph. S. (2008). "Public Diplomacy and Soft Power." *The Annals of The American Academy of Political and Social Science* 616, (1): 94–109.
Nye, Joseph. S. (1990). "Soft Power." *Foreign Policy* 80 (Autumn): 153–171.
Nye, Joseph. (2004). "Soft Power and Higher Education." In Internet and the University Forum. Available at: http://www.educauseedu/ir/library/pdf/ffpiu043.
Nye Joseph. (2010). "The Future of Soft Power in US Foreign Policy." In I. Parmar and M. Cox. (eds). *Soft Power and US Foreign Policy: Theoretical, Historical and Contemporary Perspectives.*, New York: Routledge.
Oehler-Şincai, Iulia Monica. (2011). "Brief Reflections on the Development of the FDI Theory." *Theoretical and Applied Economics* 18, (11): 35–42.
Oliveira, Pedro M., Katherine M. Ponte, and Aleda V. Roth. (2003). "Cross-Border Mergers and Acquisitions as a Tool to Transfer Knowledge and Foster Competitive Capabilities." *International Journal of Technology, Policy and Management* 3, (2): 204–223.
Olson, Richard Stuart. (1979). "Economic Coercion in World Politics, with a Focus on North-South Relationships." *World Politics* 31, (4): 471–494.
Omran, Abdel R., and Farzaneh Roudi. (1993). "The Middle East Population Puzzle." *Population Bulletin* 48, (1): 1–40.
Oskarsson, Katerina. (2012). "Economic Sanctions on Authoritarian States: Lessons Learned." *Middle East Policy* 19, (4): 88–102.
Papanek, Gustav F. (1972). "The Effect of Aid and Other Resource Transfers on Savings and Growth in Less Developed Countries." *Economic Journal* 82, (327): 934–950.
Pape, Robert A. (1997). "Why Economic Sanctions Do Not Work." *International Security* 22, (2): 90–136.
Pappé, Ilan. (2014). *The Modern Middle East: A Social and Cultural History.* London: Routledge.
Parola, Francesco, Luca Persico, and Giovanni Satta. (2013). "Time, Space, and International Diversification of Service Firms: Assessing the Abnormal Growth of Container Port MNs." *Economia e Politica Industriale—Journal Of Industrial And Business Economics* 40, (1): 89–115.
Peksen, Dursun. (2009). "Better or Worse? The Effect of Economic Sanctions on Human Rights." *Journal of Peace Research* 46, (1): 59–77.
Pells, Richard. (2011). *Modernist America: Art, Music, Movies, and the Globalization of American Culture.* New Haven, CT: Yale University Press.
Peri, Giovanni. (2002). "Globalization, Rigidities and National Specialization: A Dynamic Analysis." *Structural Change and Economic Dynamics* 13, (2): 151–177.
Perkins, Dwight H. (2012). "Rapid Growth and Changing Economic Structure: The Expenditure Side Story and its Implications for China." *China Economic Review* 23, (3): 501–511.
Peterson, Peter G. (2002). "Public Diplomacy and the War on Terrorism." *Foreign Affairs* 81, (5): 74–94.

Petras, James. (1993). "Cultural Imperialism in the Late 20th Century." *Journal of Contemporary Asia* 23, (2): 139–148.

Plaisance, Patrick Lee. (2005). "The Propaganda War on Terrorism: An Analysis of the United States' "Shared Values" Public-Diplomacy Campaign after September 11, 2001." *Journal of Mass Media Ethics* 20, (4): 250–268.

Porter, Michael E. (2011). *Competitive Advantage of Nations: Creating and Sustaining Superior Performance*. New York: Simon And Schuster.

Potocki, Rodger. (2011). "Belarus: A Tale of Two Elections." *Journal of Democracy* 22, (3): 49–63.

Pournarakis, Mike, and Nikos Varsakelis. (2004). "Institutions, Internationalization and FDI: The Case of Economies in Transition." *Transnational Corporations* 13, (2): 77–94.

Puddington, Arch. (2003). *Broadcasting Freedom: The Cold War Triumph of Radio Free Europe and Radio Liberty*. Lexington: University of Kentucky Press.

Quazi, Rahim M. (2005). "Effects of Foreign Aid on GDP Growth and Fiscal Behavior: An Econometric Case Study of Bangladesh." *Journal of Developing Areas* 38, (2): 95–117.

Radelet, Steven. (2003). "Bush and Foreign Aid." *Foreign Affairs* 84, (5): 104–117.

Rarick, Charles A. (2006). "Destroying a Country in Order to Save it: The Folly of Economic Sanctions against Myanmar." *Economic Affairs* 26, (2): 60–63.

Rarick, Charles. A. (2007). "Economic Sanctions: Failed Foreign Policy Tool and a Cost to American Business." *Economic Affairs* 27, (3) 65–70.

Reuther, David E. (1995). "UN Sanctions against Iraq." In David Cortright and George A. Lopez (eds), 121–133. *Economic Sanctions: Panacea or Peacebuilding in a Post-Cold War World*. Boulder, CO: Westview.

Rizvi, Fazal. (2011)."Theorizing Student Mobility in an Era of Globalization." *Teachers and Teaching* 17, (6): 693–701.

Robertson, Roland. (1992). *Globalization: Social Theory and Global Culture*. London: Sage Publications.

Rodrik, Dani. (2014). "The Past, Present, and Future of Economic Growth." *Challenge* 57, (3): 5–39.

Rothman, Tiran. (2007). "A State's Choice: Nuclear Policy in a Changing World between Libya and North Korea." *Defense and Security Analysis* 23, (3): 297–313.

Rowe, David M. (2000). "Economic Sanctions, Domestic Politics and the Decline of Rhodesian Tobacco, 1965–79": In Steve Chan and A. Cooper Drury (eds)., 131–157. *Sanctions as Economic Statecraft: Theory and Practice*. Basingstoke, UK: Macmillan.

Roy, Denny. (2005). "Southeast Asia and China: Balancing or Bandwagoning?" *Contemporary Southeast Asia: A Journal of International And Strategic Affairs* 27, (2): 305–322.

Roy, Denny. (1996). "The "China Threat" Issue: Major Arguments." *Asian Survey* 36, (8): 758–771.

Rubin, Barry. (2002). "The Real Roots of Arab Anti-Americanism." *Foreign Affairs* 81, (6): 73–85.

Rudra, Nita. (2002). "Globalization and the Decline of the Welfare State in Less-Developed Countries." *International Organization* 56, (2): 411–445.

Rugh, William A. (2006). *American Encounters with Arabs: The "Soft Power" of US Public Diplomacy in The Middle East.* Westport, Connecticut: Greenwood Publishing Group.

Sakr, Naomi. (2001). *Satellite Realms: Transnational Television, Globalization and the Middle East.* London: IB Tauris.

Santoro, Michael A. (2003). "Beyond Codes of Conduct and Monitoring: An Organizational Integrity Approach to Global Labor Practices." *Human Rights Quarterly* 25, (2): 407–424.

Savun, Burcu, and Daniel C. Tirone. (2011). "Foreign Aid, Democratization, and Civil Conflict: How Does Democracy Aid Affect Civil Conflict?" *American Journal of Political Science* 55, (2): 233–246.

Schmidt-Felzmann, Anke. (2011). "EU Member States' Energy Relations with Russia: Conflicting Approaches to Securing Natural Gas Supplies." *Geopolitics* 16, (3): 574–599.

Schneider, Cynthia. P. (2003). "Diplomacy That Works: "Best Practices" in Cultural Diplomacy." *Cultural Diplomacy Series.* Center For Arts and Culture. Boston, MA.

Schoar, Antoinette. (2002). "The Effect of Diversification on Firm Productivity," *Journal of Finance* 62, (6): 2379–2403.

Schroeder, Miriam. (2008). "The Construction of China's Climate Politics: Transnational NGOs and the Spiral Model of International Relations." *Cambridge Review of International Affairs* 21, (4): 505–525.

Scott, James M., and Carie A. Steele. (2011). "Sponsoring Democracy: The United States and Democracy Aid to the Developing World, 1988–2011." *International Studies Quarterly* 55, (1): 47–69.

Seck, Abdoulaye. (2012). "International Technology Diffusion and Economic Growth: Explaining The Spillover Benefits to Developing Countries." *Structural Change and Economic Dynamics* 23, (4): 437–451.

Seekins, Donald M. (2007). *Burma and Japan Since 1940: From Co-Prosperity to Quiet Dialogue.* Copenhagen: Nordic Institute of Asian Studies.

Shafaeddin, S. M. (2005). "Towards an Alternative Perspective on Trade and Industrial Policies." *Development and Change* 36, (6): 1143–1162.

Shapiro, Alan C. (2008). *Multinational Financial Management.* Hoboken, NJ: John Wiley and Sons.

Shaw, Tony. (1996). *Eden, Suez and the Mass Media: Propaganda and Persuasion during the Suez Crisis.* London: IB Tauris.

Shee, Poon Kim. (1997). "The Political Economy of China-Myanmar Relations: Strategic and Economic Dimensions." *Southeast Asia* 19, (1).

Shirazi, Farid. (2008). "The Contribution of ICT to Freedom and Democracy: An Empirical Analysis of Archival Data on the Middle East." *The Electronic Journal of Information Systems in Developing Countries* 35, (6): 1–24.

Shleifer, Andrei and Daniel Treisman. (2011). "Why Moscow Says No-A Question of Russian Interests, Not Psychology." *Foreign Affairs* 90, (1): 122–138.

Shor, Russell, and Robert Weldon. (2009). "Ruby and Sapphire Production and Distribution: A Quarter Century of Change." *Gems & Gemology* 45, (4): 236–259.

Sidani, Yusuf. (2005). "Women, Work, and Islam in Arab Societies." *Women in Management Review* 20, (7): 498–512.

Sidel, Victor W. (1999). "Can Sanctions Be Sanctioned?." *American Journal of Public Health* 89, (10): 1497–1498.

Simmons, Beth A., and Zachary Elkins. (2004). "The Globalization of Liberalization: Policy Diffusion in the International Political Economy." *American Political Science Review* 98, (1): 171–189.

Slavov, Slavi T. (2007). "Innocent Or Not-So-Innocent Bystanders: Evidence from the Gravity Model of International Trade about the Effects of UN Sanctions on Neighbour Countries." *The World Economy* 30, (11): 1701–1725.

Smeets, Roger. (2008). "Collecting the Pieces of the FDI Knowledge Spillovers Puzzle." *The World Bank Research Observer* 23, (2): 107–138.

Smith, Jackie. (2002). "Bridging Global Divides? Strategic Framing and Solidarity in Transnational Social Movement Organizations." *International Sociology* 17, (4): 505–528.

Smith, Jackie, and Dawn Wiest. (2005). "The Uneven Geography of Global Civil Society: National and Global Influences on Transnational Association." *Social Forces* 84, (2): 621–652.

Smith, Pamela Hyde. (2007). "Politics and Diplomacy: The Hard Road Back to Soft Power." *Georgetown Journal of International Affairs* 8, (1): 1–9.

Snow, Nancy. (2008). "International Exchanges and the US Image." *The Annals of the American Academy of Political and Social Science* 616, (1): 198–222.

Shin, Jongtae and Jaeyong Song. (2008). "The Paradox of Technological Capabilities: A Study of Knowledge Sourcing from Host Countries of Overseas R&D Operations." *Journal of International Business Studies* 39, (2): 291–303.

South, Ashley. (2011). *Burma's Longest War: Anatomy of the Karen Conflict.* Transnational Institute, Amsterdam: Drukkerij Primavera Quint

Spilimbergo, Antonio. (2009). "Democracy and Foreign Education." *The American Economic Review* 99, (1): 528–543.

Steinberg, David I. (2001). *Burma: The State Of Myanmar.* Washington, DC: Georgetown University Press.

Steinberg, David I. (2007). "The United States and its Allies: The Problem of Burma/Myanmar Policy." *Contemporary Southeast Asia* 29, (2): 219–237.

Stifel, Lawrence D. (1971). "Economics of the Burmese Way to Socialism." *Asian Survey* 11, (8): 803–817.

Stone, Diane. (2001). "Learning Lessons, Policy Transfer and the International Diffusion of Policy Ideas." *Working Paper No. 69/01.* Center for The Study of Globalization and Regionalization. University of Warwick, Coventry, England.

Stradiotto, Gary, and Sujian Guo. (2007). "Market Socialism in North Korea: A Comparative Perspective." *Journal of the Asia Pacific Economy* 12, (2): 188–214.

Strebinger, Andreas. (2014). "Rethinking Brand Architecture: A Study on Industry, Company-and Product-Level Drivers of Branding Strategy." *European Journal of Marketing* 48, (9/10): 1782–1804.

Stulz, René M. (2005). "The Limits of Financial Globalization," *Journal of Finance* 60, (4): 1595–1638.

Subramanian, Arvind. (2011). *Eclipse: Living in the Shadow of China's Economic Dominance*. Washington, DC: The Peterson Institute For International Economics.

Sylwester, Kevin. (2005). "Foreign Direct Investment, Growth and Income Inequality in Less Developed Countries." *International Review of Applied Economics* 19, (3): 289–300.

Takeyh, Ray, and Nikolas Gvosdev. (2002). Do Terrorist Networks Need a Home?. *Washington Quarterly* 25 (3): 97–108.

Tan-Mullins, May, Giles Mohan, and Marcus Power. (2010). "Redefining 'Aid' in the China-Africa Context." *Development and Change* 41, (5): 857–881.

Tanoos, James. (2014). "Post-Cold War State Industrialization as a Means of Economic Growth in East Asia versus Eastern Europe." *European Scientific Journal* 10, (10): 444–456.

Taylor, Michael, and Nigel Thrift, (eds). (2012). *The Geography of Multinationals: Studies in the Spatial Development and Economic Consequences of Multinational Corporations*. Abingdon, UK: Routledge.

Taylor, Philip M. (1992). *War and the Media: Propaganda and Persuasion in the Gulf War*. Manchester: Manchester University Press.

Telhami, Shibley. (2002). *The Stakes: America in the Middle East: The Consequences of Power and the Choice for Peace*. Boulder, CO: Westview Press.

Telhami, Shibley. (2006). *Annual Arab Public Opinion Survey*. Washington, DC: Brookings. Available at: http://www.brookings.edu/~/media/research/files/reports/2010/8/05%20arab%20opinion%20poll%20telhami/0805_arabic_opinion_poll_telhami.pdf.

Testas, Abdelaziz. (2004). "Determinants of Terrorism in the Muslim World: An Empirical Cross-Sectional Analysis." *Terrorism and Political Violence* 16, (2): 253–273.

Tessler, Mark. (2003). "Arab and Muslim Political Attitudes: Stereotypes and Evidence from Survey Research." *International Studies Perspectives* 4, (2): 175–181.

Thein, Myat. (2004). *Economic Development of Myanmar*. Singapore: Institute of Southeast Asian Studies.

Tibshirani, Robert. (1996). "Regression Shrinkage and Selection Via the Lasso." *Journal of the Royal Statistical Society, Series B* 58: 267–288

Tillman, Seth. (1982). *The United States in The Middle East, Interests and Obstacles*. Bloomington, Indiana: Indiana University Press.

Tomlinson, John. (2001). *Cultural Imperialism: A Critical Introduction*. London: Bloomsbury Publishing.

Tong, Hui, and Shang-Jin Wei. (2011). "The Composition Matters: Capital Inflows and Liquidity Crunch during a Global Economic Crisis." *Review of Financial Studies* 24, (6): 2023–2052.

Townsend, Janell D., Mehmet Berk Talay, and Sengun Yeniyurt. (2009). "Getting to Global: An Evolutionary Perspective of Brand Expansion in International Markets." *Journal of International Business Studies* 40, (4): 539–558.

Treisman, Daniel. (2012) *The Return: Russia's Journey from Gorbachev to Medvedev.* New York: Simon and Schuster.

Gaughran, Audrey, Howard Mollett, and Antonio Tujan. (2004). "Development and the 'Global War on Terror.'" *Race & Class* 46, (1): 53–74.

Turnell, Sean. (2008). "Burma's Insatiable State." *Asian Survey* 48, (6): 958–976.

Van de Graaf, Thijs. (2013). "The "Oil Weapon" Reversed? Sanctions against Iran and US-EU Structural Power." *Middle East Policy* 20, (3): 145–163.

Van de Walle, Nicolas. (2012). "*Foreign Aid in Dangerous Places: The Donors and Mali's Democracy.*" *WIDER Working Paper #2012/61*, available at: https://www.econstor.eu/dspace/bitstream/10419/80969/1/718476131.pdf.

VanWagenen, Paul. (2000). "US Economic Sanctions—Non-Traditional Success against North Korea." *Law and Policy in International Business* 32, (1): 239–262.

Verčič, Dejan. (2008). "Public Relations and Power: How Hard Is Soft Power?" In Zerfaß, Ansgar, van, A. A. Ruler and Krishnamurthy Sriramesh (eds). *Public Relations Research: European and International Perspectives and Innovations.* Wiesbaden, Germany: VS Verlag für Sozialwissenschaften.

Vogel, David. (2008). "Private Global Business Regulation." *Annual Review of Political Science* 11: 261–282.

Walsh, John Christopher. (2011). "Robert Gordon and The Rubies of Mogok: Industrial Capitalism, Imperialism and Technology in Conjunction." *Asian Culture and History* 3, (1): 94–100.

Walt, Stephen M. (2009). "Alliances in a Unipolar World." *World politics* 61, (1): 86–120.

Walter, Andrew. (1999) "Globalisation and Policy Convergence: The Case of Direct Investment Rules," In Andreas Bieler, Richard Higgott, and Geoffrey Underhill (eds). *Non State Actors and Authority in the Global System.* London: Routledge.

Wang, Miao. (2009). "Manufacturing FDI and Economic Growth: Evidence from Asian Economies." *Applied Economics* 41, (8): 991–1002.

Wapner, Paul. (1996). *Environmental Activism and World Civic Politics.* New York: City University of New York Press.

Wasserman, Herman. (2013). "China in Africa: The Implications for Journalism." *Ecquid Novi: African Journalism Studies* 34, (3): 1–5.

Weinstein, Michael (ed.). (2005). *Globalization: What's New?* New York: Columbia University Press.

West, Michael O. (2014). "China, Africa and the Bandung Idea, Then and Now." *Agrarian South: Journal of Political Economy* 3, (1): 111–123.

Whang, Taehee. (2011). "Playing to the Home Crowd? Symbolic Use of Economic Sanctions in the United States." *International Studies Quarterly* 55, (3): 787–801.

Whang, Taehee. (2010). "Structural Estimation of Economic Sanctions: From Initiation to Outcomes." *Journal of Peace Research* 47, (5): 561–573.

Wight, Colin. (2014). "Morphogenesis and Cooperation in the International Political System." In Margaret Archer (ed.), *Late Modernity: Trajectories toward Morphogenic Society*. 221–240. Switzerland: Springer International Publishing.

Williamson, Oliver E. (1973). "Markets and Hierarchies: Some Elementary Considerations." *American Economic Review* 63, (2): 316–325.

Williamson, Oliver E. (1981). "The Economics of Organization: The Transaction Cost Approach." *American Journal of Sociology* 87, (3): 548–577.

Williamson, Oliver E. (1998). "Transaction Cost Economics: How It Works; Where It Is Headed." *De Economist* 146, (1): 23–58.

Williamson, Oliver E. (2005). *Transaction Cost Economics*. Berlin: Springer.

Wimberley, Dale W., and Rosario Bello. (1992). "Effects of Foreign Investment, Exports, and Economic Growth on Third World Food Consumption." *Social Forces* 70, (4): 895–921.

Winkler, Adam. (1999). "Just Sanctions." *Human Rights Quarterly* 21, (1): 133–155.

Winkler, Deborah. (2013). "Potential and Actual FDI Spillovers in Global Value Chains: The Role of Foreign Investor Characteristics, Absorptive Capacity and Transmission Channels." *World Bank Policy Research Working Paper No. 6424*. Washington, DC: The World Bank Publications.

Wint, Alvin G., and Densil A. Williams. (2002). "Attracting FDI to Developing Countries: A Changing Role for Government?." *International Journal of Public Sector Management* 15, (5): 361–374.

Wolf, Martin. (2004). *Why Globalization Works*. New Haven, CT: Yale University Press.

Wong, Anson, and Xianbo Zhou. (2014). "Development of Financial Market and Economic Growth: Review of Hong Kong, China, Japan, the United States, and the United Kingdom." *International Journal Of Economics And Finance* 3, (2): 111–115.

Wood, Reed M. (2008). "A Hand upon the Throat of the Nation:" Economic Sanctions and State Repression, 1976–2001." *International Studies Quarterly* 52, (3): 489–513.

Wooldridge, Jeffrey M. (2009). *Introductory Econometrics: A Modern Approach* 4th ed., Mason, OH: South Western / Cengage Learning.

Wrobel, Ralph M. (2007). "North Korea after the Nuclear Crisis: The Future of the Economic Reforms." *Post-Communist Economies* 19, (4): 483–503.

Wyler, Liana. (2009). "Burma and Transnational Crime." *CRS Reports for Congress # 7–5700*. Washington, DC.

Xie, Lei. (2011). "China's Environmental Activism in the Age Of Globalization." *Asian Politics & Policy* 3, (2): 207–224.

Yang, Dali L. (2006)."Economic Transformation and Its Political Discontents in China: Authoritarianism, Unequal Growth, and the Dilemmas of Political Development." *Annual Review of Political Sciology* 9: 143–164.

Young, Stephen. (2001). "What Do Researchers Know about the Global Business Environment?" *International Marketing Review* 18, (2): 120–129.

Zaharna, Rhonda S. (1995). "Understanding Cultural Preferences of Arab Communication Patterns." *Public Relations Review* 21, (3): 241–255.

Zakaria, Fareed. (2011). *The Post-American World: Release 2.0 (International Edition).* New York: WW Norton and Company.

Zeng, Ka. (2013). "High Stakes: United States–China Trade Disputes under the World Trade Organization." *International Relations of the Asia-Pacific* 13, (1): 33–63.

Zhao, Hong. (2012). "China-Myanmar Energy Cooperation and Its Regional Implications." *Journal of Current Southeast Asian Affairs* 30, (4): 89–109.

Zhimin, Chen. (2005). "Nationalism, Internationalism and Chinese Foreign Policy." *Journal of Contemporary China*1 4,(42):3 5–53.

Index

The manufacturer's authorised representative in the EU is Springer Nature Customer Service Centre GmbH, Europaplatz 3, 69115 Heidelberg, Germany. If you have any concerns regarding our products, please contact ProductSafety@springernature.com

Printed and bound by CPI Group (UK) Ltd, Croydon, CR0 4YY
22/10/2026
02238259-0001